This book should be returned/renewed by the latest date shown above. Overdue items incur charges which prevent self-service renewals. Please contact the library.

Wandsworth Libraries
24 hour Renewal Hotline
01159 293388
www.wandsworth.gov.uk

Wandsworth

HOW TO

TRUE STORIES FROM A LIFE

SOLVE A

IN FORENSIC MEDICINE

MURDER

DEREK AND **PAULINE TREMAIN**

HARPER
element

HarperElement
An imprint of HarperCollins*Publishers*
1 London Bridge Street
London SE1 9GF

www.harpercollins.co.uk

HarperCollins*Publishers*
1st Floor, Watermarque Building, Ringsend Road
Dublin 4, Ireland

First published by HarperElement 2021

1 3 5 7 9 10 8 6 4 2

Images courtesy of the authors, with the exception of plate 1 (top photograph),
which is courtesy of The Curator, The Gordon Museum

Derek and Pauline Tremain assert the moral right to
be identified as the authors of this work

A catalogue record of this book is
available from the British Library

ISBN 978-0-00-840488-8

Printed and bound in Great Britain by
CPI Group (UK) Ltd, Croydon

For our children – Ross, Gemma, Rowan
and Amber – and our families.

CONTENTS

FOREWORD

BY DR RICHARD SHEPHERD

You may think, watching any of the many crime series on television, that all murders are solved by one crucial person. Who that person is will of course depend on whether you are watching a police, a pathology or a CSI television series. The thing they all have in common is that one critical person does all the jobs and makes all the discoveries. In the end there is usually a blinding flash of inspiration, a quick arrest, a confession and it's all over and time for a cup of tea. I know you know that's not how it works, but still you go with the story, even if, like me, you are always somehow left dissatisfied and think, *I wonder what it's really like* ...

Derek and Pauline's brilliant book tells you what it's really like. You certainly get the nuts and bolts of forensic medicine, but you also get the brains, bullets and bones. This superb book leads you painstakingly through the tests and the truths and the spellbinding background minutiae of the investigation of many of the murders that were dealt with in the Department of Forensic Medicine at the world famous Guy's Hospital in central London.

You'll very quickly appreciate that, despite the many famous names so closely associated with that department

– Professors Keith Simpson and Keith Mant and more recently Dr Iain West – and the many murders that were dealt with over the years in that department, it wasn't the headline names that were important, but the whole forensic team, working together in rather cramped and crowded rooms at the back edge of the least favoured wing of the hospital to uncover scientific and medical evidence, prove the cause of death, establish the identities of corpses and assailants and then produce the facts that were crucial in obtaining a conviction.

The team at Guy's dealt with so many thousands of deaths over the years – some domestic murders, some serial murders, some accidental deaths and, in later years, some terrorist related. Deaths of babies, children, adults and the aged. Each death was dealt with using specialist skills that had been built up over years. The department was also innovative – finding, establishing and proving new techniques in many areas, including microscopy, weapon recognition, serology and toxicology.

Derek and Pauline were crucial figures in the department and in the investigation of many headline cases over the years, including the Clapham rail disaster and the sinking of the *Marchioness*. These mass disasters all had to be investigated at the same time as deaths from gang violence, natural causes and tragic accidents – time just had to be found, somehow. High-profile or 'celebrity' deaths always added complications to the work, often with the media, as did deaths in high society, while deaths of the homeless in filthy squats in derelict buildings or on street corners were seldom reported by the press. However, these deaths were noticed, and were investigated with exactly the same determination by the team at Guy's. And so they were, for many years, the daily life and work of Derek and Pauline.

I remember so clearly Derek sitting in the department's laboratory – a room always humming with the noise of machinery and smelling of vaguely disconcerting chemicals, often with notes of decomposing something or other. Pauline would often be found in her office, which always smelled of coffee, i.e. much better, efficiently managing the department and controlling (or attempting to) the many pathologists who were based at this national hub of forensic excellence. Pauline was also brilliant at keeping police, coroners and sometimes even judges firmly, but politely, in their places. But she wasn't deskbound – for many years she actually worked in the mortuaries every day alongside the pathologists as the autopsies were being performed, and both she and Derek attended many murder scenes to take photographs, take samples and to make precise notes. Derek and Pauline, each in their own domain and each an expert in their own right, brought to the team at Guy's diverse assets, skills and experiences that always proved useful in tracking down a murderer.

In this book, Derek and Pauline have captured the essence of how a murder investigation progresses in a forensic department – the joys of success and the frustrations of dealing with transient evidence; the stresses of managing human bodies, or parts of bodies, knowing that personal feelings have to be kept at bay until the scientific facts are established; putting in long, hard hours, often in difficult conditions, until the job is finished, and never, ever, expecting a 5 o'clock departure, because that is simply not how forensic medicine works.

This book not only provides an insight into how forensic medicine works, it places you centre-stage as the work goes on around and about you. It leads you into strange places and will, at times, test your belief in humanity. One downside is that you'll never be able to watch a fictional crime series again without a knowing smile and an extra-large slice of disbelief!

You will be gripped, fascinated, enthralled and (as we all are when doing this crucial job) occasionally appalled – but that is the reality of the work involved when you have to solve a murder.

PREFACE

On your way to work, have you ever glanced at the person opposite and wondered what they do for a living? It's a common enough pastime. It's distinctly unlikely, though, that you would ever have guessed what our working lives entailed. You would have found nothing remarkable or odd in our appearance. You might well have wondered, however, about the unmistakable odour of decay occasionally trailing in our wake ...

You are about enter a universe in which the extraordinary is commonplace; the unmentionable, part of a standard vocabulary; chilling sights and sounds, everyday. This is the world of forensic medicine – a place we began to inhabit at relatively young ages, but one far from the common concerns of youth.

Whether you are a fan of televised forensic drama, documentaries, horror films or autobiographies, this book will not only give you a new perspective on the genre, but catapult you into a new world. This is easily the stuff of nightmares, and we do share hair-raising events and experiences. We also convey what it was like to occupy a workplace where there was a constant focus on the darker elements of life.

The subject of death still retains its rather taboo status. In Western society there is an attendant fear of the unknown, as science has no comforting answer about what happens to our personality after we die. All we can be sure of is that our physical body will no longer function. That is unsettling. Understandably, we choose not to think about the subject if we don't have to.

Some people find it unacceptable to dwell on the fact that there are professionals who willingly play a part in the investigative process of death. Nor can they tolerate the thought of work that entails pieces of human tissue, body parts or photographs of injury – items which are standard in our work setting. For these people, no explanation of the need to establish a cause of death, or uncover evidential proof and mete out justice, will provide sufficient reason to engage with death. But when you face the subject of natural death every day, it tends to lose its power to strike fear into you. For one thing, it is not as daunting, as you have already come to terms with it as a concept. It is not always welcome to contemplate, but the fact is that death is an unavoidable part of the living process. The physical breakdown of the body is a sign of having lived, however long. As a result, how you live becomes important. Working closely with death challenges your perceptions of life and urges you to constantly re-evaluate priorities and what is of significance to you.

There is no doubt that death quickly becomes more normalized when you regularly see the dead, who have, in the vast majority of cases, arrived at the mortuary due to natural causes. This can have its advantages. Being able to switch into 'professional mode' can be of benefit when having to deal with the organizational aspects of the death of a close friend or relative. It creates order from the chaos and prevents descent into an emotional maelstrom. Naturally, though, the death of someone close will have exactly the same impact on us as it would on anyone else.

This is worth stating, because there are people who are so repulsed by anything forensic that they will go so far as to suggest that anyone working in our field of investigation clearly has no sense of decorum and must be in some way deranged; that we must have no empathy, no compassion. For readers who fall into this category, we are hopeful that this book will go a long way towards proving otherwise.

Forensic work is clearly not your 'average' job, of course. But it can be a bit of an adventure – though one for which there is arguably no adequate preparation. Elements of it are awe-inspiring: for instance, knowing that a recently deceased body will, given the right conditions, retain the tell-tale anatomical features that form the clues from which a pathologist will arrive at the cause of death. This is true whether these clues are retained in the tissues and organs of the body or result from deliberately inflicted trauma. Both can involve specific technical investigations by a forensic medical scientist in order to contribute to the given cause of death, as you will learn here.

Equally, there is fascination in watching a pathologist at work. It is even more satisfying if you happen to be one of the team assisting them and can learn from the experience. In such a workplace, curiosity is encouraged and freedom of thought accompanied by freedom of speech. The conversations that take place are, for the most part, incomparable to any found in a standard business environment. The people who choose to work in this field tend to be remarkably open-minded, largely because they have either seen everything or will do at some point.

Our book has been written to open up the world of the forensic pathologist and reveal the team who work behind, or alongside, them and to inform you of how the scientific aspects of forensic medicine can often form a crucial part of the forensic evidence given in court. Our hope is to broaden public perception of the lesser-known aspects of murder investigation, the importance of correct photography of the body, both at the scene and later, in the mortuary, and how the smallest and most insignificant-seeming detail might be one of the most crucial elements in solving a murder.

Welcome to our world. We hope you enjoy sharing it with us.

CHAPTER 1

A NIGHTMARISH RESTORATION OF IDENTITY

At the end of a working day, when everyone around you has left and is probably almost home, the forensic department at Guy's Hospital in London isn't the ideal place in which to find yourself working late. But as a forensic medical scientist I would often be there as the light faded.

As shadows appeared, my perceptions were heightened. The lights in the corridor outside would begin a series of erratic clicks as they cooled down following the departure of my last colleague, leaving me in a dimly lit environment. I would pick up on every footstep as staff vacated the other floors, their welcome human presence fading into the distance, leaving me feeling even more isolated and alone. Instinctively, I would work more quietly, hyper-aware of every sound I made, as well as the sounds around me, the hum of the constantly running fridges and freezers …

I would have more awareness of processes which, in daylight, would give me little cause for alarm, but which, as night fell, became just that little bit spookier. The familiar smells I would breathe in warmly and comfortably every morning, as I reached my daily workspace, would become less reassuring: remnants of chemicals now safely stored away for the night, warm wax used to coat and fix tissue specimens, musty old cupboards full of distinctly strange objects.

The occasional flecks of dust that had filtered through the shafts of sunlight during the day had long since settled, leaving stillness in the air. Everything had shut down for the night. Except me.

During the day, the Department, as we called it, was a busy and industrious place, full of the humour and vigour of people who loved their jobs and couldn't wait to get to work. But as night fell, that light and carefree environment gradually darkened and became an entirely different place.

Everything took on increased significance. A lone skull on a nearby desktop, an otherwise everyday sight, and part of the head pathologist's collection of curios, now took on a more ghoulish aspect. Indulged as a quaint, even appropriate feature for a forensic department by day, it gradually turned into a more menacing escort into the night, as shadows passed over it, highlighting the empty eye sockets and the presence of two holes: entry and exit wounds from a bullet. A reminder of murder. A reminder that this skull had once served as the shell covering the brain of a living human being.

A skull, of course, has always been viewed as the ultimate reminder of mortality. However, in our department, a skull was viewed as evidence, highlighting the fact that so much of our workload was directly associated with violent endings. In the dim laboratory, this one also reminded me of why I felt such a huge amount of job satisfaction. I played my own part in these investigations. I had skills which contributed to solving violent crime. But such visible reminders still sent the occasional chill down my spine.

'Here, Trogg, have a look at what I've got!'

Dr Kevin Lee, our second-in-command pathologist, had returned from working in the Thames Valley during the last hour of my working day, as he tended to do. His long journey in from St Peter's Hospital in Chertsey, Surrey, took several hours.

On this occasion I was just taking off my white lab coat and collecting my motorcycle helmet from my locker, ready

A joy to be around, Dr Kevin Lee (left) and Dr (now Professor) Stephen Cordner (right).

to make my half-hour journey home by motorbike. But that would have to wait.

'I need your help,' Kevin said, setting down the extremely large white 'brain bucket' he was carrying.

As the chief scientific officer, I was used to receiving anatomical items by bucket. A bucket usually indicated a messy job. This particular job would turn out to be a highly unexpected departure from any of my more routine laboratory processes. To say it required skill and anatomical knowledge would be an understatement.

Inside the bucket was the extremely mangled head of a female murder victim. There was no body, just the decapitated head. The body, with the head still attached, had been placed on a railway track the previous afternoon, with the apparent intention of it being run over by a train, rendering the face unrecognizable.

The railway track in question was located on a busy link between Surrey and London, and in due course an Intercity 125 smashed into it at great speed, causing catastrophic damage that had rendered the face almost unrecognizable. *Almost*, but not quite. This was the basis for the unexpected task I was about to be given that evening.

What remained of the external structure and skin of the head was a mass of large splits and shreds. The exterior of the head itself was covered in blood, and very little content remained inside, as any remnants of brain had already been preserved at the mortuary for further scientific reference. The skull had mostly been shattered upon impact with the train and some of the more splintered remnants had also been left at the mortuary for observation at a later time. So the head I was looking at resembled a bloody, shredded, mangled empty sack ... and Kevin wanted us to reconstruct it.

He was well known in our department for his pranks and, looking at the head, you could be forgiven for thinking that this was another of them, but I automatically knew he meant business. His request had a highly practical and necessary purpose. Once we had a more recognizable structure, the idea was to photograph it so that the injuries could be recorded, given a description and allocated a numbering system which could be used as a reference. From this, a post-mortem report could be produced for a murder trial – assuming the police investigation ever reached that point. This would depend on whether it was possible to find any further evidence, or indeed witnesses, and whether the police could track down the perpetrator. Meanwhile, I found myself involved in one of the most surreal experiences of my life.

First, we cleaned the skin. Then I realized we needed a base on which to mount the head, so that there was something solid to hold the scalp in place while we rebuilt it. For this, I used one of my larger laboratory beakers. Then I decided that a brain would be useful as a prop around which to shape the head. In a forensic department there were always items of this nature around, and I was able to locate an old one fairly easily in one of the tubs on the shelving behind me in the cutting room. Fresh brains are very soft and yielding, but the brain I chose had been pickled in formalin, the preserving liquid I routinely used at work, for a very long time, so it had a certain firmness, which created the ideal full and oval shape required for our purposes. We began to manoeuvre it into the cavity inside the head, wrapping the deflated remains around it as best we could.

Having got the overall shape of the head, we now began work on the more specific features of the face, painstakingly stitching together the remaining pieces of skin strip by strip, like a grisly patchwork quilt.

This was an unnervingly ghoulish task, but the fact that Kevin and I were very much at ease with each other meant that it was not completed without a lot of banter. There's no doubt that, to an outsider, we had the appearance of your typical mad scientists. There we were, at night, in a tiny, artificially lit lab surrounded by a dark and deserted larger laboratory, laughing and joking as we reconstructed a human head. It started out as surreal and became rather macabre as the identity of the deceased emerged. Let's face it, it's not every day you are asked to rebuild someone's head. If we hadn't kept each other's spirits up, I suspect we would have become increasingly sad at the thought of the victim's unfortunate end.

It took several hours, but in due course we were able to observe, with a sense of great satisfaction, that every last strand of flesh had been joined up. All we could go on was skin, as no bony remnants of the skull remained, but we had produced a recognizable face. Certainly one which would have been identifiable from a photograph.

I then proceeded to take shots of the head with the departmental camera, capturing every injury from every possible angle. These photographs, if necessary, would accompany Kevin's post-mortem report, which he wrote the next day.

Once I had finished the photography, Kevin made notes on all the injuries. One was due to the metal bar that acts to clear any debris from the line before the train runs into it. The forehead had received a particularly hard blow from this, making a very deep laceration. Kevin's notes also included the direction of impact, and he took and recorded measurements. This took at least another hour. We finally totally immersed the head in a large specimen container filled with formaldehyde, which would preserve it as evidence pending any future murder trial.

I was still reeling from the experience the following day. It had been particularly macabre, even in my line of work, and had the quality of a dream about it – though not one you would welcome if it returned to you in the middle of the night.

Amazingly, further police investigation did bring the case to a satisfactory conclusion. Very quickly, the husband of the murder victim became of interest to the police, not least for being the person closest to her. His position as prime suspect solidified when a neighbour came forward to report seeing him in the vicinity of the railway line on which the body had been discovered. The railway, in fact, bordered both their properties.

At his subsequent trial, the husband was found guilty of his wife's murder and received a sentence of life imprisonment.

CHAPTER 2

MUSEUM OF THE MACABRE

Even today, I still regularly ask myself: 'Why do I perform such a gruesome job?'

It all started quite by chance, when I was 15, which was then the school-leaving age, and I bumped into a friend who lived a couple of hundred yards along my road in Belvedere, north Kent.

'Hi, Shovel, how's your job going?'

In my neck of the woods, everybody had a nickname and I knew that Shovel had been working for three years at Guy's Hospital's medical school.

'Well, Trogg, I'm really enjoying it. I'm working in the biology department at the moment and it's really interesting.'

Immediately fired up by what I was hearing, I joked, 'Got any jobs going?'

'Yes, actually, the museum next door's looking for a student technician.'

'Ooh, well, put a word in for us, then. I love biology. I wouldn't mind getting into something like that.'

Within days, the museum's curator had given my friend the task of offering me a date to attend for interview. I hastily borrowed my eldest brother's smart suit and took the half-hour train journey into London.

I knew I really wanted the job even before I'd walked through the grand square colonnade of the hospital, down the stone steps, across the large square park, with its flower borders and ancient trees, and over to the far right-hand corner, to a magnificent building covered in ivy, which took on a range of vivid dark pinks, even in the spring. This was the medical school.

I walked up the steep, wide, white limestone steps, flanked at the bottom by two old-fashioned tall black lampposts, to the imposing entrance. This was where it became real.

The heavy wooden double doors opened onto a cool, grand, marble-floored entrance hall. On a series of pedestals stood a variety of marble and bronze busts of Guy's most famous surgeons and physicians, serving as a reminder,

The imposing view greeting us every morning at Guy's Hospital Medical School. For much of the year, the frontage was enveloped in beautiful fuchsia-coloured ivy.

for staff and visitors alike, of the eminence of the place they were about to enter, and the part these alumni had played in its history.

As there was no reception area or security officer at that time, I simply took a route to the right, following the signs to the Gordon Museum.

Once inside the museum office, I was introduced to the chief technician, Joe, who had been given the responsibility of interviewing me. Friendly and personable, he was the ideal person for the task. He tried hard to sell the job to me, although I didn't need any persuasion.

At the end of the interview I was taken to the third floor of the medical school to meet the museum's curator, Professor Keith Simpson, who was a slim, athletic, balding man with a very professional, respectful 'old school' manner, who called everyone by their surname.

'Aaah, Tremaiiiin, pleased to meet you.'

The job was mine, and a start date was agreed for a few weeks later: 15 October 1964.

I have no idea where my interest in medical science came from, but it certainly wasn't from my parents. During the Second World War my father had been a welder, working on tanks and military equipment in the Royal Arsenal at Woolwich, south-east London, and my mother had driven a crane, loading and unloading at the Erith docks. Later, they worked at our local pub, the Leather Bottle, while my two elder brothers and I lived a free-range existence, making camps and climbing trees in the ancient woodland behind Lesnes Abbey, at Abbey Wood, which dated back to 1178.

Now, on my first day in the job, the presentation of my first white laboratory coat brought home the fact that I was a student technician, joining the three technicians already working in the museum. There was actually no job description for me; my working day would be dictated by Joe as it unfolded.

It was on only my second day of work that I was asked to go over to the mortuary. To be honest, I found the idea really rather daunting. I was still only 15 and hadn't had many opportunities to experience anything significantly challenging, especially on an emotional level, and I didn't quite know how I felt about this type of environment and how it might affect me. I went over to the mortuary in great trepidation.

If you were to imagine someone dressed for the role of working with the dead, chief mortician Len Beaney would be that person. As I shook his proffered hand, he seemed to embody what I had expected. A very short man in his early fifties, he was dressed in a black suit and tie, beneath which was a crisp white shirt. You could see your face in his highly polished black shoes. His style of clothing seemed to have come straight from the undertaker's.

I had never seen a dead body before, especially not one on which a post-mortem had already been conducted and which was therefore open, awaiting some final stitching before being slid back into a fridge. I was intimidated just by that sight alone, but Len went to great lengths to make my visit to the mortuary so involving that my aversion and fear were quickly replaced by overwhelming interest.

Of the four bodies in view, one in particular stood out: that of a boy of only about 10 years of age, who had been run over by a lorry. At not many years older myself, I felt such sadness – and alarm, because of the degree of flattening to his head. Tyre marks were still present down one side of his face. The whole image was a stark reminder of the worst scenarios that can befall a child, and his devastated family. But I have to credit Len with making the whole experience a far less harrowing one for me than it could have been.

One thing I later learned about Len came as a total surprise. He showed me a card game he was attempting to sell and explained that he was a bit of an inventor in his spare time and had had a degree of success in selling similar games to a range of companies. I wouldn't have guessed that this quiet and unassuming man, with his sombre and formal way of dressing, was a highly creative inventor. If ever there was a reminder never to judge a book by its cover, it was Len Beaney.

I would spend seven years, in total, in the Gordon Museum, an awe-inspiring square structure housed to the right of the medical school. It covered several floors – both upwards from the entrance level and downwards into the basement – linked by a central spiral staircase, with large skylights in the ceiling aiding the huge glass chandeliers in lighting the interior. It was divided into four square areas running off this central staircase. The higher floors consisted of walk-around galleries complemented by a series of small square glass tiles in the flooring and decorative curved wrought-iron railings, inset into which was an occasional official Guy's crest. The basement floor was more like a standard museum.

Shelving along the galleries housed specimens in clear square Perspex boxes of various sizes and ages. A second stairway was set deeply into the interior wall, leading upwards from gallery to gallery over three consecutive floors. This was less conspicuous than the other staircase and was used mainly by the technicians.

The museum wasn't open to the public. Some form of connection was required for a visit, whether by way of conducting work at Guy's or training there, either as a medical student or an affiliated medical trainee, usually a visiting St John's Ambulance candidate. It was a place for study and research.

On the ground floor there was a rather arresting series of life-sized anatomical wax models that had been stunningly fashioned by wax artist Joseph Towne (1806–1879). They were beautifully detailed, and revered as being strikingly anatomically correct. These lifelike 'bodies' were disconcerting, though, if you happened to be the last person in the museum at night and were required to turn off the fuse box in the basement. The trip to the basement always seemed to take less time on the way back up.

Another section of the museum housed wax models designed to demonstrate dermatological conditions. Many of these were gruesome to behold. One depicted a face which had been eaten away by a nasty bacterial infection typical of the effects of syphilis at the time. Another demonstrated the disturbingly swollen limbs of elephantitis. Yet another showed a face covered in black boils; others, red or yellow pustules. There were so many models – well over 100 – that if you spent too long among them you would begin to forget that they illustrated conditions which had largely been eradicated in the outside world.

A student lecture theatre was located on the ground floor, as was an original series of paintings by Lam Qua (real name Guan Qiaochang). Painted between 1836 and 1852, they illustrated a range of medical conditions which had been encountered by a leading American medical missionary of his day, the Reverend Dr Peter Parker (incidentally, not Spiderman), prior to corrective surgery. I knew that there would have been no form of anaesthetic available to the patients undergoing the procedures, even if those involved tumour removal, or the amputation of a limb. The operations would have been performed in the quickest possible time – certainly within minutes – so that the requirement to endure extreme pain would have been minimized, but I still felt my buttock cheeks clench every time I saw the paintings.

The final section on the ground floor housed a series of glass display cases on a par with any standard scientific museum. The exhibits ranged from antique medical instruments to microscopes and other examples of early surgical equipment. In pride of place was the velvet-lined surgical box used by a ship's surgeon at Nelson's Battle of Trafalgar. Equally noteworthy were Lister's antiseptic spray and some early anaesthetic equipment.

The upper floors of the museum were dedicated to 'wet specimens', i.e. specimens of human tissue and/or organs which had been preserved in fluid-filled Perspex jars. There were some very arresting sights. When browsing through this broad range of anatomical curios, it was only natural to progress from the more mundane to the truly revolting.

The sections were organized according to the body's anatomical systems, and each took up as many as two sides of an entire floor, according to the availability of space within each category. It seemed that just about every possible medical condition was represented. Every jar on display was assigned a reference number, and a nearby catalogue gave the visitor as much detail as was known, by way of a corresponding entry and description. Where available, a full case history was provided.

Most specimens arrived in the museum as the result of a surgical extraction; some arrived direct from the mortuary. In the time I worked there, the museum housed hundreds of them, a few dating back to the era of Joseph Towne. The more ancient were mounted in glass, having already been preserved in a combination of alcohol and glycerine. Black bitumen, or tar, had been used as a final seal for these jars.

One of the experiences I will never forget at the museum again occurred on only my second day there. The task of enforcing the museum's 5 o'clock curfew was given to me. This was designed to root out any stragglers, ready for closing for the night, and to ensure that the rules were enforced in relation to our opening hours. It had the added benefit of ensuring that all the museum staff could leave on time.

Joe, as my supervisor, gave explicit instructions that I should make sure everyone left immediately and not take any nonsense from anybody, because, he said, 'Some of them will try it on.' So, 15 minutes before closing time, I walked around the whole museum, telling everyone I encountered that they should leave because we would be closing soon. What I didn't know on my second day was that one of the most senior surgeons at Guy's was giving a tutorial to a group of medical students on one of our balconies. As I gave my command to his party, his shock was palpable. Looking back, I can see his point. A cocky young technician was walking up to him and, in front of all his students, rather unceremoniously throwing him out.

Of course he rounded on me and said, 'Don't you know who I am?'

Remembering my very specific instructions, I didn't flinch. 'No. And I don't care *who* you are. You've got to leave. Now! Go on, out!'

I later learned that the surgeon had taken up this professional embarrassment with a friend at the most senior level – the museum's curator, Professor Keith Simpson. I was therefore relieved, and quite proud, when I learned that the professor had stood up for me and apparently confirmed that I had just been doing my job in reaffirming the closing time. I hadn't expected this. It shows the measure of the man that he would support a junior member of his staff rather than pander to the sensitivity of a top surgeon and friend. (It also goes some way towards explaining why I have never since been fazed by anyone's sense of their own rank or self-importance – particularly in the medical profession.)

My first few weeks were spent mostly in the curator's office, which doubled as a preparation room. Accessible from the main entrance to the medical school, this room also had a hidden internal entrance via a door in the museum's main gallery on the top floor. It was my destiny to start work there, alongside a very specific assortment of specimens: the penis gallery.

The penis gallery was, as might be expected, an area given over to exhibits of this type. One of them in particular seemed guaranteed to elicit considerable giggling from visiting nurses. It dated back to the 1800s, and had belonged to a man who was understood to have undergone a 'religious epiphany'. Full of remorse because he had used this part of his anatomy to 'commit a sin', he had decided that in order to atone he would excise the organ responsible from his body. He immediately cut off his entire genitalia and threw them into an unlit furnace for destruction. They were discovered, peppered with bits of carbon, and someone thought of conveying them to the museum for display. Another penis gallery exhibit showed a metal ring punched through the foreskin. Dating back to the 1800s, it was one of the earliest exhibits of this kind of body art.

The prep room/curator's office, lit only by ordinary incandescent lighting, was always dark and dingy. Long and narrow, it had a couple of laboratory sinks at one end and a huge oak table in the middle, which we used for cutting. That was, if we could find a space, as there was never a time when the table wasn't heavily stacked with specimens. Modern plastic Tupperware and glass containers mingled with antique copper-lidded glass jars, and at one end of the table was our huge red 'Day Book', in which specimens were catalogued on arrival.

Beneath the wooden table were large white enamel containers housing items of particular interest and thereby rendering them retainable indefinitely. One of these contained a huge benign ovarian tumour. It was an eye-watering 60cm x 40cm in size and apparently its owner had used a wheelbarrow to cart around her extended abdomen prior to surgery. Another housed a uterus containing a pair of non-identical twins. This exhibit was useful to teach first-aid students who might otherwise have remained generally unaware that non-identical twins were supplied by separate placentas, rather than a single one.

To the left, rows of shelves were stacked from floor to ceiling with specimens awaiting display. On the window ledge above the sinks were two huge 50-litre aspirators, or huge jars. It was from these that we obtained our specimen mounting fluid.

To the right, a fluorescent strip lit a long bench on which we would mount the specimens. The only natural light came from a bank of high square windows, and as the room was in a well, it was always a relatively dark area in which to work. As a student technician I would spend most of my day there, handling specimens, learning to photograph them and finally mounting them in Perspex jars for exhibition in the museum, working alongside colleagues performing similar tasks. I don't remember a time when the shelves or surfaces weren't loaded with specimens awaiting comple-tion. This gives some indication as to how busy we were.

One of my favourite areas of the museum was a room just off the first-floor gallery. Part way through the morning or afternoon we would take a tea break there. It had been an old anatomical demonstration room and had remained in its original form. Entering it was like walking into another world. I could imagine medical students from the previous century peering down through the central gap, approximately three metres square, as they watched demonstrations performed by their more qualified superiors. Perhaps they leaned slightly forwards, pressing up against the decorative wrought-iron railings in order to peer into the 'workshop' below, trusting that no one would faint and fall through the gap.

It was always fascinating to browse this area in between sips of tea or coffee. It gave such an insight into days gone by. I managed to find ancient specimens which, for whatever reason, had never been moved on. I found a range of differently sized antique glass jars with thick bases, oval in shape, whose lids would have been sealed into place using bitumen before being hung up for display. I found antique projection equipment, a series of old picture frames, Joseph Towne models which had never quite made the final cut to be transported downstairs for public viewing, for whatever reason … With its old musty chemical smell, that demonstration room was a treasure trove, and one of which I became very fond. As soon as you entered, you had the tangible sense that you were occupying the same space, touching the same things and breathing in the same air as had been inhaled 100 years before, by similar staff, working on identical tasks to those I was now performing. As a 15-year-old, this gave me a real sense of connection, not only with the Gordon Museum, but with Guy's itself.

CHAPTER 3

THE ANATOMY OF MURDER

A s my macabre surroundings grew on me, the section of the museum dedicated to forensic medicine very quickly became my favourite. I defy anyone not to gravitate towards the chilling theme of murder when they have a choice between viewing standard anatomical specimens and items that have been critical evidence in the most notorious murders in recent history. There was no comparison.

This section displayed weapons and body parts that Professor Simpson had collected during the course of his work as consultant Home Office forensic pathologist. In his personal memoir, *Forty Years of Murder*, he had written about the many cases of his long and very distinguished career. So it was a bit surreal, looking at the exhibits with which he had been personally connected and recalling the gory details of the crimes and the names and fates of their perpetrators.

One of Professor Simpson's most noteworthy cases, in which his evidence had been of vital importance, related to a serial killer of the 1940s. John George Haigh would become notorious as the 'Acid Bath Murderer' or, more dramatically, courtesy of the newspapers of the day, 'Acid

Bath Haigh'. Following a series of petty crimes in his youth, he had spent a period of time in prison, during which he had taken the opportunity to learn from other criminals how to commit murder. More specifically, how to commit the 'perfect' murder. In prison it was fairly easy to obtain acid, allowing Haigh to perform experiments on dead mice and observe the length of time it took for their small corpses to completely break down and dissolve away.

On his release from prison Haigh acquired a workshop, and it wasn't long before he began looking for victims to fleece. A very charming and attractive man, he circulated among the wealthy, carefully picking out his victims and learning to falsify their signatures in order to fraudulently claim insurance pay-outs for his own financial gain. But he had greater ambitions ...

Having secured premises to rent, Haigh procured a large metal drum and filled it with acid. On a pretext, he would arrange for his victim, usually a woman, to visit him at his premises. There, he would club them or shoot them and lower their body into his acid bath, where it would dissolve. Later, he would return to run off the liquid remnants. However, not all the contents would be reduced to a liquid. It was necessary for Haigh to discard the silt that remained at the bottom, which he disposed of by throwing it into the disused yard at the rear of the premises.

When Olivia Durand-Deacon met John Haigh, he was referring to himself as an engineer. This led to a discussion about engineering a design she had devised for making false fingernails. Once he had enticed her to his premises to 'develop this concept', Haigh shot her as soon as her back was turned. Placing her body into his acid bath overnight, ready for disposal the next day, he took the expensive fur coat she had arrived in and made immediate enquiries about selling it. This action, however, was to lead to his downfall. As Mrs Durand-Deacon's absence became apparent, one of her friends became so concerned that she implored Haigh to accompany her to the police station to report her friend missing. As he had been the last person with whom she had come into contact, the police became suspicious of him and, as a result, his premises were investigated. Unfortunately for him, the gun he had used to shoot Mrs Durand-Deacon was still where he had left it. Nor was it long before the police discovered the acid bath and Mrs Durand-Deacon's false teeth. Convinced they had a murder on their hands, they immediately arrested Haigh and put their evidence to him.

However, Haigh had become very familiar with the law and, convinced of his own safety, he taunted them, saying, 'Mrs Durand-Deacon no longer exists. I have destroyed her with acid. You can't prove a murder without a body.'

He then gave them the names of eight more victims, knowing that their bodies had also been destroyed in his acid bath. As far as he was concerned, there was no evidence with which to charge him.

As the pathologist who covered the area in which the murder had taken place, Professor Simpson was called out. Once he had viewed the workshop, he showed particular interest in the area outside it where the slurry had been poured. Bending down to inspect it, he was able to identify small pieces of bone and a hard lump of fat. When it was suggested that the lump of fat was a lucky find, he astounded everyone by claiming that he had, in fact, been looking for it. In his view, a heavily-built woman such as Mrs Durand-Deacon would undoubtedly have gallstones.

This physical evidence was added to the already incriminating evidence of Haigh's attempt to sell Mrs Durand-Deacon's fur coat, and he was convicted of murder and hanged in 1949.

Some 15 years later I was viewing the gallstones, which had made their way into Professor Simpson's forensic collection in the Gordon Museum. Today they are still present, in their glass case, from where they testify to Professor Simpson's expertise in identifying a piece of physical evidence that was crucial in the successful conviction of a serial murderer.

A few of the exhibits in the forensic section of the museum were of great historical significance. For instance, we happened to have in our possession Himmler's false teeth, which had been retained for posterity when, as a way of avoiding capture at the end of the Second World War, he had committed suicide by biting through a glass vial containing cyanide. What was distinctive about the teeth was the fact that it was still possible to identify the pieces of glass ground into them.

Some exhibits required a strong stomach, while others could just fill you with horror. One jar displayed the head of a London stockbroker who, suffering financial difficulties, had put a shotgun into his mouth and blown away the front of his face. It was as gruesome a specimen as you could imagine, but it had its uses in demonstrating the internal impact of a shotgun injury to the human head, from the perspective of a suicidal shooting.

If you could overcome your feelings of reluctance or revulsion, a range of specimens were available demonstrating various anatomical injuries as a result of murder. As you moved along the selection of cases, with their increasingly grisly exhibits, it was impossible not to be drawn to them and to read the accompanying information about their origin. Therefore, before you knew it, you were viewing some pretty nasty items, but being propelled along almost without turning a hair.

The exhibits included, for instance, the wrists of suicide victims who had cut into major arteries. One jar contained a throat which had been cut. Other specimens showed the effects of gunshot wounds beneath layers of skin. These were joined by examples of broken bones, stab wounds to skin, and skulls which had been shattered by a heavy blunt weapon such as a hammer. Almost every conceivable forensic artefact associated with death or murder was there.

In our current politically correct age, the display of such a collection might seem at the very least unnecessary, and possibly inappropriate. You have to remember that, first and foremost, the museum was designed to educate medical personnel about injury. Every exhibit deepened the knowledge of up-and-coming surgeons and of ambulance staff who might be attending at the scene of just such an injury. Together, they brought about a greater understanding of anatomical detail. For instance, who can now forget that the hardened fat of gallstones cannot be destroyed by acid?

There was one item in the collection, however, that would definitely not have passed muster today as an appropriate exhibit. Why? First, it was housed in a display cabinet fronted by thin glass, and secondly, it was quite accessible to members of the public. It was a service revolver. It had been retrieved from a murder scene by Professor Simpson and it wasn't until some years later, when the Irish Republican Army (IRA) was a threatening presence on the mainland, that anyone gave particular thought to the fact that our glass cases wouldn't be immune to a smash-and-grab raid. Joe arranged for the gun to be housed more securely elsewhere and, instead, a photograph of it to be put on display.

The museum was an enthralling place, especially for a 15-year-old, and I felt very lucky to work there. I would happily browse the specimens and catalogues during my lunch break and soon found myself remembering the specifics of each specimen and artefact. Over time I became personally responsible for pickling some of the specimens as they arrived, and this extended my knowledge base and paved the way for a more precise, and far-reaching, association with forensic injury in the future.

Away from the museum, I helped out at the Leather Bottle occasionally, doing jobs for the owner, and one day discovered an ageing set of drums in an outbuilding. I was told that if I worked for free through the summer I could have them. So, at the age of 15, I was a largely self-taught drummer and formed a rock band with my mates. If you think my nickname, Trogg, is bad, spare a thought for the rest of the band: Stig, Mogg-man and Bonehead. Al (Alan) got off lightly with Algernon. Despite this, we can't have been too bad, as in time our band, the Stonehouse Band – named appropriately after the local psychiatric hospital! – began to play the blues, and even performed at London's Round-house.

Within a couple of years I became a guide for parties of first-aiders who had booked a private tour at the museum, hoping to become more familiar with human anatomy and to learn to recognize specific features relating to all kinds of injury. As staff, we would perform this service out of business hours for a small fee – £2 in the Sixties – and tips were often given to us as well. It was an enjoyable way to spend a couple of hours after work, and I found that passing on the knowledge I had acquired was not only satisfying, but gave me an invaluable opportunity to hone the presentation skills I would later use in lecture theatres.

A few items, in particular, drew an excessive amount of interest from visitors. The penis rings were, of course, guaranteed to raise a nervous laugh. Then there were the more unsettling items: the aberrations of nature. People often had a sense of bravado that made them think they were capable of viewing anything, but that all changed when they were, over the course of an hour, exposed to gory and unusual sights. Even St John's Ambulance trainees weren't always prepared for everything they were shown. Perhaps the worst of the aberrations was the two-headed baby, which was a disturbing sight for anyone who hadn't had much exposure to medical abnormalities. Passing through the range of unusual exhibits in the lead-up to this sight gave visitors time to adjust. But occasionally they would begin to feel decidedly off-colour. On one occasion I found myself with my hands full when six people became simultaneously unwell, two of them fainting at the same time.

CHAPTER 4

BODY PARTS

One evening I was waiting in the museum for the arrival of a tour party when the phone rang and I found myself taking a call from one of Guy's surgeons, who asked if a body part could be delivered to me direct from theatre.

The part happened to be an arm, and it had a shocking and sad history behind it. During rush-hour at the nearby overhead railway station, a man had fallen onto the tracks. As he had landed, his hand had made contact with the live rail. Fortunately, he had landed on only one side of his body, the right, and this meant the live current had travelled straight up his arm, back down his leg and out safely to earth. It had therefore not crossed his heart or his brain, which would have killed him. He had been rushed to Guy's by ambulance and hastily conveyed to theatre for surgery to his injuries.

The surgeon who related the story to me was fairly graphic in his description of what had followed. The fact was, the man's arm had been 'cooked' by the electricity, and apparently in theatre the surgeon had been able to, quite literally, pull it away from the body 'like a piece of cooked chicken'.

It was a relief to later learn that, having had his life saved first by, some would say, fate, and then subsequently by the surgical team, the man went on to make a full recovery.

His arm, though, was still warmer than average body temperature when it arrived at the museum. It was also giving off a very distinctive aroma, which quickly permeated the whole area. Singed human flesh bears an uncanny resemblance to a favourite meat used in a traditional British Sunday lunch, and it was a long time before I could face roast pork again.

Body parts came to us in many ways, but I didn't expect to have to transport one across London by train. This task fell to me a couple of years into my time at the museum, when a hospital on the outskirts of London got in touch concerning a body part they thought we might have an interest in. I was sent across to collect it.

When I arrived, I didn't need to take the word of the technicians that the black plastic package contained half a leg; there was little disguising the fact. A noticeable thickening part way along its length indicated a bulging calf muscle; added to which, the foot was forming a perfect right angle at the end.

The story behind it was that the surgeon supplying it to us had found an unusual tumour on a patient's leg and, during surgery, had removed the leg just below the knee. He had given us a call because he had recognized that it might have value as a teaching aid.

Carrying the body part back to Guy's was easier said than done, because the size and shape of the package unfortunately indicated what it contained. And yet, at peak lunchtime rush-hour, I did my best to look as though I was carrying something very ordinary. Commuters in London always do their best to avoid direct eye contact and will usually scan a person or object rather than overtly staring, but still I found myself attracting more than a few inquisitive glances. Perhaps it was just as well my fellow travellers didn't know what would happen to the contents of the suspicious package when I reached my destination.

Back at the lab, the more creative aspects of our enterprise came into play. As the leg was to be retained indefinitely as one of our specimens, good preservation was essential. First, it was necessary to find a tank large enough to take an entire lower leg. Then we poured just enough 70 per cent clear methylated spirits into the tank to entirely cover the limb once it was added. Something more dramatic was now required: cardice. Cardice consists of large chunks of solid white carbon dioxide (CO_2). It is a chemical you are likely to know by its common name: dry ice. On stage it is used to create fog-like visual atmospherics for the theatre or musical acts. In a scientific capacity we used it as a freezing agent, similar to liquid nitrogen, to immediately lower the temperature of whatever object came into contact with it. Cardice was more easily available than liquid nitrogen at the time, as a solid delivered in a large tub, rather than a liquid. It was necessary to use it on the same day it was delivered, in order to prevent its temperature degrading and being lost to the atmosphere. Therefore we immediately put on gloves and goggles and, using a hammer, began to break up the huge chunks of cardice into smaller ones, which were loaded into the tank of methylated spirits. At this point the lab began to resemble a scene from a Hammer Horror film, as massive clouds of dense dry ice billowed up into the air, rolling outwards in every direction across the worktops. As they died down, we added the leg itself to the mixture, dramatically boosting the flow of rolling clouds. The leg remained in this combined concoction for some hours, while we waited for it to become rock hard.

I could see why the surgeon had thought the tumour would be a valuable resource: it was the size of my fist. It was now necessary to open it up so that its internal structure could be viewed by visitors to the museum. We used a band saw, running it straight through the centre of the entire leg to give an internal view of both lower leg and tumour.

As a 17-year-old, not only was this one of the more unusual tasks I had ever been asked to perform, but the processing of the leg had been eye-opening. The leg also proved to be a very interesting exhibit.

I began to study histology at college, as a day-release student over a five-year period, to achieve an ongoing promotional status. First, I completed a general technical course over three years, then I spent two years specializing in the histology processes I was now using at work. Initially, Joe had performed all the histology for the museum, but he had begun training us all. Histology involves the processing of a 3mm-thick square sample (approximately 1cm x 1cm), taken from a piece of human tissue or an organ, using specific chemical stains and techniques. Any pathology, i.e. disease process, shows up as a different colour when accentuated by the stain, and the cells will generally be a noticeably different shape or colour than the surrounding non-diseased tissue. Once a pathologist has viewed the processed slides under a microscope, the findings allow them to give an accurate cause of death.

When it came to my final examination after the five years of study, rather worryingly I finished early and walked out an hour ahead of everyone else. I was concerned that I had forgotten something really important, but fortunately I hadn't, and I qualified with distinction, gaining a full technical certificate. I was delighted to gravitate from junior to full technician, which coincided with my acquiring a steady girlfriend, Jackie, who had been one of the Stonehouse Band's entourage.

My spell of being the youngest and lowest-ranking member of the museum officially came to an end when there was a reshuffle and one of my colleagues transferred to another medical department. Alongside his work in the museum, he had been performing analysis on the organs of drowning victims that were brought in by Professor Simpson on a fairly regular basis. It was impossible not to know when my colleague had returned after one of these investigations, as he trailed a pungent, very unpleasant odour in his wake: human decomposition. With his departure, it fell to me to perform these investigations in my new role as histologist in the museum.

On one particular day I performed analysis on not just one, but three drowning cases simultaneously. All three were extremely badly decomposed by the time they were recovered from the Thames. The thing about decomposition is that the deeply penetrating, lingering smell knows no bounds. You don't get used to it, and the more time you spend in its presence, the more unpleasant it becomes. It sinks so deeply into your nasal passages and the pores of your skin that you can't smell anything else for the rest of the day.

Despite the fact I had worn a face mask to perform my task on this particular day, there was no escaping the awful smell, which had penetrated my hair, my skin and the fibres of my clothes. That evening, I sank into my seat in the enclosed compartment of an old-style 12-person train carriage and looked out of the window as usual while the carriage became increasingly packed with London Bridge's busy commuters. However, a few minutes later, as the whistle was about to blow, I turned my head and realized I was completely alone. I had no trouble guessing why everyone had left in such a hurry. I would have got away from the revolting smell myself, if it had been possible.

Histology rapidly developed into the foremost part of my technical working life. As I enjoyed it so much, I would set myself targets as to the number of specimens I could process within a given time-frame, which I would then aim to beat. My exposure to a wide range of disease processes naturally increased, due to the large number of tissue samples I was handling on any given day. In fact, I became so enthusiastic about my job, and had such an apparent flair for staining techniques, that I earned something of a reputation as an expert in this field within the medical school.

An unfortunate side-effect of performing so much histology was about to strike, though. We used formalin to preserve tissue every day, with no idea it was toxic. Soon I began to suffer with 'contact' industrial dermatitis – a painful condition which was also extremely debilitating, given that it caused swelling of the fingers. The creases in my knuckles would develop deep, painful splits, and any skin which made contact with the formalin would become scaly and flake away. Eventually the skin on my hands was splitting whenever I put any weight or pressure onto the objects around me.

It was not then generally known that formalin created this painful condition. Nor was there any Health & Safety advice relating to the wearing of protective rubber gloves when moving specimens, so I struggled on regardless. Until I eventually had a dedicated cutting room in the forensic department, where it was natural to don rubber gloves before embarking on the handling of specimens, my contact

A treasured photo: Champagne on Primrose Hill at sunset on the hottest night of the year. Pauline with Professor (Cedric) Keith Simpson.

dermatitis had to be regarded as an unfortunate occupational hazard.

In 1972 Professor Simpson decided to amalgamate the histology that was being carried out in the Gordon Museum with that being performed in his own department, and asked me if I would like to transfer over to the forensic department permanently, as a full scientific officer. I was excited to be asked and keen to perform the work. From this point on, my remit would expand dramatically into several areas of expertise.

It was a time of change. Jackie and I married just after I left the museum, and would go on to have two children, Ross in 1976 and Gemma in 1979.

Professor Simpson also semi-retired, having already given up his post as curator of the Gordon Museum, and Professor Keith Mant, his second-in-command, took over the reins as head of department.

CHAPTER 5

PARTIES, DRUGS
AND ALCOHOL

In 1977, at 28 years old, I was promoted to senior laboratory scientific officer. I was now responsible for the departmental accounts, including the ordering of chemicals and equipment, and took responsibility for the department in the absence of the pathologists. However, I knew that I wasn't going to become a millionaire overnight. It was always understood that any reward associated with working in the forensic department came from the work itself, not the money going into the bank. It was therefore very tempting to join other technical staff from throughout the hospital whenever the call went out for volunteers to undergo a drug trial. The £100 payment seemed good compensation for our trouble and was always useful money for a family man, so it seemed perfectly reasonable to give up the occasional weekend at home, in order to spend it voluntarily hospitalized with my workmates. If nothing else, it was a great opportunity to get to know each other better, trade banter and revel in spending time out of our white coats and in a less formal setting.

These trials preceded, by some years, the disastrous 'Elephant Man' drug trial in which the volunteers developed agonizing symptoms, ranging from critical swelling of their bodies to organ failure. One volunteer even lost parts of his fingers and toes to vascular degeneration caused by his body shutting down. Speaking for myself, and, I'm sure, for all those I volunteered with, we had absolutely no qualms about becoming human guinea pigs. We all signed up willingly enough, and obviously led charmed lives, as not one of us ever experienced even the mildest of negative reactions.

Once we were installed on the ward, there was great camaraderie between us. As the nurses checked our blood pressure and vital systems, we chatted them up. We put up with any discomfort without a second thought and bluffed our way through the occasional feeling of soreness or irritation. No doubt, if any of us had felt like complaining, they would have been at the mercy of everyone around them throughout the remainder of the drug trial, baited for being a wimp.

If the trial took place on a weekday, often we could return to work straight after the drug had been administered. It felt like easy money when our only inconvenience was to ensure we kept an eye on the time, so that we could report back for blood to be taken in the final monitoring process. Not having to take a day's leave was helpful. We didn't lose any money and we didn't have to conduct our home lives around the trials, only our normal working lives, which was relatively easy by comparison.

* * *

I have little memory of one drug trial, as it became increasingly hazy as time went on. It also happened to be the most fun to take part in. You may understand why if I confide that it involved a lot of alcohol. And I do mean *a lot*. The drug we were testing was similar to Zantac, which is a standard treatment for stomach ulcers. The purpose of the trial was to detect exactly how the drug would react, once it was in the blood circulatory system, should it be combined with alcohol. As it was inadvisable to mix this type of drug with alcohol, whether by accident or design, you can imagine that we were first warned that we might experience more than the usual sense of inebriation. Being young and up for this type of scenario, we were only too happy to take up the offer of free drinks all round!

The staff supervising the drug trial worked just along the corridor, in Pharmacology, so we knew them well. It didn't escape their notice that, instead of the usual paltry three volunteers, there were six, word having got around that Pharmacology was about to become 'party central'. We reported at 7 a.m., two hours earlier than usual, as directed, and were each poured a total of *six* vodka and oranges ... on a totally empty stomach. By 9 a.m. we were all completely plastered and congratulating ourselves heartily on the fact that we were being paid to do this. As we sat around, becoming increasingly loud and giggly, the instigators of the trial seemed to be getting as much amusement from us as we were from one another.

I have no idea how we managed to find our way back to our desks that morning, and I seriously doubt whether any of us performed any real work that day. Our only requirement, over the course of the trial, was to report back for monitoring of our blood alcohol levels. Do I remember any of these trips? Absolutely not! Fortunately, by 5 p.m. we had all sobered up enough to make our respective journeys home. Another great day at the office!

A later trial required three full days of hospitalization while we underwent testing of a blood-thinning drug. This involved a cannula being inserted into the arm and a series of injections being administered ... in the buttocks. So it was as embarrassing as it was painful, and the lack of alcohol was a bit of a downer too.

I am constantly reminded of the apparatus that was used to take our blood, as it consisted of a series of three sharp double blades. These were pressed onto the skin and sliced in one motion into the flesh, leaving a tell-tale series of two regular-striped incisions. This all sounds very scientific, but it was actually quite painful and, unhappily for us, the blades were applied as often as three times on the hour. Our blood flowed readily from the wounds, which were used to monitor the length of time it took to clot. The nurses would mop it up using filter paper, and the notches on our arms are still visible today. However, we received the excellent sum of £400 each, which seemed more than adequate compensation – a lot of money, then – for taking three days' annual leave to be repeatedly sliced into.

Another trial involved eating fish for every meal for a whole week. Fortunately, as a keen fisherman, I enjoyed fish and had no objection to being given a bag full of it to take home.

In the freezer were skate wings, chunks of cod and plaice, and prawns, which they gave us 'for snacks'. Fortunately, we were able to supplement the fish with vegetables and potatoes (even chips), as long as we completely avoided meat and poultry. Seafood was expensive at the time, and I considered it a bit of a luxury to eat like this for a whole week; plus, it saved significantly on my household bills for that week.

There was a disadvantage, though. We were required to collect all our urine during that time, which required carrying a screw-top bucket with us everywhere for the purpose. This wouldn't have been so bad, but for the overpowering stench of fish! That was a trial in itself, and I couldn't wait to replace the lid each time I added to the contents.

The drug trial itself was designed to record the levels of mercury in our urine, and also to test our blood for it. It wasn't generally known in the 1980s that fish contained significant levels of mercury and heavy metals, so our enforced seafood diet was presumably an early experiment to prove the point.

In the end, I was glad to see the back of that trial. With my 'O' blood group, I couldn't wait to return to a carnivorous diet.

One drug trial had unexpectedly funny consequences. This trial entailed swallowing radio-opaque pellets. The idea was that these pellets would be viewed during their journey through the alimentary canal (i.e. mouth to anus) via the use of X-ray, and the medical staff would check on the length of time it took for the drugs to be digested. There would be one final X-ray to ensure the pellets had all passed out of our bodies.

It might sound easier than having to submit to blades and needles. However, this trial involved the considerably less welcome prospect of having to collect all our faeces over a 24-hour period, adding to a sizeable plastic tub every time we went to the loo. It was unpleasant for everyone, as these buckets were inspected periodically, the staff X-raying our pile of faeces in order to gauge how many of the pellets had passed through. Twenty-four hours is a long time when you're collecting your own waste at work, and it doesn't get any easier when you're at home.

One of our colleagues, Tim, hadn't even reached the laboratory one morning when a dramatic complication arose. At the time, the IRA had been particularly active on the British mainland and the police were on high alert for any suspicious packages, and for persons carrying any unidentifiable luggage which might denote the presence of a bomb. They were especially vigilant in a city as important as London.

Tim had dyed his hair into bright multi-coloured stripes, which always drew the wrong kind of attention, and as he carried his white bucket, complete with a magnificently full collection of faeces, across the railway station forecourt on his way to work, he drew the attention of the police. He was immediately apprehended, and naturally the police wanted to know exactly what he was carrying in his suspicious-looking tub.

His 'far-fetched' tale of being involved in a drug trial didn't pass muster. The police gathered round.

'Come on, son. Open the lid.'

Bad idea. The police scattered in all directions, recoiling from the horrifying contents, and their stench. Unsurprisingly, there was no further objection to letting Tim continue on his way – so long as he headed in the opposite direction as soon as possible.

To return to alcohol for a moment, it wasn't only useful in trials, or for oiling the wheels in any setting, it also happened to be one of the most useful chemicals in our labs. We used it regularly during my time in the Gordon Museum to enhance the coloration of our specimens; by this, I mean adding definition to the signs of pathology (disease) in organs such as the brain, kidney or lung. Also, our tissue specimens first needed to be fixed in formalin. This had the unwanted side-effect of turning the colours darker and dulling them. For instance, blood would no longer show as red, but brown. So, after using the formalin to preserve the tissue, we would have to dip the specimen straight into alcohol in order to turn it back to its original colour, before finally mounting it and putting it into glycerine in a Perspex jar. As a consequence, we used alcohol for virtually every specimen, generally in large quantities.

After a few weeks' use, the alcohol would lose its efficacy through the continual dilution process, whereby it lost its ability to return colour to the specimens sufficiently well. We therefore used to pour the weakened alcohol out of its container and let it settle for a while, generally overnight, after which we would pour the clear liquid off the top and dispose of the murkier liquid at the bottom.

Professor Simpson caught on to this and, rather than let it go to waste, used it as antifreeze in his rather large Rover.

So, the museum ordered a fair amount of alcohol for preservation purposes, and we were required to state that it was to be used for medical purposes only. We favoured methylated alcohol, also known as methylated spirits, which was relatively cheap to buy in. The reason for its lower price was that it had been rendered effectively undrinkable by the addition of methyl alcohol, a substance which is highly toxic. The more recognizable version, generally available from hardware stores, contains a blue dye and pyridine, a chemical known for its distinctive smell and very much associated with methylated spirits. These additions were designed to make the alcohol smell repulsive, and therefore be unpalatable to all but the most desperate of drinkers. Mostly the process was to ensure that, as methylated alcohol wasn't subject to customs and excise duty, it wouldn't be sold cheaply on the black market. Not that there would be many repeat customers. Methylated alcohol is definitely not biologically compatible. It is poisonous and doesn't break down once it is inside the body in the way of normal alcohol. If you were committed enough to drinking it, you would, over time, go mad and at the same time pickle yourself on the inside.

Therefore, whenever the museum wanted any alcohol for more social purposes, we would order only the best – 100 per cent absolute ethanol. For the medical school Christmas party we would order it by the 20-litre drum. It was of vastly superior quality, on a par with neat vodka, and, being scientists, we made proper scientific dilutions of it with water, which seemed to pacify any concerns when suspicions arose as anyone entered the medical school and was hit by the alcoholic fruity aroma. The fruity smell came from the fresh lemons, limes and oranges we used to make a phenomenal knock-out punch in a very large metal surgical bowl. Every year we looked forward to brewing up in our unofficial 'alcohol workshop' (the prep room in the basement). The aroma would permeate the entire lower ground floor of the medical school and leave us all feeling very Christmassy.

Everyone enjoyed the fruits of our labours. Whether you were a governor of the hospital or the lowliest technician, for one night a year your rank and position were forgotten ... as was everything that happened that night.

You would always know a successful party by the aftermath. Highlights were the unconscious body I stepped over in the gents' toilets and the grunting and groaning overheard from one of the front benches of the lecture theatre. My train journey would be followed by a half-mile stagger up a steep hill back to my home. I have almost no memory of ever doing this.

From a scientific viewpoint, I found that alcohol could be counted on as a solution to other issues which arose. For instance, in parts of the museum the cleaners would use a final coating of polish to buff the floors, which were kept pristine to maintain a professional appearance. Over time it became a bit of a problem, though. The polish couldn't reach the edges and corners, which therefore received minimal attention and became grimy and sticky. Despite the fact that it was unlikely anyone would ever have cause to be looking down at the floor in the museum, this mattered to us. We were very proud of our working environment.

Once again, alcohol came to the rescue. We discovered that pouring a huge drum of methylated alcohol over these areas and applying a scrubbing machine could bring them up like new. What never occurred to us at the time was that if someone had lit a match there would have been a sizeable explosion.

On the other hand, I had a close call when I was over in the chemistry department one day. A technician was distilling alcohol, using an upright condenser, and I was standing directly in front of his bench, deep in conversation with another colleague. An upright condenser separates pure ethanol alcohol from water. As the liquids are heated together in a glass flask, the ethanol vapour cools first and condenses, forming a more concentrated liquid. However, the liquids have different boiling points and it can therefore be a potentially hazardous process and requires a high level of concentration, due to the flammability of the alcohol.

That day, the cooling condenser tube somehow became trapped in a drawer, making the pressure inside soar. Suddenly the apparatus took off like a Saturn V rocket! As we all instinctively dived for cover, the glass condenser hit the ceiling and shattered into thousands of fragments, showering the floor with slivers of fine glass.

As it happened, it could have been far worse. We could have been in harm's way and sustained chemical burns. A powerful explosion could have ripped through the room. There could have been a fire. As it was, we nervously laughed it off.

CHAPTER 6

INTRODUCTION TO AN EXTRAORDINARY WORKPLACE

How does a relatively naive 20-year-old woman become embroiled in the seamier side of life forensic medicine can often represent?

It was at 10 years old that I discovered my love of medicine, through spending a memorable week on the children's ward of Harold Wood Hospital, in Romford, Essex. It was even a happy week if you discount the pain leading to an appendectomy and its subsequent recovery. To me, the hospital environment had a magical quality.

I would happily have stayed on, had I been able. I didn't want the magic to end, or to forget what it had felt like to be a patient, around whom all activity centred and whose every whim was catered for. As I left, I impressed that feeling on myself. I also had a sense of premonition, of joining the ranks of hospital staff one day. My intuition told me that it wouldn't be as a doctor or a nurse, but at that point I knew of no other way of achieving it. My father was the assistant director of a large accounting firm in the City, in which my mother also worked as a comptometer operator. We had no medical connections in our family other than my older sister, who at the time had just qualified and was working as an occupational therapist.

I was 15 when my class tutor, Mrs Kidd, informed me about the role of medical secretary, which fired up my interest. This was it – my way into the hospital environment. *And* it was paid. So I embarked on the official two-year diploma at a local college.

On that course, not only did we reach great speeds in shorthand and typing, we also qualified in first aid, studied medical terminology and procedures, and were given opportunities to observe surgery (a tonsillectomy). We were also given three work-experience placements, a fortnight in each, giving us experience of three possible environments in which we might like to work, once qualified: a hospital, a polyclinic and a GP's surgery.

For me, there was no contest: the hospital placement still felt so enthralling. The London Chest Hospital, in Bethnal Green, east London, gave me the chance to observe a heart catheter being placed in a still-conscious man, and to watch as a range of tests were given to assess debilitating lung conditions. It was there that I learned that some medical secretaries sat alongside their consultants during patient clinics, witnessing patient–consultant interactions and noting the advice and treatments recommended. This was a revelation. For me, there was no substitute for witnessing first-hand how symptoms became diagnoses and remedies were suggested.

However, there was one side to clinic attendance that I hadn't reckoned on: the human agony that might attend a diagnosis. Still aged only 16, I was totally unprepared for the enormity of one particular tragedy. An elderly gentleman had attended a clinic with a relative, unaware of the seriousness of his medical condition. On being told of the need for an immediate admission for surgery, both he and his family member were so concerned for each other's inconvenience that the scene of selfless compassion, on both sides, that followed overwhelmed me. I had no idea that tears were streaming down my face until I noticed the consultant nodding meaningfully at his secretary, who was overseeing my placement at the clinic. I just knew that as soon as the clinic ended I would be sent packing, having shown insufficient professional poise. So it was a complete shock to find that their concerns were all for me and my welfare, and that they felt guilty for having been overly enthusiastic about involving me in the clinic. This was totally unexpected, and in fact their generosity helped me quickly recover and I was much better prepared for the afternoon session, which went without a hitch.

I felt privileged to have been shown such consideration. What stayed with me, though, was that the experience had offered a very valuable early appreciation of the clinic scenario. Not only did I now understand the anxiety patients might be feeling when attending a surgical clinic, but I also knew there was a possibility that events might unfold beyond their control. It was a lesson in empathy I would remember when I administrated clinics myself.

Having temporarily been 'let out' of college for my placements, I found the few remaining months interminable and it was a relief when I found my first job at the National Heart Hospital in the West End, in 1977, as junior secretary to Professor Sir Magdi Yacoub. This is a name some will associate with the late Princess of Wales, who was captured by a press photographer watching him perform heart surgery. I not only sat in on clinics, but also attended ward rounds. This patient-facing part of the role proved as fascinating as it was educational.

There was one more bonus: encouragement to witness open heart surgery itself. I took every opportunity to visit the viewing gallery, and somehow, over the course of my tea breaks, managed to view the entire process as the chest was incised, the ribs were ratcheted open and the beating heart itself was revealed – a phenomenal sight. Viewing heart surgery linked the highly complex surgical terminology with the procedures, and what could have been a routine job became infinitely more interesting.

When I moved to St Bartholomew's Hospital in the City a few months later, I found greater fulfilment in the larger teaching hospital environment, with its broader scope of specialisms and, of course, the social opportunities it offered. In time, I was asked if I were willing to offer my shorthand services to a child specialist dealing with ADHD and autism. It was an almighty stretch to fit an additional day's work into an already full workload, but I enjoyed the variety. It also had the benefit of singling me out as highly capable when a higher clerical officer position arose. I was consequently offered my own department, Diabetics, to manage. This, I thought, was the pinnacle of my career. I had reached the top level in my career progression in the NHS before I had even turned 19.

*   *   *

Just before I took on the higher role, I was spotted working in Urology by one of their consultant surgeons, Mr John Wickham, a real gentleman, highly regarded, and a leading light in renal surgery. He asked if I would consider becoming his private PA and running his Harley Street consultancy in a few months, when his current PA was due to leave to have a baby. I jumped at the chance, though it was with mixed feelings that I left Diabetics – a position (and team) I really loved. Still, the idea of progression was always a strong driver for me and I had also set out after college with the intention of working in the private sector. Glamour, a smart location, an elevated salary … I would have a long Tube journey, but I didn't mind. In fact, rail fares and lunch were perks of the job. And who wouldn't mind being asked to walk down and hand-deliver communications to patients staying at Claridge's, while doing a bit of people-watching and sight-seeing at the same time?

Number 149 Harley Street was located right at the top of the street and also incorporated Devonshire Place, to its rear, where the London Clinic conjoined it via a hidden doorway. This allowed private access to visit our surgical patients. My days now included celebrity gossip and the arrival of royalty, as all traffic stopped in the street outside. In the main, our patients hailed from the Middle East and/ or were titled or well-known household names. I had considered the society gossip of Nigel Dempster's column in the *Daily Mail* required reading for years, and the environment in which I now spent my days included many names from those pages.

My responsibilities extended to organizing the correct quantity of blood for the week's various surgical procedures, as well as the flow of patients; by any other name, cash flow. Although I already had a very driven work ethic, there was a whole other level to performance in this arena. One lovely lady, writing from her country estate on embossed coat-of-arms notepaper, taught me, in an entirely kind and understated way, that the three days of phone calls from her would continue until I managed to acquire the results of her tests, which meant pushing the person I in turn had been ringing every day for them. A mental light bulb went on as I realized that I was now in a place where, if you pushed kindly and appropriately, results would be given almost as instantly as they were expected. I should point out that at the time there was a major gulf in efficiency between private practice and the NHS, though thankfully computerization has transformed this somewhat. Everyone around me in Harley Street worked with a sense of urgency, and although it could put the pressure on at times, it was an atmosphere in which I felt very much at home.

It was while I was working in Harley Street that Professor Simpson's autobiography, *Forty Years of Murder*, came to my attention and transformed my expectations. I had never heard of a secretary routinely accompanying their boss out of the office and 'into the field' – both figuratively and literally. Professor Simpson's secretary had become as familiar a sight at the scene of death as he was, and, together, they would crouch over the body of the deceased as he dictated his findings. She later typed these up either in the forensic department or at a collapsible table in the mortuary itself.

This was an eye-opener. *This* was what I wanted. I had never been content to be purely office-based. I knew instantly that a job like this would suit me and I was fired up to find a job just like it; because I couldn't imagine anyone ever willingly giving up the role at Guy's.

The synchronicity and speed with which the pieces of my life were then rearranged was mind-blowing. Only three months later I opened the free weekly handout *Ms London*, available at all London underground and overhead stations, to discover an advertisement for a senior secretary to the professorial head of the forensic department and his team at Guy's Hospital. This wasn't a job *like* my dream job; this *was* my dream job.

Looking back, had I missed that week's advertisement for any reason, I might not only have missed the career step of a lifetime, but also meeting my future husband.

Given that it was such an unconventional job, perhaps I should have been prepared for my interview to follow a completely different format from any that had gone before. Without HR representation, the interview was with Professor Mant himself, who thrilled me with the offer of a guided tour of the department.

The opportunity to see inside the department about which I had read so much was riveting. I visited laboratories and was introduced to everyone – 'everyone' being only three permanent staff, including the senior laboratory technician, Derek, as the pathologists were on location at their various mortuaries that morning. It all looked relatively ordinary, if you excluded the occasional skull on a desk or grouping of bones in a glass case.

We finally rounded a corner and paused on the periphery of what I soon learned was the cutting room. At first glance, it appeared to be a storage space. I took in the stacks of white tubs packed tightly against one wall from floor to ceiling and guessed there were over 100 of them, diminishing in size as they rose in precarious white towers, somewhat reminiscent of the stacked plastic bricks of a child (sorry, Derek!).

Then I noticed the labels, hastily scrawled in black pen: *kidney*, *liver*, *brain*. I guessed – correctly – that the majority

Professor (Arthur) Keith Mant. Derek would work alongside four departmental heads, while Pauline would work for two.

had been there for years and might remain so far into the future.

One object had already caught my eye and I distinctly remember the overwhelming compunction that inexorably drew me back to it. I couldn't imagine its use, so I moved to walk away, thinking that we were about to resume the tour. Professor Mant, on the other hand, settled himself in the doorway, by which I gathered a second reconnaissance of the room was expected. So I studied the object in more detail. It was a tub in the deep laboratory sink, from which its top third protruded, but its contents were buried beneath a dense layer of enormous static creamy bubbles, a thick scum rising several inches over the top and disguising whatever was lurking beneath.

As I contemplated the bucket's size and the likely nature of its contents, I sensed that we had been standing in the doorway for a while now and I didn't want to take up any more of Professor Mant's time. But ... I was beginning to feel that there was a particular significance to this 'centre-piece' and knew, without doubt, that it was something I was being actively encouraged to observe. I also sensed it was not going to be a pleasant revelation when it came. So I allowed myself to begin making mental calculations and assumptions, whereupon the romanticism of being so close to my dream job began to diminish, as cold, hard logic began to take hold. After all, we *were* standing on the threshold of a medical laboratory, and we *were* surrounded by what could only be described as body parts of various sizes and descriptions ... and this *was* a pretty sizeable bucket.

'*There's a head in there.*'

It was an entirely matter-of-fact pronouncement, delivered somewhat *sotto voce* almost directly into my ear, but it was still utterly shocking to me. I must have jumped, but it made utter sense, given our surroundings. However, this revelation was immediately superseded by other concerns. *What if this a bluff? Could it be Professor Mant's idea of a joke? Is he teasing me to gauge my level of naivety?*

But there had been no amusement in his voice and, turning my head in his direction, I found him serious and resigned.

The fact that we remained static in the doorway, in a kind of limbo, gave me my answer. He couldn't have failed to have seen my reaction. Perhaps he could also hear the deafening roar of my heartbeat. Was this the point at which I should turn and run, screaming?

My thoughts were already scattering: *Seriously? Who keeps a head in a bucket and* melts the flesh off ... *with acid? What kind of* normal *person would do that? Are they keeping it as a kind of trophy? In that case, are the people in this department all psychopaths?!*

These all seemed perfectly logical explanations at that moment. They still do. But, as I was later to learn, no one working there would have been unduly bothered by the discovery of a head sitting in a bucket containing a destructive chemical. In a department of this nature, that was 'business as usual'. In this particular department, it was 'one of Derek's projects'.

CHAPTER 7

FIRST ENCOUNTERS

My first glimpse of Pauline was when I was making my way out of the medical school and spotted an attractive young woman being chatted up by our postgraduate pharmacologist/toxicologist colleague, Paul Morrison. He had noticed her looking a bit lost in the foyer and offered help with directions to our department for her interview. After that, I was briefly introduced to her when Professor Mant was showing her around.

Later, we all discussed how the candidates' interviews had gone. In fact, there were only two applicants, which seems unbelievable today. Maybe no one wanted to work in a place which dealt with the deceased. Also, the job advertisement had only been run in one magazine and hadn't gone through an agency. There was no social media to take it further than *Ms London*'s circulation. Fortunately, we had all seen Pauline's application and been impressed by her shorthand and typing speeds, and now we were impressed by Pauline herself – she was young, attractive, well spoken (even though she came from Essex!) and dressed well. We knew that we would be delighted to welcome her to the department.

* * *

Wide-awake with eager anticipation, I left the family home for the train journey from Gidea Park into Liverpool Street and the long walk over London Bridge to Guy's, and arrived an eager 50 minutes early for my first day's work.

At that time, I had no idea that the pathologists spent all morning in their respective mortuaries. The cleaner, Millie, was surprised to see me, but immediately made me welcome while we awaited the arrival of the first member of staff that day. Mike, a technician in serology (blood testing), joined us 15 minutes later, and we all got chatting over a cup of tea. Every once in a while, one or the other of them would glance optimistically at the clock and murmur, 'Derek will be here in a minute,' before continuing to amuse me with a variety of anecdotes. Mike, in particular, was a very gifted storyteller.

Obviously, I thought, they were waiting for one of the bosses to take ownership of me and to pass on some work to keep me occupied. So it was a bit of a surprise when Derek waded into the office in his motorbike gear and helmet. This wasn't the picture I had formed in my mind's eye.

But with his arrival there was a noticeable rise in energy in the room, as well as a visible relaxation on everyone's part as he sat down, having made himself a cup of instant coffee. Having only spoken at a distance previously, I now took in his appearance: quite tall, with dark eyes and dark curly hair, courtesy of a perm – which was all the rage then, even for men. After a quick slurp of his drink, he half-sat, half-reclined with practised ease into the dark plastic chair and moved effortlessly into informative and enquiring conversation. Apparently, this was why he was so important: he was at ease with strangers, kept the conversation flowing, took the onus off everyone else; he injected more levity and could be relied upon to give a boost to proceedings. That's what I noticed that first morning, in a place where I had yet to feel at home: his social ease and innate friendliness, his confident, easy banter. He was direct with an outlandish sense of humour, evident warmth and kindness, and an ability to laugh at himself.

Within half an hour of his arrival Derek had already spoken the immortal words: 'You'll find all of life here' and 'If you don't see it coming through this department, it isn't worth thinking about.' Over the next few months I would discover just how right he was.

The role of one medical secretary is now sometimes carried out by no fewer than three in some hospitals. My previous work had, though, been based on handling a heavy workload, rather than oral and visual information which might turn the stomach. It soon became apparent that my work was beginning to vary considerably from what had gone before.

As always, the number one priority was a combination of speed and accuracy. These were required in order to convey information to the pathologist when a call-out to a suspicious death was received. A time for their attendance would be agreed and conveyed back to the referring senior investigating (police) officer (SIO), then the pathologist would be out of the door and on his way to the scene as a matter of urgency.

Formerly, one of my most time-consuming responsibilities had been retrieving patients' notes from a filing repository the size of an aircraft hangar. Here, filing was one sheet per case, accessed by swivelling my chair around. Every aspect of my job was conducted in my own room, allowing me to speed my way through large numbers of reports.

Another change was the difference in contacts. These were no longer hospital staff, GPs and patients, but investigating detectives, coroner's officers and mortuary staff, as well as those from the wider Guy's community.

For now I was office-based, and was so busy integrating into the department that I temporarily forgot that I had wanted to accompany the pathologists to their crime scenes. Whether I would remain as enthusiastic about my job once I had taken on the full mantle of scene and mortuary attendance with the pathologist was, for now, still open to question.

At this stage I was, however, routinely exposed to descriptions that were impossible to forget, because I felt a strong compunction to stop typing to read the case histories of the deceased. I felt it appropriate to acknowledge the deceased person in this way. The case history was always cause for consideration, no matter the type of death.

Within days, I became aware of how relatively sheltered my life had been. In this job it didn't matter how much enthusiasm and fascination you could muster; they could only take you so far. You needed a certain amount of grit, and the ability to go beyond what you were seeing and hearing, to go deeper, to ask questions. There could be an otherworldly quality to this workplace: hushed conversations; their relationship to murder. Not to mention some seriously questionable stories from my new colleagues. It was unnerving, yes, but it was surprising how quickly it all began to feel normal.

There were also surprises in store for the other staff, who hadn't been familiar with an empty in-tray in the secretary's office at the end of the day. Derek began referring to me as 'Super Spink' because I was so fast in clearing my workload.

My first encounter with Professor Keith Simpson did not disappoint. He was, for many, an icon in the world of forensic pathology, and I was happy to discover that he lived up to the hype. He held himself in a certain way, conducted himself as a true gentleman, and had charm and charisma in spades. Added to this, his manner was entirely unassuming, while commanding the utmost respect.

I will never forget the day I first met him. He breezed into my office, spotted the newbie and, holding out his hand, politely asked my name. As we shook hands, I gave my first name, as always. However, this was clearly insufficient, as it was met with a pregnant pause, our handshake floating in mid-air while I grasped that what was required was my surname. From that moment on, I was 'Miss Spink'.

Professor Simpson had officially retired from Guy's in 1972, but returned to collect his post every day. This required some effort on his part, as he lived in Belgravia – perhaps 40 minutes away, if traffic was reasonable. If I didn't see him, I wouldn't be aware of him; such was his quiet way that he largely arrived and left unobtrusively within the space of only three minutes.

He only ever began a proper conversation if there was anything of significance to say, which added to his gravitas. When he was around, whoever you were, you knew you were in the presence of greatness.

We remained on formal terms for years, until we both attended a departmental social event to mark the departure of Australia-bound Dr Kevin Lee. This coincided with the hottest day of the year and, on a sweltering evening, we all congregated at the top of Primrose Hill. As we sipped champagne and took in the breathtaking sunset over London, Professor Simpson began chatting to me. Later, after we had all finished our first course, instructions were given that everyone should move six places to their left, whereupon dinner would recommence. This placed me directly alongside him. This was the first time we had really had any kind of in-depth personal conversation. He was incredibly attentive and, I thought, seemed very well informed about me. He expressed a real regard and extended his own thanks for the way in which I had been conducting my work in the department and the value I had brought to my role. I hadn't been aware that he had made it his business to learn of the impact I was making, though perhaps I should have been. What shocked me most was that he used my first name from the outset of our conversation and, warmly, through the remainder of the evening.

The following day, when we were once again in a place where business was conducted, he returned to the usual formalities – as though the previous evening's break with protocol had never happened.

* * *

As I settled in to the Department I became aware that Derek's popularity throughout the medical school was very apparent. His working life was punctuated by frequent visits to or from his many longstanding friends, both in the scientific community and throughout the medical school's various departments. In 1985 he was promoted again, to chief scientific officer, and it was, of course, his office to which the pathologists would return from their morning's post-mortem lists with items for further investigation.

With such a close professional relationship with the pathologists, we both spent a good deal of time in their company. Lunchtime, for us all, often meant decampment straight to the Boot & Flogger wine bar, tucked just off Borough High Street. Derek and I consequently felt very much the pathologists' *de facto* back-up team, whether at work or at play. If it sounds like a close-knit community-within-a-community, that's because it was. This inclusivity created a great connection and loyalty between the pathologists and ourselves, which was demonstrated by the many invitations for drinks, lunches and occasionally dinner. Additionally, trainees on annual sabbatical from global locations included us in their plans as soon as they saw the extent of our integration. On top of this were the social benefits of a large London teaching hospital; teaching and training naturally lending themselves to the celebration of every academic achievement.

In time, however, we were to discover that acceptance of these social invitations came with baggage, in the form of envy from those who weren't so prominent on the patholo-gists' radar, given their relatively lower level of contact with them. Our conversations were very rarely the 'shop talk' which would have disadvantaged any absent staff, but there came a time when we did feel duty-bound to contemplate lessening our involvement. It would have required bowing to the whim of detractors, though, and ultimately been counter-productive, especially as we had formed close bonds over many months (or years, in Derek's case). The fact is, these breaks from the office were a welcome respite from the subject of death or murder. They were also great levellers, as all sense of hierarchy was put aside, though rank was never really an issue among the staff, whatever position we held.

Due to its location on the south bank of the Thames, our department not only offered forensic pathology cover to the immediate area, Southwark, but to other areas, extending both north into Essex and south-west into Surrey. It also covered Oxford and spread out across the whole of the Thames Valley. Given the enormity of this area, call-outs to a suspicious death were routine occurrences. On a monthly basis there might be half a dozen of them, occasionally more. Within four years our department merged with St Thomas' Hospital, and when Dr Iain West joined us from St Thomas', replacing Professor Mant on his retirement, his areas of cover came with him, adding the whole of West-minster, including Soho, and Sussex.

When there was a pathologist call-out everyone responded at once, and the pathologist would be out of the department within minutes, heading for the scene of death to perform crucial observations and give an estimated time of death. Such call-outs could arrive at any time of the day or night. It was not uncommon to find a pathologist had spent the better part of the early hours of the morning in a location miles from home, describing anywhere between a dozen and 100 or more injuries in concise, complex detail, despite a serious lack of sleep.

My own first encounter with a dead body did not, in fact, take place at Guy's. It had occurred 18 months earlier, at Bart's Hospital. Advised by my consultant that an item needed to be collected from the pathology department – a place with which I had no familiarity – I walked across the campus until I reached the dim interior of the farthest-flung part of the hospital. As I arrived, I heard sounds of banging and clanging from the further recesses of a corridor. These were as yet unrecognizable to me, though they would become very familiar over the course of the next few years: a mechanical saw, perhaps a band saw, I thought, and a heavy implement hammering out blows. I suspected renovations were taking place somewhere. Perhaps a workman could point me in the right direction?

At the end of the corridor, one of a set of double doors was propped wide open. Knocking politely produced no response, so I started to lean forward, in full expectation of catching someone's eye. Meanwhile, the mechanical sounds continued.

The sight that greeted me will forever be etched on my memory: the lower legs of a prone, pale, lifeless male body lying on a sturdy stainless steel table. Recoiling with a physical jolt of sheer horror, I realized that this building was the mortuary. I was surprised that its door had been open.

Should I leave? But then I would still have to collect the item at some point and I was too busy to do all this again, so I determined to brazen it out and try to find someone within hailing distance.

Once more I leaned forwards and my eyes travelled along those pale legs, and along the abdomen to the chest, and up to the top of the breastbone. I felt a bit guilty for being an uninvited observer – normally mortuaries are out of bounds to all but those who have business there – and my heart was racing. I had the creeping sense I was viewing something I shouldn't be allowed to see, but I felt committed now. Gathering my courage, I stepped closer to the door in the hope of making myself visible to whoever was inside, hoping to distract whoever was operating the equipment I could hear.

Once again, my eyes took in the pale body and, this time, as they reached the head, I finally took in the full remit of what was on view ... and literally shot up into the air, my heart thudding out of my chest, while my mind kept repeating the words: *'But that person has no face!'*

It was true, in a way. Apparently the electric saw I had been hearing had removed the top of the skull to give the pathologist access to the brain. The head had been propped up by a wooden block which angled the chin forwards, and there was clearly no brain in sight. Added to which – and a far more arresting sight – the scalp had been inverted and pulled down over the face. So I was looking at a reversed flesh-coloured expanse of skin, beneath which a bulge of nose was just recognizable. The body was, indeed, faceless.

This was a gruesome enough sight, but the situation was infinitely worsened by the acute angle at which the scalp dropped away, flapping downwards from just above what I guessed to be eye level. I was therefore observing a faceless, dramatically shortened head of only half the normal proportions. It was deeply disturbing, and for several seconds I felt terrified, wondering what monstrous aberration I had uncovered. I had only recently viewed the unnerving film *Coma*, a futuristic medical thriller which had completely tuned into the anxieties of the public concerning hospitals, mortuaries and dead bodies. The horrific scene before me seemed to embody my – and the physician writer Robin Cook's – worst fears about what might be committed behind mortuary doors in a hospital setting.

The sudden upwards trajectory of my body must have finally alerted one of two morticians to the fact that they had company ... and a witness. Suddenly, a man in a white coat breathlessly presented himself, with what seemed to be a hint of smugness. Somehow I managed a coherent sentence, and he returned quickly with the item for which I had come.

It was an unnerving introduction to the world of the mortuary and I was left shaken for some while afterwards. In fact, this could so easily have marked both the beginning and the end of my association with a mortuary. But clearly fate had other plans in store.

My second visit to the mortuary took place approximately two months into my tenure at Guy's. Our newly arrived Australian pathologist, on sabbatical from Melbourne, Dr

– now Professor – Stephen Cordner, had swiftly spotted, and subsequently fostered, my thirst for more knowledge about forensic medicine. In fact, it was thanks to him that my off-site role as a travelling PA even became established. He invited me to join him in the mortuary at Guy's one day, so that he could dictate directly to me, rather than into a handheld audio-recorder. Taking shorthand directly was infinitely preferable to me, but there was no doubting my reticence to enter the mortuary after my previous experience at Bart's. However, Stephen was gently insistent, and at just before 2 p.m. that day we were making our way across the hospital complex towards the mortuary and he was chatting to me about life in general, no doubt in an effort to allay any fears about what the experience might entail this time.

It had been one thing to see a dead body in a mortuary with only a partial skull remaining; it was quite another to envisage a mortuary *full* of them. Which is what I was doing. Thoughts of escape were already going through my head as we surreptitiously entered the low, innocuous-looking building located off a busy thoroughfare. No one would have guessed its real nature, as is so often the case with a mortuary.

When I next saw Stephen, he was 'gowned up' and ready for work. Following him into the circular mortuary, which already felt a little claustrophobic, I found myself standing in the middle of a sea of dead bodies. Every available table seemed to be occupied. As I looked at them, Stephen glanced towards me and paused to kindly say, in his guttural, broad Australian accent, the immortal words: 'See, they're not going anywhere … are they?'

I had to agree. I took notes for him as he made his way around, but it wasn't an easy afternoon. I was deeply affected by the sight of a very young baby girl. Lying there peacefully, in an exquisite white satin and lace outfit, she looked for all the world as though she were only asleep. Being overwhelmingly maternal from almost the earliest moments of my own infancy, I could barely stop myself from rushing over to pick her up for a cuddle. It took several moments of serious restraint to get past this response and understand that this wouldn't make the slightest difference to her. Nothing could bring her back. On multiple levels, it was a challenging sight for a first day at the mortuary.

Word obviously filtered through to Professor Mant that I had survived the mortuary experience and he began to invite me to take notes for him at Southwark mortuary. I performed this role for weeks at a time until he retired six months later. I also attended a call-out with Dr Kevin Lee and helped Stephen out occasionally at Guy's mortuary.

Pauline always seemed very composed, whatever the circumstances, and struck me as quite sophisticated in the way she handled herself, but she could also be a little bit accident-prone at times. I didn't find out until we came to write this book about one incident which took place when Professor Mant was retiring from Guy's. Despite Pauline's embarrassment, I think it's too good a story not to include. I'll let her tell it ...

* * *

1983 ... an era well before Channel 4's *Frasier* had intro-duced Britain's heathens to real coffee, and the snobbery surrounding it in Seattle, birthplace of Starbucks. Admit-tedly, several of us would share the contraband of coffee beans we bought freshly ground. But for those not in this bespoke coffee club, departmental coffee came freeze-dried in a glass jar with a screw-top lid, and any flavour was immediately contaminated by the diabolical London tap water.

We were about to receive our first visit from the highly regarded Professor Hugh Johnson. A professor of forensic pathology, he had arranged to reconnoitre the department, in view of a possible transfer across to us from his headship at St Thomas' Hospital, to take over from Professor Mant. Our hospitals were amalgamating, and this, for us, was the beginning of the process. As it happened, Professor Johnson ultimately did not take up the headship, having very sadly died of a heart attack before the amalgamation could take place. Instead, the position fell to his second-in-command, Dr Iain West. But of course that afternoon we were not to know this, and our colleague Ian Bradbrook, who made it his business to quiz Professor Mant and pass on any nuggets of importance, had warned us that Professor Johnson was 1) a tall, imposing man who seemed unlikely to encourage any low-key, humorous behaviour; 2) known not to suffer fools gladly; 3) the owner of a very short fuse. So we were all out to make a good impression. Fortunately, we had good form in social engagement at all levels throughout the forensic arena. There were a few nerves, but what could possibly go wrong? Well ...

I happened to be wearing my favourite dress of the moment. It was a brushed-cotton tartan shirt-dress with a low-set microscopically-thin band of softly gathered rubberized elastic holding it in place on the hips. Below the elastic was perhaps no more than 15 centimetres of skirt. I remained unperturbed by this. The only disadvantage was the readjustment required every time I stood up or sat down. However, I was prepared to put up with a bit of unpredictability for the sake of fashion.

I launched into my task of making a good impression by offering a hot drink to Professor Johnson and Professor Mant, who were standing in conversation behind me, less than two feet away. The teabags were already on the countertop at the ready, but it turned out that a cup of coffee was required. I have an indelible memory of that jar of Nescafé. I can see it now: its label, content level, height and width, and its position, at the back of the top shelf of a high cupboard. At 5 feet 3 inches, *I* hadn't put it there and had to reach up for it very carefully. The extra effort put significant pressure on the delicate sliver of elastic around my hips, pinging it straight up to my waist.

Now, this shouldn't have been a problem. I *should* have pulled the elastic back down, uttered a face-saving quip and laughed off the incident. But I was 23 years old, under pressure, unfamiliar with the new visitor, acutely aware of the importance of his visit and of his supposed temper … and I panicked.

Precious seconds ticked by as I stood rooted to the spot and finally reasoned that, were I to readjust my dress now, the incident would take on infinitely more embarrassing proportions than if I just carried on as normal, and hoped that Professor Mant managed to draw Professor Johnson's attention to the library on the other side of the room.

Behind me, Professor Mant, obviously more used to my clothing choices, was actually gamely trying to carry on, but it wasn't happening. The deafening silence told its own tale. And all I could think of was that I was letting Professor Mant down. His possible humiliation was more unbearable to me than my own.

Then the realization hit me: I was wearing a thong!

My mind went blank, my cheeks burned even more furiously … Time stood still. Thankfully, my hands were still mechanically going through the motions of lining up mugs, spooning coffee or tea into them, turning on taps and loading the kettle.

That kettle seemed to take forever to boil. The wait, with my back resolutely turned against the silent professors, felt *interminable*. The minutes were filled with a jumble of arguments whizzing through my brain. If I made a readjustment now, the professors would know that I had always been aware of my clothing malfunction … and had done nothing but let them watch it: *awful to contemplate*. If I left it, and anyone else came along the corridor, they would wonder what on earth was going on: *even worse*. So I just carried on: *the only available option*.

But now another problem arose. To make a hot drink to most people's taste, milk is required. The milk was inside the door at the bottom of our small fridge, which happened to be located far beneath the laboratory bench at my side. More panicked calculations raced through my brain.

Crouching would create even more of a tug on the elastic, potentially hiking the dress up even further. If that happened, I would have *no* skirt. At the same time, if I turned even a fraction of an inch in their direction, the professors would catch sight of my face and see the red-hot glow of my cheeks. This, inexplicably, felt like the worst possible humiliation of all. Should I swoop down, even though swivelling on five-inch heels might result in ending up in an ungainly heap on the floor? Yes, I really had no other option. Before I could change my mind, I fastened my gaze on the fridge door handle, swooped down, yanked it open, making the contents rattle furiously, grabbed the milk and flung the door shut. Had I achieved all this in one swift balletic manoeuvre? No, I had bent from the waist – revealing worse than the cheeks on my face.

Drink-making mission completed, after what felt like several hours, I turned and, with more distance between us than was ideal, held out the mugs to the professors. Did I dare look up to gauge what expressions were etched into their stunned faces? Shock ... embarrassment ... bafflement ... or worse?

No way!

Both professors mumbled their thanks and headed for the door.

Heading shakily for the comfort of my desk, I now had the chance to contemplate the impression I had made on my bosses, old and new. I sat down heavily in relief ... though not, of course, before firmly tugging my errant hemline back into place.

CHAPTER 8

SUSPICIOUS DEATH

The skirt incident apparently didn't harm my professional reputation, as Dr Iain West arrived and, almost immediately, I acquired my off-site/on-site split day, which, of course, was what had originally drawn me to the role. What's more, it happened within the space of a week, which may have been due to word having already spread of my willingness to become involved in the mortuary. Perhaps Kevin had passed on the information, as he and Iain were friends. In any case, I was soon spending the majority of my time off-site with Iain, taking a taxi across from Guy's to meet him at Westminster mortuary every morning. I would then accompany him, should he receive a call-out to somewhere in the south-east, in the afternoon.

Spending the day off-site with a pathologist turned into the dream job I had thought it would be: enthralling, exciting and so professionally rewarding. What I discovered was that there was no substitute for being at the epicentre of events.

Since Iain, as the pathologist, was central to police investigations, he would be treated with great deference, and a certain amount of this very kindly extended to me. I was thrilled to be standing alongside this leading authority as he heard the details of the incident preceding death and determined the cause of death for everyone present. What's more, I was able to add something of value to this set-up. Taking shorthand dictation alongside Iain, I brought adaptation and immediacy to the working alliance. Iain had recently invested in an electronic typewriter for me and I used it at any mortuary we attended. I could now type transcripts of his dictation up into witness statements while off-site. The senior investigating police officer, and the coroner's officer, were glad to receive a freshly typed post-mortem report 'hot off the press', rather than days, or

The weight of this recently whitened
skull was surprising.

weeks, later. This was a vital document, giving them a necessary lead and freeing them up to concentrate on other important aspects of their inquiry.

I suspect Iain saw my interest in off-site attendance as a huge advantage in terms of the time it ultimately saved, but it worked both ways. I considered myself extremely lucky, as he had no interest in audio dictation, which meant all our work together was conducted in shorthand. I had never particularly enjoyed the boring, faceless detachment of audio-dictation. On a practical level, the clangs and bangs of the mortuary could obscure much of it anyway, and shorthand led to far greater accuracy and speed in transcription.

Still managing a pathology team, on catch-up days at Guy's I now received a lunchtime phone call from Westminster mortuary as Iain dictated his PM reports. He would then zoom across in his sports car from Westminster to London Bridge. In those 20 minutes or so I would drop everything else to type up his dozen or so reports. He generally didn't stay long before making his way back down to his Surrey home, but the coroner's officers at Westminster would have those reports to hand the following morning and our workload would be bang up to date.

Now that I was becoming a regular feature at Westminster mortuary on a weekday, I was able to view a huge number of post-mortems close up. The pathologists were, by now, showing me hardened arteries, blood clots in the heart and brain, tumours, fractures, deep bruising to the muscles, and so on, and this gave me a huge bank of mental images on which I would draw 20 years later, whenever I was required to graphically recreate anatomical injury as a forensic graphic artist.

The first time I attended a suspicious death investigation with Iain was a revelation, though shocking too, as I witnessed the investigation become much more involved than I had originally expected.

I had hardly sat down one morning when Iain rushed in to announce that we were leaving within five minutes as he had received a call-out in the south-east. After a two-hour drive, we were met at the gate of a property in a respectable neighbourhood and shown into the back door of the house by the senior investigating officer, who had been awaiting our arrival. It was 11 a.m., and although I don't remember seeing any curtains twitching I definitely had the sense of being watched. A large number of scenes of crime officers (SOCOs) were present, walking to and from a van outside. Their white outfits looked starkly out of place in the idyllic sun-drenched neighbourhood. In the gloomy interior of the house they were busy everywhere. This was the first time I had watched them in person; until then, like most people, I had only ever seen them in crime dramas or news bulletins. Their busy sense of purpose quickly brought home to me the reality of why we were there.

Iain was immediately taken through to another part of the house in order to make his observations regarding the scene and the body. In view of this being my first suspicious death attendance, he gave me a kindly smile and asked me to wait in the open-plan kitchen and living-room we had accessed through the rear of the property. I found a corner where I hoped I was sufficiently out of the way and began to take in my surroundings.

What struck me first was the obvious disarray: a kitchen sink and countertop piled with unwashed dishes, a lounge cluttered with toys. It dawned on me that normal family life had been unfolding in this space only a few hours before. Judging by the toys, it had involved small children. But it had come to an abrupt end.

Becoming aware of Iain's voice in the hallway, I found my thoughts turning to what might be going on elsewhere in the house. I looked out into the hall and was surprised to see a body lying near the bottom of the stairs. It was that of a woman in approximately her late twenties or early thirties. She was lying face-down, her face darkly congested. Something about her position seemed slightly off-kilter. She was unnaturally arched away from the stairs, her right arm flexed backwards, not making contact with any of the surfaces surrounding her. I would have expected outstretched arms if she had tried to interrupt her descent. Certainly her body position didn't look natural.

The senior investigating officer had initially informed Iain about an apparent altercation between the woman and her husband which had taken place the previous evening at the top of the stairs. At some point she had apparently lost her balance, fallen down the stairs and possibly hit her head, as her husband had been unable to wake her.

A post-mortem examination was set for 2 p.m. in the local mortuary and we headed off for a bite to eat before returning at the agreed time. I settled into a chair which had been placed for me a couple of yards from the mortuary table and prepared to take Iain's dictation. He was just within audible distance as half a dozen senior detectives closed in around him, almost blocking him from view. I remember a feeling of particular anticipation. By now I had typed several thousand PM reports and been present at a great many post-mortem examinations. However, this was the first time I had witnessed a post-mortem in suspicious circumstances yet to be verified. I didn't know what to expect, but the death would undoubtedly fall into one of two categories: an accident or suspected homicide.

I was acutely aware of the rigor mortis in the body, which was, at first, lying face down, exactly as it had been discovered, the upper back arched upwards to the right and not making contact with the table. This was recorded in the external findings and the body was then turned over. The acute angle of the flexed right elbow was now so prominent that I could see that it was pulled almost protectively inwards, across the woman's chest, with the right palm open, in very close proximity to her face. It looked as if she was in a position of supplication, or trying to ward off blows. Both arms now blocked access to the front of her body and gave Iain no possibility of examining her face, neck or chest for any signs of external injury, old or new.

What happened next surprised me as, with a resigned smile to all those around him, Iain suddenly raised his own arms high into the air and pushed with all his strength down onto the body, prising the woman's arms apart. This brought forth a series of loud cracks as the rigidity of the limbs gave way. The sight was unnerving, as was the sound, echoing in the quiet mortuary. It was the first time I had ever encountered a situation where rigor had to be broken.

As the arms flopped to the sides of the body, there was a collective gasp as we saw what they had been hiding: a conspicuous row of large oval-shaped bruises at the lower end of the woman's neck. Rather like a macabre necklace, these large marks curved around to encircle the entire front of her neck – four distinct blue-grey fingerprint-shaped marks. An apparent large thumbprint also became visible, as Iain turned the body slightly, to note all the marks on the neck. In that single moment we all knew how the woman had died, and how compromising this evidence was for the last person to have seen her alive. As Iain went on to perform dissection of the neck, the very distinctive external marks of manual strangulation were confirmed, and internal examination revealed deep bruising of the neck structures and fracture of the hyoid bone – a classic sign of manual strangulation.

I was thunderstruck to learn that this case did not have quite the open-and-shut conclusion everyone present would have expected. It was dropped due to a technicality and the husband was released.

As someone new to murder scenes, I had found the day a very involving though emotionally draining experience. At the same time, there had been something strangely compelling about witnessing the events that transpired. Learning the cause of death at the same time as the pathologist was a uniquely educational experience, though the awful tragedy of the case lingered in my mind long afterwards.

There was an otherworldly feeling to being present in ordinary, homely surroundings marred by a sudden act of violence – actually being present in the home of the deceased while their body still occupied a part of that home, the site where their life had ended. The atmosphere of the house had been forever changed. The home would henceforward be remembered by the family, police and community for tragic reasons. However, without a doubt, my last and most overwhelming impression on arriving home, 12 hours after arriving at the scene, was of the young children who had lost their mother. It must surely have been in violent and terrifying circumstances. I couldn't bear to think about the fact that they might not only have overheard an argument, probably not for the first time, but also been witnesses to it. That very morning they had been carried down the stairs, directly past their mother's body, by local police officers whose job it was to remove them as quickly and compassionately as possible from the crime scene their home had so suddenly become. One moment of violence had shattered the comfort, the routine, the normality of these young children's lives and denied their mother her very right to life.

I would never forget the circumstances of my introduction to the crime scene … and to the fundamental remit of the pathologist.

CHAPTER 9

TALES OF THE UNEXPECTED

In my early days in the department my gradual adjustment centred on the strangeness of this new environment. As time went by, I got used to expecting the unexpected.

One unmistakable sound would float regularly along the corridor, garnering a few laughs, or jibes, from any technical staff or pathologists who happened to be passing. When I first became aware of it, I reasoned that perhaps it was the result of something particularly unpleasant taking place. What I would never have guessed was that it not only came from the *lair* of the senior scientific officer, but that it *was* the senior scientific officer – Derek – making it. Yes, the very man who spent so much time up to his elbows in horrible gunk was regularly retching.

It turned out that gagging was never Derek's response to a repellent sight, but a hair-trigger response to nauseating smells. Items originating from drowning cases in particular were never going to be fresh, and if the body had spent any time in the Thames, or body of water elsewhere, even opening the lid of the tub was enough to set Derek off.

So retching was a fairly common occurrence. However, there was a sound which indicated something arguably far worse was taking place in Derek's lab: whistling. Whistling I initially believed to indicate absorption in an enjoyable task; but before very long I realized that as a rule *any* sounds coming from Derek's cutting room signalled unpleasant things best avoided. In short: gagging meant a stench; whistling meant a horror scene. We all learned to avoid Derek's vicinity when he was whistling so that our own gag reflex didn't kick in.

In fact, I never really got close to the smells, as Derek would frantically wave us all away. But it was the sights that usually proved infinitely worse, as there was no real way to avoid them if you walked quickly into the cutting room. In my earliest weeks at Guy's, I had no awareness of the number of unpleasant tasks relevant to Derek's line of scientific

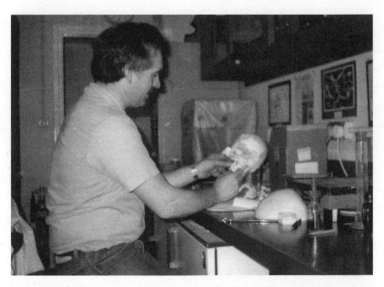

A typical day for Derek, seen here reconstructing a skull so that injuries can be documented for trial.

medical expertise. They did, however, constitute a routine part of his job, so when work-related issues required a visit to the cutting room I stood on the periphery. Even then, I had to become quite adept at averting my eyes, training them beyond or above whatever object was the focus of Derek's attention. Otherwise, I was definitely in for a shock.

The focal point in the cutting room would often be a white bucket and involve a large knife and the chopping board. This was, after all, the workspace of the person responsible for organs, body parts, dissection and reconstruction; in other words, blood and guts. The removal of flesh from bone, for example, was a process which formed a routine part of Derek's workload. It gave the pathologist a much clearer indication of any bony injury, and the cleaned item might be retained as an exhibit if there were an impending trial. The head in the bucket at my interview had been undergoing this process. As it turned out, though, my assumption that it was 'acid' being used as a defleshing agent was slightly wrong. This head had been submerged in hydrogen peroxide, a form of bleach. A bleaching agent, he told me, would not only dissolve the flesh, but render the bone simultaneously whiter. This was preferable for retention purposes.

When I next encountered an appalling sight, I was intent on conveying an urgent message to Derek and didn't at first pay particular attention to what he was doing. However, as I was about to leave I became distracted by movement. Derek was up to his elbows in what appeared to be several layers of the thick, clear plastic of a bag. However, the movement had come from *inside* the bag. Given that this was likely to contain a part of human anatomy, I was rooted to the spot.

'What the heck is that?!' I spluttered.

The object inside the bag was very large and appeared extremely heavy and unwieldy. I peered closer, and spotted blood of a deep red hue running freely between the folds of plastic. Blood was also heavily smeared across the object itself.

Without batting an eyelid, Derek said, 'It's a head.'

'Yeah, right, that's funny,' I said. So that was today's prank. A disembodied head … still moving! An excellent joke, except there was no way I was buying it.

'No, really. Look!'

I looked, but the blood was the only thing I could take in. It seemed to obscure every detail.

'Wait, I'll show you.'

With that, Derek slowly and carefully unwrapped the object.

I wished I hadn't asked. I now found myself looking at a very bloody and fleshy human head … absolutely crawling with maggots! I took a hasty step back towards the relative safety of the doorway – in case I needed to run.

'Oh no! How can you *stand* having to deal with all those maggots?'

Derek was unruffled. 'I put them in there myself.'

'*Why?*'

'Look …' Derek held the head out for my inspection.

I had never been this close to maggots before, but despite my revulsion I could now actually view what was happening. While Derek was struggling to hold the head aloft, I was becoming increasingly fascinated by the squirming hive of activity. I was almost disappointed when he had to lower it back down to rest its weight on the sink.

The hordes of fattened maggots were wriggling their way across the head and in and out of the eye sockets, nasal passages, mouth and ears. It was absorbing to watch, but I had to ask myself whether it really constituted science. Plus, I realized with a jolt, I had almost been distracted from the fact that I was looking at a decapitated and bloody human head! But even this was of no consequence now that I had become intrigued by the speed at which the maggots were chomping through the flesh, which disappeared even as I watched.

It turned out that things were set to continue in this way until all the flesh had been eaten away. When I had arrived, Derek had been in one of his checking phases, seeing how things were coming along. He now explained that the constant movement and activity of the maggots produced a level of heat which speeded up the process of flesh removal in an enclosed space such as the bag provided. Apparently, so long as the maggots were kept in warm conditions, the flesh removal would take approximately two to three days. I also discovered that maggots were considered an extremely efficient – and thorough – way of achieving this. The most shocking part of all this was the fact that Derek thought it was a perfectly normal way to spend an afternoon!

* * *

Derek's take on this is far simpler:

Of course it *was* a perfectly normal – for me, at least – way to spend an afternoon. I was often asked to reconstruct a skull if there had been an impact to it from a heavy implement and I quite enjoyed the opportunity of working with maggots. It was fascinating to watch these small creatures as they worked their way through flesh and cleared away all the tissue, so that other forensic work – such as my reconstructing the area of injury to the skull – could be performed on the bone beneath.

I had been using this process all my working life, having first been introduced to it at the Gordon Museum. Being a keen fisherman, I wasn't averse to squirming maggots. Depending on their age when I acquired them, some of them might turn into a chrysalis before their few days' work was up. But it wasn't a bad life for a fishing maggot-turned-forensic-assistant. After becoming the unexpected recipient of a hearty feast – rather than the object of one – they would be released safely into the wild, onto whichever piece of waste land was the most convenient stop on my journey home.

From my secretarial perspective, though, in no time at all, so many bizarre things began to make sense to me and the forensic department began to feel like a 'normal' working environment. This happened very much more quickly than you might anticipate. To explain further, when we arrived at work we were immediately cocooned in a world which was so far removed from the ordinary and mundane that actually leaving the department, for any reason, began to feel like stepping outside our comfort zone, rather than the other way around. At times, the shock to the system was emerging into the commuter frenzy and London life, rather than the nature of the forensic work itself.

We were always conscious of our fellow commuters, and how appalled they would be, were they to learn that we had spent our day in a mortuary. In Derek's case, who would even believe that the person next to them on the train had just been using maggots, or chemicals, to remove human flesh?

I loved my job, but once I left the office in the evenings I didn't delve back into the details of my average work day. It was apparent that they would be outside the realm of comfort for most. Certainly, there was no way my family could have aligned my work experience with their own accounting environment. They showed an appropriate amount of interest in my job, but the finer points of it would naturally have been uncomfortable for them, especially so close to dinner. Conversation about what I had been exposed to would have required careful preparation, and often I had minimal energy left to give.

Also, more than once I returned home with a head full of images it was desirable – if not important – to forget. Some of my worst days involved being shown photographs of scenes of suicide or murder. I was never prepared for this; the images played on my mind and I can even recall them now, all these years later. Our department certainly had the capacity to generate horror. I had no desire to inflict this on my family. Added to which, the subject could be broad and complex, as well as depressing.

My friends, younger and less shockable, therefore became my sounding board. To their credit, they took everything they were party to completely in their stride, never doubting the veracity of what they were hearing, even though the occasional grisly tale would have made lesser mortals' hair stand on end.

Everyone in the department not only shared a keen interest in forensic matters, but also had a good working knowledge of the medicine and science behind them. There was a pleasing openness to information-sharing, and if the pathologists were deep in discussion over a case history, the rest of us always felt welcome to remain in the vicinity to learn from their experience. In fact, I was incredibly lucky, as much of the discussion took place in my office, as the central meeting point. There was no barrier to asking questions, and explanations were freely given, and often culminated in the demonstration of a particular point. Thus Christine, our junior toxicologist, showed me how she used gas chromatography to determine levels of drugs and alcohol in the blood; Mike explained paternity-testing procedures while he dispensed blood into a series of test tubes; and Derek allowed me to have a go at using a microtome blade to cut a few slides of human tissue from a wax block into which they had been mounted, ready for histology. Our culture was open-minded and inclusive about teaching others, far more so than any workplace I have been in since.

A wide variety of information was passed on to us by the enthused pathologists. We were, after all, an audience of eager listeners, ready to hear tales of that morning's experiences. As new – and, often, disturbing – facts were passed on, we would gain a new understanding of the world of forensic medicine. This quickly became our barometer of what passed for normal at work. In our world, a grisly tale could be replaced by something infinitely worse from one day to the next. In this way we acquired our own departmental folklore. And so it was that, over the weeks, months and years, what I heard gradually became more disturbing, though I actually became less disturbed by it and took it, largely, in my ever-widening stride. However, a few stories definitely took on the mantle of weirdness – they were the real tales of the unexpected.

There is a recognized phenomenon in forensic circles called 'Silly Season'. The term arose in response to a noticeable increase in murders and suicide brought on by certain weather patterns.

It might be natural to assume that these related to the colder months of the year. The prolonged darkness of winter, coupled with a cold climate, can lead to feelings of physical isolation and depression. Then there is the recognized impact of seasonal affective disorder, caused by the lack of sunshine, and the health risks associated with reduced vitamin D. For some, what might be the unwelcome arrival of Christmas can be a trigger, or the reminder of an impending New Year, which there is no joy in celebrating.

You might be surprised to know that, despite all the above, 'Silly Season' is actually defined by a sudden and extreme rise in heat and humidity: it takes place in summer.

* * *

Weirdness could, of course, arise at any time of year, often in Derek's cutting room. For the most part, I was pleased that I had so little reason to call in to it. Added to which, the outer laboratory was a dark, forbidding room containing dark, forbidding objects, many of which were connected with dark thoughts. And I was never particularly keen to be too close to anything anatomical, largely because of the aroma. Even the freshest of human organs had an unmistakable odour, which was a little unnerving at first.

On one particular day, a tall, round, dark blue drum appeared close to the doorway of the cutting room. Petite myself, I found it was almost chest height, with a circumference of around 18 inches. At first, the fact that it was slightly in my way was my only observation. I didn't think it was particularly out of place; it even managed to blend into the background. Looking back, how I didn't ask questions about such an unusually *large* tub outside the cutting room, of all places, I do not know. But it didn't seem to merit any discussion at the time.

Later that week I had reason to walk past it again. This time I noticed that its lid was now missing. In fact, there was also something sticking up out of the centre of the drum, pointing upwards into the air. Naturally, I couldn't help but take a closer look. I'm not sure what I expected, but the first thing I saw was a floating cloud of large yellow bubbles forming a thick, floating scum. I recognized this sight from the head in the bucket ... and, believe me, it looked even more revolting close up.

Worse was to follow. Emerging from the froth was ... a human foot. It might have been less disconcerting had it not been for the row of shrivelled, white, uneven, bony and deformed toes, culminating in long, overgrown yellow toenails, rising in a pyramid-like point out of the hydrogen peroxide.

Utterly repulsed, but nevertheless intrigued, I braced myself, stuck my head round the door of the cutting room and asked, 'Derek, why is there a foot sticking out of the top of that drum? Is there something beneath it?'

'Oh, that,' he said, casually. 'There's a body in there.'

'There can't be,' I gasped. 'There's no room.'

'Yes, there is. I've cut it up. It's headless, anyway. You must have already seen the head. It was in the sink, in a bucket, when you had your interview.'

Aha! But I was still thunderstruck.

'*Really?* Why is it headless, and why did you cut it up?'

'It was easier to put the head – which was decomposing and partially mummified – into a separate container. I'm rendering the whole body down to bone.'

I was still mystified. 'So where have all those bubbles come from?'

'That's the effect of hydrogen peroxide meeting human flesh, or anything organic. It creates large bubbles of scum.'

'That's *disgusting*!'

At least it didn't smell. I was grateful for that. Basically, the hydrogen peroxide was bleaching the contents of the drum and neutralizing any smell there might otherwise have been.

Up to that point I hadn't thought dismemberment was one of Derek's tasks. However, I learned that that particular body had been found in a partly skeletonized state.

Derek described some parts of it as 'gooey' (what an image) and some of the major bones as 'in a disarticulated condition'. In other words, the body had fallen apart as it had deteriorated over a period of time. Our Australian pathologist, Stephen, had brought the remains into the forensic department and handed them over to Derek, to break them all down further and remove all the flesh and other substances, while simultaneously whitening the bones.

I also learned that the owner of the head and body had been an unidentified, homeless, elderly man. His body had been discovered in the lower, disused part of a stairwell in a multi-storey car park and conveyed to the mortuary. His identity remained unknown, and the authorities, unable to trace any relatives, were set to have the body buried in an unmarked grave, until Stephen reasoned that it could be given purpose and value if used for education. The situation might be handled differently today; at that time, what Stephen had in mind was a skeletal teaching aid for the medical students at Guy's.

I remember that the tub remained by the cutting room for around six weeks, the extruding foot reminding us all of its unusual contents every time we passed. Eventually, it occurred to me that it had quietly disappeared. The medical school had obviously acquired its new teaching aid.

There were no groundbreaking outcomes to the following stories, but they do illustrate the mindset I was fast acquiring. If no pathologist was present when an enquiry came my way, I felt it obligatory to keep an open mind, as I never knew what might turn out to be important.

A woman I would have guessed to be in her mid-thirties arrived unexpectedly in my office one morning. She was attractive, slim and athletic in appearance, well spoken, smartly dressed. I did sense an air of melancholy about her, but she sat confidently on the edge of the chair opposite me and began to ask me questions about the nature of the work conducted in the department. She had a particular interest in the types of investigation we could perform. It transpired that she was looking for a pathologist in the hope of initiating a series of tests on herself – toxicology tests. More specifically, she wanted to be checked for signs of poisoning. Eventually, she named the person she suspected of poisoning her: her husband.

I was shocked. I knew of many tales of Victorian poisoners, as many of the pathologists of that era had worked on a few of these not uncommon cases. Poisoning had earned a reputation as 'a woman's crime', given the relative ease with which women could obtain arsenic, which was freely available from the pharmacist in the form of rat poison. In Victorian society the woman was central to the home, taking responsibility for buying food, cooking the family meals and preparing drinks. So it was relatively easy for a seemingly devoted wife and mother to slip poison into a drink or meal undetected. Arsenic had little detectable aroma or identifiable flavour; besides which, many of the symptoms it engendered in its victim were similar to those of the major diseases of the time, including cholera and typhoid. Initially, swallowing became difficult; then there would be an inability to retain water, let alone food. Diarrhoea and vomiting were accompanied by severe abdominal pain. If the poison continued to be administered, the victim would sweat profusely, demonstrate mental confusion and suffer from severe convulsions, before lapsing into a coma and ultimately dying. But this was the mid-1980s. Poison *was* still relevant; I was aware of its use, even then, in Soviet-linked defections. However, this was a woman from the Home Counties, and her allegation was of a domestic nature.

Still, I felt obliged to give her the benefit of the doubt, and was keen to put her in touch with someone who could give her immediate help. If she managed to speak to a pathologist, I imagined she would find herself redirected immediately to A&E, or even the toxicology department adjoining our own. If she was right in what she was saying, her life could depend on it.

There was an immediate problem, though: it was mid-morning and no pathologists were available. So I asked if she had notified the police of her concerns. She told me she had, though they had expressed very little interest in them. This was a surprise. She was equally adamant that my next suggestion – visiting A&E – would be of no value to her. She knew it was a pathologist she wanted to see. She felt sure only a pathologist would be able to help her.

From my work with Harley Street clients I knew resolve when I saw it. And this woman was clearly lucid, intelligent and very eloquent. In fact, she seemed a little embarrassed about the circumstances that had brought her to the department. We talked a bit more about her situation and she admitted that her primary concern was to know that she wasn't imagining this. She was also desperate to avoid disclosing personal information to anyone in authority, in case it tipped off her husband, of whom she was clearly afraid. It was evident she believed her life was at serious risk.

Frustratingly, I could only advise her to come back later that day, preferably at lunchtime, when a pathologist would have arrived and would be available to take things further. She hurried away, head bowed.

I later recounted the details to our senior pathologist, who told me to alert him as soon as she came back.

I fully expected her to come back at lunchtime that day, but as the afternoon wore on she didn't make another appearance. I was concerned, but she had refused to leave contact details, so there was no way to communicate with her.

The next morning, she returned. But at exactly the same time – 10.30 a.m. This was, in one way, a relief: it proved she was still alive. But I was also exasperated by the fact that the circumstances hadn't changed: we were still two hours away from seeing a pathologist. That day I sensed more agitation on her part, which I put down to paranoia. I knew how I would feel if I were convinced someone close was trying to poison me. Her appearance had become somewhat more dishevelled and I noted her hair looked unwashed and unbrushed. She was wearing exactly the same outfit, and in fact her clothing was crumpled. Perhaps she hadn't returned home, but had slept somewhere in her day clothes overnight. She didn't seem to have used a deodorant that morning either.

As before, I had to ask her to come back later, and for the remainder of the day I watched and waited, willing her to return. It was a little confusing, then, when she did reappear … the next day. The good news was that she arrived at lunchtime, coinciding with the arrival of our senior pathologist. At the same time, her appearance was more alarming. In fact, it had deteriorated significantly. Her hair was practically dripping with grease, her skin sallow, greasy and clearly unwashed. Her increasing level of personal neglect seemed out of character for the smart person I had met only two days earlier. Her clothes were now excessively wrinkled and she trailed a strong smell of body odour. I took all this to be further indication that her claims carried weight. Perhaps our pathologist would immediately refer her to our toxicologist for a sample of her hair, or a swab from the surface of her skin. Maybe this was why she wasn't bathing – so that any samples would provide more reliable evidence.

Once she had disappeared into the pathologist's office I waited on tenterhooks. Expecting a sudden flurry of activity, I was perplexed when I heard the door to his office open and then, after a few minutes, he breezed back into my office alone. When I asked where the woman was, he told me that she had left quietly, walking in the direction of the toxicology department.

'Ah,' I said, 'so is she having some form of test?'

His answer was as unexpected as it was short. 'No. I've told her to go and see her doctor. I think she's got some sort of mental health issue.'

Of all the ways this scenario could possibly have played out, this wasn't the result I was expecting; certainly not in a forensic department.

The woman never returned and I never found out what happened to her. It is my sincere hope that she was able to get the help she needed.

* * *

One of the more unexpected associations within our department concerned one of the most secret branches of the British forces. You may well ask what possible connection a forensic department could have with the SAS. We certainly asked ourselves the same question more than once.

As it happened, one of our pathologists had connections in high places. We were blissfully unaware of this until he arrived at work one day accompanied by a man we were led to believe was an officer from the SAS. Day after day, we saw him with the same person in attendance. This continued over the course of approximately 18 months, though the head count would vary from time to time. At one stage the pathologist introduced me to seven men with, it seemed, a certain relish. The visitors were in plain clothes and their appearance was neither overly smart nor especially casual. There seemed to be a preference for darker colours, but otherwise there was nothing distinctive about what they wore. By extension, it is fair to say that they made no specific impression on me, as an observer; as was, no doubt, the intention.

However, although these men blended effortlessly into our department, in truth we were unaware of their actual purpose in being there. We would find ourselves contemplating the situation and wondering whether the pathologist was in mortal danger and required specially trained bodyguards. This was perhaps a rather more dramatic conclusion than the situation merited. What was certain was that, whoever happened to be with him on any particular day, they clearly had a free pass to be there. Where had they come from? While some, we knew, had travelled direct from their Herefordshire base, the generally early starts and constant accessibility implied a closer location, such as Chelsea Barracks. It still seemed an unusual lifestyle choice for the SAS to follow a pathologist around at work every day, though clearly it had its benefits. Once any pressing work was complete, all headed straight to the pub.

By extension, I found myself performing my role as PA alongside them as though nothing was out of the ordinary. If I stopped to think about it, taking dictation alongside SAS officers was all very surreal, although it worked if you thought about it in terms of anything being possible in our department. Added to which, it became the norm. We no longer questioned it. The fact that the visits had been sanctioned by the pathologist was sufficient authorization. We reasoned that perhaps the SAS were learning about wounding processes in the mortuary. However, whatever the reasons for their continual presence, we were witnessing what we perceived to be an emerging 'Boys' Club'.

One morning, two very senior officers arrived from Hereford, one of whom asked to have a quiet word with me. This was disconcerting. What on earth could they want? Had I done something offensive?

We sat down opposite each other and I prepared myself for the worst. The officer began to speak.

'We would like to welcome you, as Dr West's PA, to our base at Hereford for the weekend. Dr West has been invited to speak to us in a couple of weeks' time, and we would very much like it if you could accompany him.'

Wow! This was a turn-up for the books! I had a similar

reaction to Jane Austen's fictional Lydia Bennett, expressing her wide-eyed admiration for 'a whole *campful* of soldiers!'

However, I had already booked a holiday which clashed.

'I'm so sorry,' I intoned, absolutely gutted that I couldn't accept this tempting invitation. 'I have holiday plans which I can't change.'

We looked at each other for a few long seconds, and I could almost see his thoughts in an air bubble above his head: *Really? You really want to pass up this opportunity of a lifetime? Some people would kill for this. Are you sure you know what you're doing?*

I was teetering on the brink, but my own thought bubble was becoming more resolute: *I can't let my friends down. We're away for a whole week. I can't cancel because of a week-end engagement I've just been offered.*

As it turned out, fate did, in fact, have other plans. On call that weekend, the pathologist was forced to cancel the trip because of a call-out to a suspicious death. And so it was that I was saved from kicking myself for the rest of my life!

It must have been the SAS presence that gave Dr Iain West the idea. Over a departmental lunch in a pub garden one day, he announced: 'I've had an idea for a team-building exercise.'

This was met with wonderment, as the words 'team-building exercise' had never been heard before in the department.

'I've decided that we should do an activity in which we all take part.'

We waited expectantly.

'We're going to do a sky-dive!'

Our initial excitement came to an abrupt end.

'Come on, what's the problem?'

He'd been watching for a reaction, and he certainly got one. I, for one, had turned extremely pale, underneath the table my legs had turned to jelly, and I was having visions of my *life* coming to an abrupt end, as I plummeted to earth wrapped up in a broken parachute!

'Don't worry about it,' he said. 'The SAS will be training us, and they'll be giving their time for free.'

Nope. I was still not on board with the idea. Worse, it was starting to sound like a done deal!

'We're going up … in a plane … to 1,500 feet … and when it's your turn to jump, you *will* jump … or you will be *pushed* …'

He was watching me intently, with glee, by that point. I was visibly shaking, the blood pounding through my ears was now deafening, and I knew that if my colon responded as it was now when I was up in the air, there was no way I'd last the distance! The worst of it was, Iain's decisions were always final, at least as far as he was concerned. And he was head of department. How on earth was I going to get out of this?

Thankfully, though Iain seemed to enjoy our squirming, none of us wanted to do it, and someone somewhere along the line managed to shelve the idea. Perhaps the SAS weren't going to give up their time if we weren't entirely on board.

When I found out, to say I was relieved would have been the understatement of the year.

* * *

Approximately 18 months after the SAS had integrated themselves seamlessly into our department, another unexpected situation arose.

Given the regularity with which we were entertaining this branch of the military, I wasn't particularly surprised when a man in his mid to late thirties called in to my office, claiming to be SAS. He asked for the pathologist connected to the SAS by name and I rang across to the mortuary to notify him of his visitor. He was busy, so he asked me to keep the man entertained for a couple of hours until he was free.

So the man settled down to wait. He made an impression on me from the outset, though not the one he might have been hoping for. I wasn't sure if his forceful and dynamic bearing signalled super-confidence or a sense of entitlement; I instinctively felt it was the latter. What made the biggest impression, however, was his watchful intensity. As in literal in-your-face scrutiny. I expected the SAS to be observant, but this was an unnerving and unrelenting gaze.

While he talked, I contemplated how very differently he came across from every other member of the SAS I had encountered. They had had a casual, laid-back air; in fact, personal ease seemed to be a default setting. This man was clearly very intense. The other soldiers had always treated me with unfailing politeness and professionalism, even though there was a certain amount of aloofness too. There was nothing aloof about this visitor, and immediately taking over my office indicated a certain lack of manners, I felt.

Over the preceding years, not one of the SAS had voluntarily parted with even the slightest personal detail about himself. Twenty minutes into this man's visit he had already divulged details to me which, I felt certain, must have broken the code of secrecy I expected him to be under oath to maintain.

Perhaps he sensed my interest was waning. While maintaining the extreme level of eye contact, he stood up and began to pace slowly around my room, demanding all my attention. At the same time, I felt him becoming agitated. He couldn't sit still; up on his feet one minute, he was stalking around my office the next, then sitting directly opposite me again and leaning across to talk at me in conspiratorial tones, while rolling up the sleeves of his cut-off T-shirt so that I could appreciate his super-sized muscle-bound arms and shoulders.

After around 45 minutes my congeniality was spent, but he became even more animated, launching into an account of travelling the world on top-secret missions. Then all of a sudden he changed tack. Sitting forwards once more, he talked of not receiving the support he should have received from the SAS hierarchy when he was out in the field. His anger increased as he gave me the specifics of how badly he had been treated. Then, just as quickly, he put down his drink and, leaning towards me again, maintained unbroken eye contact as he gave me a non-stop, blow-by-blow account of how he had been captured and tortured.

If he was hoping for a reaction, he was disappointed. I was actually surprised not to feel more moved by his story, though working in a forensic department prepares you, to a certain extent, for horrific detail. Added to which, although it may be a little unfair, my thinking at the time was that if you wanted to impress someone, surely you would be more successful if you recounted how you managed to *evade* capture. Furthermore, I was beginning to doubt his stories, wondering if they were just ways of getting attention.

Maybe it was my indifference that finally made him move on. I certainly had no energy left to give. He managed to find an audience elsewhere, in Derek, then Christine. This inadvertently gave us the opportunity of later comparing notes. We found he had told us all identical stories – same details, same events, in the same order. I wondered if perhaps I had been too judgmental, after all; possibly he had been 'on autopilot' as he recalled the details and this had been responsible for the fact that I had been so unmoved. On the other hand, we collectively agreed that his openness was a direct departure from the level of secrecy we expected from the SAS, and had hitherto experienced.

Within a couple of hours he was back, as was the pathologist. Their meeting seemed to go well. I could hear loud conversation, punctuated by bursts of laughter, as I opened the door to deliver hot drinks to them. In fact, they seemed to be getting on famously. Surely, then, I had been too harsh in my own assessment; maybe we all had.

Later that evening the pathologist passed on to his high-level contacts the details of the man's visit, including the name he had given, and they could find no evidence of his existence in the SAS. As a matter of fact, unless he had given a fictitious name, no one had any idea how he had come to know so much about the connections between the pathologist and the SAS. A red alert was raised and we were all advised to keep a lookout for the man and let certain people know immediately if he returned.

With the absolute confirmation that he was not – and never had been – a member of the SAS (at least under this name), we were left with only one conclusion: that he was a fantasist who had been rejected by the army at some point, which had spurred him on to berate them at every available opportunity and do his best to show them in a bad light to anyone willing to listen. If it hadn't been such a waste of our time I might have felt sorry for him. After all, he had tried so hard to convince us all, on so many levels. He just hadn't been able to satisfy that most valuable criterion of all: human instinct. In any case, he never returned.

'Ah, Derek, I've got something for you.'

Professor Mant held out an ominous-looking plastic bag. He had just returned from a wood in the Thames Valley area, where the body of a woman had been found. He informed me that the bag contained a human skull with a significant amount of flesh still on it, and asked me to remove the flesh so that he could examine the injury to the skull in finer detail.

I called into my local fishing tackle shop the next morning on my way to work and bought two pints of maggots. Maggots were sold either by the pint or half-pint, and even dispensed using the typical pub half-jug or pint glass. They were poured into a box containing air holes, which I placed in the carrier of my motorcycle before heading into work.

I planned to start work on the head the following day, so I needed to find a secure place to confine the maggots for the evening. I hit on the idea of using the laboratory fume cupboard. This allowed me to pull down the glass at the front to keep them in a safe and enclosed space. I didn't, of course, expect anyone else to go near the package.

The next day I arrived at work, put on my white lab coat and headed straight over to the fume cupboard. I lifted the glass and took hold of the bucket, expecting to see the maggots inside ... but it was empty. I searched everywhere in the lab, to no avail. Finally, I realized that the only possible explanation was that their warmth had lifted the lid, which perhaps hadn't been closed as tightly as I had hoped, allowing them to escape. The only way they could have disappeared completely was by wriggling up the inner wall of the fume cupboard, up the flue, and out beyond the roof panel to some unknown destination in the medical school.

The mystery was never solved. There were no reports of any unforeseen infestations of flies. Thankfully, neither was there news of a sudden deluge of maggots dropping on someone's head ...

What did I make of being left alone for a few moments – while Iain West changed – in the mortuary at the end of a morning's session of note-taking? Perhaps strangely, I didn't find it intimidating. First, a mortuary is usually very brightly lit, and secondly, I was there during the day and never at night. Most importantly of all, neither of us has ever seen the slightest sign of life in a dead body.

However ... it wouldn't be honest not to disclose having heard accounts of at least one heart starting to beat again when someone has woken up in there. In which case, it's debatable who will have suffered the biggest scare: the morticians or the recently declared deceased!

Then there are other tales of the unexpected we have been party to, those you couldn't make up. It is a hot late summer's afternoon, for instance, and one of your colleagues has had a brainwave: it would be very pleasant to visit the pub after work for a cold pint or two. As you arrive, you see only one available table. At the bar, you find yourself lazily scanning your surroundings as you wait for the drinks to be poured. You spot the social drinkers, there for the same reasons you are. You spot the regulars, too: those familiar enough with the bar staff to pull up a stool and chat with the landlord.

As you sit down with your drinks, you begin to understand why your particular table was free: the couple at the next table are overly loud, ruddy in the face and slurring their words. It's not especially late, but it's obvious they've been here for a while. What you cannot possibly know, of course, is that this is their second heavy drinking session at this pub today. You smile tolerantly as their boisterous outbursts infiltrate your own group's conversation. Casting a brief look in their direction, you think they seem happy enough. In fact, the clink of their glasses indicates a toast. Perhaps whatever has brought them here is a cause for celebration.

'*Listen!*'

All of a sudden, the person in closest proximity to them is leaning into the centre of your table, eyes wide.

'Listen to the people at the next table!'

Now everyone in your circle is straining to hear the couple's conversation. It's not difficult. They aren't whispering, even though their words are of a distinctly dark and troubling nature.

Though your knees are weak, your legs somehow propel you to the bar, where you commandeer the landlord's attention. To all intents and purposes, you just appear to be in a hurry to request another round of drinks, though you've lost interest in everything but the importance of the message you need to communicate to him. There is just time for one swift, unobtrusive glance in the couple's direction. It's not so much their talk of murder that worries you, it's their heavily bloodstained clothing.

It all began with a heavy drinking session for three pub regulars: two men and a woman. They had been friends for some time, and one of the men felt confident in confiding to the other two that he had a growing stash of benefit payments, which had accumulated into a tidy sum. He was persuaded to detail where he kept the money.

That particular lunchtime the three were drinking heavily, as they always did. Fellow patrons observed them to be merry and talkative. At some point they all returned to the soon-to-be-victim's home. What initially started out as a straightforward robbery quickly escalated. The victim put up a considerable fight, despite his intoxication, but the attack by two assailants, with a knife, soon overpowered him and he sustained a fatal injury.

The murderous couple now faced a problem: they had an unwanted dead body on their hands. Disposing of it would have to be conducted secretly, if they weren't to attract attention and incriminate themselves. Discussion of the available options led to an agreement that there was only one possible solution: dismemberment. Being so heavily inebriated, they recognized that a single knife between them would be insufficient for the task. Heading to the kitchen, they happened upon the most recently introduced labour-saving gadget of the day: an electrically operated Moulinex carving knife. This was just what they needed. So, between them, they carried the body into the bathroom, found a means of plugging in the electric carving knife and began their grisly task.

It was one thing to have a cutting implement to lessen the burden of the undertaking, but quite another to continue with this gruelling task in the stifling heat of a summer's afternoon. Having built up a considerable thirst, they made a decision: what was needed was more liquid refreshment. Though not water, of course. Downing tools, they left the heavily bloodstained scene to make their way back to the pub. The rest you know.

There were a few inconveniences facing the couple on the arrival of the police at the pub to arrest them. For a start, the number of witnesses didn't help. Neither did the fact that they were still covered in the blood of their victim. And back at the scene, the incriminating tools were still where they had left them, along with the partially dismembered body in the bath.

There was never going to be any contest to a murder charge; neither was the judge lenient when it came to sentencing them both to life for murder.

*　*　*

There is undoubtedly an element of darkness to forensic work, dealing as it does with murder, suspicious death and suicide. For us, this dark undertone was often shrouded in what may have appeared to be frivolity and high-spirited banter, but we all implicitly understood what lay just beneath the surface. As a rule, we tended to have a similar outlook on life; non-verbalized, perhaps, but evident in our constant tendency to draw out the humour in any given situation. It was far preferable to the alternative: bleakness or depression. A natural by-product of our work was developing what might have appeared to be a 'harder shell'. A blasé attitude was a way of protecting ourselves from the less desirable emotions.

Did the humour ever go too far? Well, for us, it was a very necessary and welcome way to disperse a low mood. It was a great leveller, everyone being in on the joke. It served as a distraction and lifted us out of tense situations. Given a choice between tears or laughter, laughter was universally better for morale.

So, though our workload originated in the investigation of death, the atmosphere at work was palpably light, from the pathology team down. Pranks were played at every opportunity and no joke was left untold. When I joined the department, even teasing held no malicious intent. In such an atmosphere a low mood was unlikely to settle for long.

Dr Kevin Lee in particular, though a busy pathologist, was very generous with his time and brilliant at creating an enjoyable atmosphere as soon as he entered my office. He was invariably in a lively and upbeat mood. You would never have believed he had just come from a morning in a mortuary. His interesting and amusing stories made my day, while his quick wit and wicked sense of humour transformed every moment. Afternoons would pass in a haze of hilarity, and those days were always the most memorable.

He even had a knack for making questionable remarks in the most natural, inoffensive way. I happened to be out in the field with him one day after a call-out at lunchtime. We had travelled by train to Chertsey, Surrey, where he was to perform a post-mortem on a person who had apparently been suffocated by having a plastic bag placed over the head. There was now a question of whether it was an act of murder or, possibly, suicide. That would be confirmed by any signs of a struggle, and any defence injuries suggested by scratches, or fingernail indentations around the neck where the bag had been tightened. These would indicate an effort to remove the obstructing article and a fight for life.

Kevin donned his protective clothing and snapped on his laboratory gloves. I joined him standing to one side of the body, shorthand notepad and pen at the ready. I was expecting his initial external observations, followed by a dissection of the neck, which would confirm the external findings and lead to the definitive cause of death. For the post-mortem, Kevin required the instruments of his trade: a pair of forceps for holding skin and tissue, and a scalpel with which to cut. As he perused the surfaces around him, in search of these implements, he delivered one of his magnificent quotes: '*Now, where's my knife and fork?*'

Totally unexpected, highly irreverent ... and in really bad taste, I know. But the inappropriateness shocked me into a fit of giggles.

I hadn't yet recovered my composure before his next quip was delivered only seconds later, on examining the condition in which the body had arrived at the mortuary. I need to explain that at the time there was a popular television advertisement for a supermarket chain. It cleverly drew the viewer's attention to certain measures which had recently been introduced with the aim of retaining maximum freshness in their products. This was apparently Kevin's first thought as he gave his full attention to the body. In fact, the deceased had suffocated themselves – which came as a complete surprise to me, as I hadn't been exposed to this type of suicide before. As Kevin turned his attention to the head, which was wrapped in not only one, but two layers of clear plastic, he observed: '*Aah ... double-wrapped ... for freshness!*'

Whenever he appeared in my laboratory, there was a chance that Kevin might turn my scientific equipment into missiles. If we weren't too busy, one or the other of us would frequently ponder how we could spend that day's lunch break improving on the previous day's projectiles.

Part of my training at college had involved glass-blowing. This may sound unlikely, but it was advocated as being a useful skill, as you could make your own test tubes out of glass. Some technicians felt inclined to do this and made a fair amount of their own scientific equipment.

When I discovered a series of redundant long glass tubes, which had been used in the creation of test tubes many years previously, a plan formed in my mind. My predecessors, and some of my more enterprising contemporaries, would cut a piece of a length of metre-long glass of approximately 5mm in diameter by heating it and pulling a piece off, or using a diamond blade to score around the tube and snap it off, before fashioning a closed-ended test tube. For Kevin and me, however, these tubes were to find a far more pleasing recreational purpose.

I discovered that a large syringe needle of 6cm in length would fit snugly into this type of outer test tube. First, I had to remove the burrs present on either side of our sterile plastic syringe needles, but once the needle was positioned inside the long tube we were ready to fire our 'darts' at their target. Blowing hard down the outer tube, we would see the sterile syringe needle flying out. We even created a target out of a specimen tub lid for our own in-house alternative darts contests. Fortunately for us, the syringe needles were made of highly durable plastic and lasted as long as our interest in playing this game. Fortunately for everyone else in the vicinity, our games took place in the confined microscope room – a small inner office inside my laboratory – where no observers would ever come to any harm. As we repeatedly aimed our tubes into the inner room, 15 feet from the target, a whole hour's lunchtime passed very quickly.

Kevin had a particular fondness for deconstructing and reassembling items of equipment and, as a result, was able to devise an even riskier device for us to use. Fashioning a cone from the tip of a plastic pipette, he would push it onto the end of the syringe needle. All that was then required was to fill the needle with his favourite chemical explosives and shoot the needle down the tube. Genius! Whistling down the tube, the tipped syringe would hit the target and explode loudly, bang on cue. Result: one grinning and very smug pathologist.

Next it was my attempt … which was when things took a slightly different turn. I blew down the outer tube as Kevin had done, but halfway down the tipped syringe somehow became snagged on the side and exploded too early, while it was still in the outer glass tube. The impact blew the end off the outer tube and the whole apparatus shattered into thousands of pieces, showering the entire lab with them. There was no way of topping that.

Over time, our explosive devices became something of an art form. There was no going back, and inevitably we became quite adept at practical jokes with them. And if playing explosive pranks on each other ever became boring, someone else would become our target. For instance, Pauline sometimes found that, when she sat down on her chair in the morning, the loud bang would quickly propel her back out of it!

One morning I came into work and went to put my motorbike gear away as usual, in my locker. Unbeknown to me, Kevin had been busy the previous evening, devising a simple but extremely effective trap. On my locker door was a horizontal row of long vents, to which Kevin had fixed an elastic band with the aid of a paperclip. The other end of the band was stretched halfway across the inside of my locker and fastened securely to the bar at the top, on which clothes were hung. Kevin had had the presence of mind to use a lubricant on the small door handle outside, and had also smeared two reactive chemicals all around the outer edges of the cabinet, for maximum explosive effect when they connected. Of course, all this was cleverly hidden from my view.

As I innocently opened my locker door, it simultaneously slipped from my grip and was pinged forcefully backwards, straight onto the explosives. The deafening bang that resulted really got my blood pumping first thing in the morning. It was just a shame for Kevin that he wasn't there to see how high I jumped.

Moving up a gear, we somehow made the – some would say inadvisable – decision to mix glycerine with another chemical, which was known to react violently with it. We put them into a tube and sealed them inside one of my large white-lidded specimen jars. I then lowered the jar into my deep laboratory sink. There was just enough time to take cover before the lid was blown off the container and the contents, which were stained purple, were blasted all over the ceiling. The result was some permanent purple dents. Later, the evidence of our scientific achievement was sadly lost when the laboratory was treated to a new coat of paint.

Occasionally we sailed a bit *too* close to the wind with our experiments, with dramatic and unexpected consequences. My next explosive mix was smeared onto a piece of filter paper, which I left to dry on the window ledge on a hot, sunny afternoon. Unfortunately, I got distracted – by the real work I was conducting! – and forgot all about it. A few minutes later Professor Mant arrived in our shared office and sat down at his desk just as a sudden gust of wind whipped up. Neither of us saw the breeze catch the filter paper, which flipped over, causing a loud explosion a little too close to where Prof was sitting. I jumped myself, but Prof's startled reaction was so comical that I had trouble containing myself … and even more difficulty explaining it away.

The occasional prank was an absolute necessity to take our minds off the distressing situations we encountered in the course of our work. We needed this balance, otherwise we could find ourselves upset for weeks. Just a few minutes of fun went a long way towards creating a bit of welcome light relief. We wouldn't have lasted long had we not found such outlets when dealing with tragic and heartbreaking situations.

These were even worse if they related to a child. I once had the thoroughly wretched task of having to photograph multiple deep bite marks all over the body of a 4-year-old girl, inflicted by her stepfather. As departmental photographer, I was asked to go over to the ward to photograph her injuries, as it was likely the photographs would be used in court, as evidence against the parent. But it was known that she wouldn't survive her injuries, and was expected to die soon after. She had been subjected to such an inexplicable level of abuse that it was difficult to control my emotions, and I came back burning with rage. It upset me for weeks. The feeling is still there if I happen to recall that case at any time.

Another time we were told about a young mother who had enticed her two reluctant young children up onto the roof of a nearby housing block. Despite their anxiety and pleas not to, she jumped, taking them with her. It was especially harrowing hearing about the aftermath of the fall, which didn't immediately kill all three.

We felt exactly the same as anyone else hearing about such cases: distressed, enraged, unable to understand the thought processes of the perpetrator. We felt frustrated, powerless. Sadly, we were exposed to this type of situation too often in the course of our work.

Working in the laboratory, I would regularly encounter Home Office forensic pathologist Dr Alan Grant, a very diminutive, stooped, elderly 'old school' gentleman, who had had an accident when younger which had resulted in a curvature of the spine. He couldn't have reached 5 feet in height and would shuffle along the corridor to his office next door, head down. I would hear him call out to me as he passed by, on his way to take patients' blood for one of his areas of expertise: paternity testing. We always felt it was unusual that a forensic department – associated with the investigation of the deceased, rather than the living – offered paternity testing, but it was Dr Grant's specialism and came with him.

The paternity testing was performed weekly on a Wednesday afternoon and occasionally provided a few edge-of-the-seat, heart-stopping moments. We welcomed couples, whole families and the occasional high-profile celebrity. What they all had in common was the fact that they were largely at loggerheads with each other and, by extension, their ex-partner's wider family. Mothers and fathers invariably arrived separately, which was just as well, as this was vital to keeping the peace. As they waited in the department, a queue would usually build up and there would be a gradual increase in the anxiety levels of those present. Much of this related to having to give blood in the first place, but our patients also ran the very real risk of bumping into the person who was causing them to spend an afternoon in this unpleasant way.

The arrival of Dr Grant was detectable from the overwhelming aroma of pipe tobacco that followed him around. I found him to be a real character, and was very amused by his unexpectedly coarse vocabulary. Intermittently I would hear the odd expletive escape from his office if something wasn't going his way. This would often catch me off-guard, and I would double up in hysterics at the sound of this quiet and unobtrusive gentleman suddenly letting off steam. He was always pleasant, but not particularly communicative. As soon as he had arrived a steady flow of patients appeared, usually around half a dozen cases per week.

Being in his eighties, Dr Grant had a pronounced tremor in his hands. The consternation of those undergoing blood extraction became increasingly intense as he bore down on an arm, his needle wobbling furiously. Almost without fail, I would be interrupted and forced to abandon whatever laboratory work I was performing so that I could assist him. This meant holding still a struggling child or baby while he took their blood. In comparison to the size of the child, the needle looked huge. It wasn't helped by the fact that Dr Grant was really quite doddery. Naturally, the child I was holding would be desperate to escape from the threat of this old man they didn't know and this needle they knew was going to hurt them. There were times when I would have to put a child into an arm-lock.

Dr Grant somehow managed to overcome his tremor

and hit his intended target every time, but there was one incident which I'm sure the child, and his mother, will never forget. I know I haven't. The boy was very young and thin, and he began to struggle so much that when Dr Grant pushed the needle into his arm it came straight out the other side! Did the boy bleed a lot? Actually only slightly, given the speed at which Dr Grant withdrew the needle.

Another time, I suddenly heard myself being summoned urgently. As I arrived at the door to Dr Grant's office I was greeted by the sight of a very large, unconscious man who was slumped forwards, and a tiny doctor trying, unsuccessfully, to keep his patient from collapsing all the way down to the floor. He turned out to be a docker, and was built like a battleship. It was as much as I could do not to explode with laughter at the sight I was greeted with. I rushed in to help, just as Dr Grant peered at me over the top of his horn-rimmed glasses and muttered, impatiently, 'F***ing stupid prat's fainted!' That set me off, and I was almost incapacitated with laughter. Despite this, I somehow managed to prop the man back up and haul him into a chair. I brought him round, but was still so hysterical that I had tears running down my face. He must have wondered what was so amusing, but fortunately wasn't so offended that he decided to knock me unconscious with one swipe of those enormous hands.

As a rule, no great concern was shown in the event things turned ugly – which was fairly unsettling for me as a young female, and Wednesday afternoons were never my favourite. It is one thing knowing that summoning help will bring a posse of technicians running to your aid, but quite another to find yourself in the middle of warring couples. Looking at it from our current perspective of Health & Safety, it is apparent that there was considerable potential for a serious incident to erupt at any moment. Shouting, swearing, punching, kicking, ABH, GBH – in the event of an escalation in tempers within the confines of our corridor there would have been nowhere to take cover. To prevent things from getting out of hand, male visitors were given a seat in the corridor outside Dr Grant's office, and I was encouraged to ask female visitors, along with any children and supporting relatives, to wait in my office. They would sit there patiently on uncomfortable plastic chairs, and it was a challenge to type or make a phone call with a row of upturned faces as a backdrop, inevitably eavesdropping on conversations about forensic matters and watching everything I did, bless them.

Gradually, they would have no option but to encroach upon my office space, as multiple members of the family lined up. Young children would sit playing with their toys on the office floor. I had no problem with this, until I was required to get to the door, usually to prevent an unwelcome encounter, which presented me with navigating a row of legs of varying sizes. Naturally, couples would recognize each other's voices, as might the children, which was rather sad if they were missing their daddy, and sometimes the hostility felt intense in my enclosed office space. On the whole, though, equilibrium was maintained, though it was very uncertain how things would transpire on any given afternoon.

There was little we could do if patients decided to hang around outside the office, as every patient ultimately gave their blood sample in the same room – Dr Grant's. We just hoped that warring couples would leave by different corridors and exit the hospital premises without incident.

What I recall most about those afternoons is the way the atmosphere could change in an instant when a patient heard a familiar male voice at my office door. Our continual state of high alert didn't always prevent the occasional aggressive encounter and more than once a couple had to be physically restrained. Fortunately, this mostly pre-dated my involvement. I also knew that if a fight broke out elsewhere in the department it was someone else's responsibility to defuse it. This was the reality to which I clung and from which I gained a measure of reassurance, as Wednesday afternoons rolled around with dreaded certainty.

Unlike Pauline, because I was technical staff dealing with tissue and body parts, the time came when the giving of my own blood was required of me. It eventually happened when Dr Grant decided to test it, out of interest, and discovered that I had a very common blood group, O Rhesus positive. For those who are unaware, an 'O' blood group can be given to anyone in an emergency, but it is the Rhesus negative blood group that is universal and in demand for blood transfusions. My own group, 'O' Rhesus positive, does not come into this category. However, for Dr Grant's purposes, having a Rhesus positive type meant I could help him in checking the Rhesus type of his patients. Using my blood as a control, he could discover a child's or baby's

Rhesus blood type by testing whether there was any reaction by their blood to my blood. If there was clotting in their blood in reaction to mine, they would be Rhesus negative. If there was no clotting, their blood would be compatible with mine, confirming it as Rhesus positive, identical to my own.

So I was suddenly in demand every week for fresh blood. Having my arm punctured every Wednesday wasn't really something I looked forward to, but it was a sacrifice worth making. This does, of course, predate all the genetic advances of recent years and the computerization of blood testing that takes place now. Back then, I did, at times, feel a bit like a pin cushion.

CHAPTER 10

SPERM DONOR

There was another, much less commonly known, area in which Dr Grant specialized: sperm analysis. We would both have an occasional visit from a male client alleging that his female partner was cheating on him. More often than not, the man would offer up a pair of her knickers, having retrieved them from the wash basket. Once, I was even offered an entire bed sheet. I would test these items for the presence of sperm. It was an unusual investigation for a forensic medical scientist to perform, so I had no idea how people knew about the fact that I was testing materials for sperm, but word must have got around somehow.

Once particular day, a man knocked on my door, seeming to know exactly who it was he was looking for. I had barely confirmed who I was before he told me he thought his wife was cheating on him. As we got into conversation, he suddenly pulled a plastic bag containing a pair of his wife's knickers from his pocket and asked if I could test them for him.

At that time I was performing research on sperm identification on materials. I therefore always had the appropriate reagents made up for use, which considerably speeded up the process that day. The man waited in my office while I performed the test for him, which took just over half an hour, and I was able to identify the presence of sperm on the knickers.

I felt sorry at having to give him bad news, especially when he was clearly upset by having his worst fears confirmed, but, despite this, he had the presence of mind to ask what I charged for my work. When I declined to take any payment, he kindly pushed a tenner into the top pocket of my white coat.

There were occasional negative results from these tests, but it was never pleasant having to disappoint someone with a positive result.

The investigation for the presence of sperm required the performance of an analysis for the presence of prostatic (i.e. originating from the prostate) acid phosphatase, an enzyme which is strongly present in seminal fluid. The way I conducted this analysis was to check first whether the area of staining was dry or still damp. If dry, I would administer a few drops of a weak saline (salt) solution, by pipette, onto the stain. This facilitated the pressing of the dampened area on the item of clothing (or bedding) onto a sterile filter paper. I could conduct my experiment from this point forward without having any direct contact with the original stain, thereby crucially maintaining the integrity of the sample in case further testing was required.

I would spray the filter paper with a chemical reagent, which led to a straightforward positive or negative result for the presence of acid phosphatase. If negative, the chemical reagent would remain clear when introduced to the sample on the filter paper. If positive, within a few seconds the filter paper would immediately turn a dark magenta or purple. I could then take any positive outcome further by conducting a follow-up test to identify the presence of sperm within that seminal fluid. This provided incontrovertible proof for the complainant.

If sperm had been positively identified, the second part of my test involved dabbing the original damp stain onto a small glass microscope slide. Onto this I would drop a reagent called haematoxylin. This reagent reacts with any individual sperm present by turning them a two-toned shade of blue. Specifically, the sperm head will be very light and the blue will darken along the length of its body, reacting to the arrangement of DNA in the sperm and ending with a dark blue tail. There is the chance a sperm might break down over a period of time, or as a result of the conditions it has remained in for a while; for instance, it will decompose in damp or exposed circumstances. Or its tail might separate from its body, or it might appear fuzzy and less well defined under the microscope. Whatever its condition, though, a single sperm head will still retain its light-to-dark deep blue colour once it has been exposed to the haematoxylin staining agent.

As with any enterprising scientist before me, and much like the fictional Dr Jekyll, I performed a control test using myself as the subject. This involved using my own live, viable sperm to devise a method for comparison purposes. At the outset, I prepared the way by transferring some of these sperm onto a shirt, which I chemically tested to ensure the live sperm showed up, which they did. I then air-dried the stain on the shirt and put the whole thing into a plastic bag, labelled and dated it, and put it into a cupboard in the microscope room at work. Over the next few days I became caught up in more pressing work and completely forgot about the results of the test. When I discovered it, 53 months later, the shirt was still perfectly sealed in its original evidence bag.

During that time, things had moved on a bit in our department. For one thing, I had acquired an ultrasonic bath. I used this to clean glassware more effectively. So I now had an idea: perhaps I could use a combination of ultrasound and the millipore filtration method I was using for drowning analysis to extract the sperm cells from the shirt. If so, it could prove a valuable method of enquiry concerning the longevity of sperm.

I cut off a small piece of the stained shirt and placed it in a few millilitres of saline solution in a universal tube. I placed this into the ultrasound bath and set it to vibrate at an extremely high frequency for a few minutes. This successfully shook off any sperm present into the liquid solution. This sperm-containing solution was pushed through one of my millipore filter papers and I then dried the filter paper on a hotplate. If any sperm were now present, they would stick to the filter paper.

Once dry, I stained the filter paper using the haematoxylin method, simultaneously staining any sperm present. As the final part of the process, I mounted the dried stained paper and any sperm on a microscope slide, to which I then added a chemical known as a mounting media, which turns an opaque millipore filter completely transparent. Finally, I added a cover slip in order to preserve the final results intact.

Examining the shirt material, with its 53-month-old sperm, under a microscope, I was amazed to discover that the sperm were not only still present after all this time, but that there seemed to have been no decline in their condition, whole sperm still being present with their tails fully intact.

A Greek colleague and good friend, Professor Panos Epivatianos, who was on sabbatical with us at the time, reasoned with me that this must have been due to the fact that the evidence had been preserved in optimal conditions. After all, the shirt had been dry and had been immediately transferred into a plastic bag, which had been placed in a warm, dry drawer.

Still, we had not been expecting to find sperm which retained all of their characteristics, let alone their tails, after such a long time. In fact, we were so impressed that we wrote a paper on the subject, and it was published in a French forensic journal.

An interesting early sperm-testing case involved a separated couple. The woman was accusing her former partner of having got her pregnant, even though the man himself was adamant that it had nothing to do with him, as he had been sterilized through a vasectomy.

We first performed paternity testing, as this would establish whether there was a match between his and the child's blood. There was. This categorically proved him to be the father. However, this only complicated the issue, as he was insistent that the test was faulty, given his previous vasectomy.

Dr Grant asked him for a sperm sample, which I tested, again using the haemotoxylin stain. There was a significant quantity of viable sperm cells.

As a result of these findings, the man investigated further, only to discover that his vasectomy had been performed incorrectly. No cutting had taken place, only tying-back of the *vas deferens* tubes. Therefore, sperm had leaked through the tie-back.

These circumstances were very unusual, and the results unwelcome. However, the stain was able to prove to both parties without doubt that the man was the father of the child.

Dr Grant continued with his paternity-testing practice at Guy's for many more years. He also continued to work in the mortuary as a pathologist. We were saddened when we learned that he had unexpectedly dropped dead in the middle of a post-mortem. However, knowing him as I did, I always felt that this was the way he would have wanted to go.

Forensic exhibits in Guy's Hospital's Gordon Museum. The top shelf of the left-hand cabinet shows bone fragments, dentures and gallstones from John Haigh's acid-bath murders. An early photographic/negative superimposition is displayed on the shelf below. To the right are exhibits of asphyxia, gunshot injuries, abortion and infanticide. Even now, the museum seems as gruesomely shocking as it is compelling.

No fume cupboard would be complete without fumes. Highly corrosive acids are used to dissolve human tissue in drowning analysis.

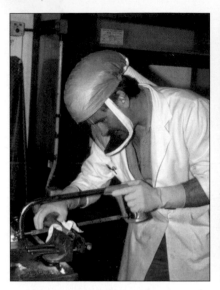

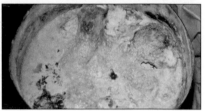

Derek cutting a femur to acquire uncontaminated bone marrow for drowning analysis.

I liked to call these Derek's 'primordial soups', his infamous tubs used to reduce human flesh to bone. Top: Parts of a fleshy skeleton beneath the surface. Above: The infamous 'blue tub'. See if you can spot a hip bone and a foot (right and centre). The lower tub has been exposed to the hydrogen peroxide for longer.

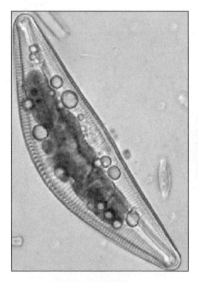

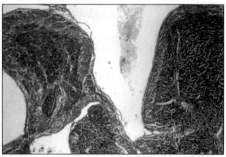

Viewed under a microscope, diatoms are stunning. To date, over a thousand species have been identified.

Derek's Rhodanile Blue stain technique on a piece of heart tissue following heart attack. The dark blue areas indicate reduced oxygenation compared with the paler pink, healthy heart tissue.

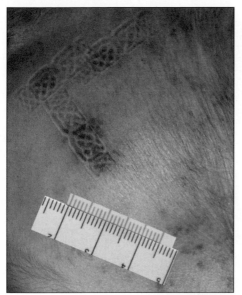

A good example of how patterned injury can be overlaid with a suspected weapon – in this case a ring – to provide evidence that this object has very likely caused the child's injuries.

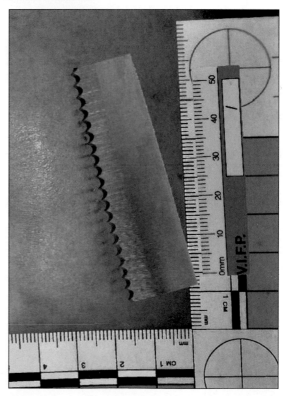

Using our own bread knife, you can see the identically spaced serrations to an actual injury caused by a similar knife blade to skin.

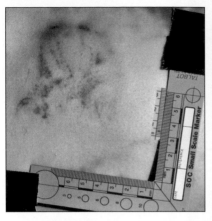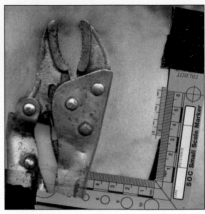

These images give a clear indication of how a patterned injury to skin can be traced to the suspected implement, in this case the outline of a wrench (left), including its jaws and rivets. All are identified in the scaled weapon and wound overlay (right).

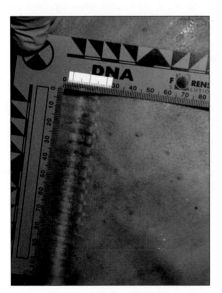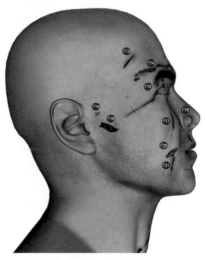

Scaled overlay showing parallels between dumbbell bar (top layer) and patterned injury to skin (base layer).

A typical example of how body mapping sanitizes injury for the jury. All our injuries are hand-crafted, not cut and pasted, in order to prevent the real injuries from being shown in court or to the viewing public.

Typical defence wounds from a knife attack. Juries receive replicated injury well when compared with the real injury from a post-mortem photograph of the deceased.

We use bespoke Hollywood film-industry software to demonstrate internal anatomy, in this case replicating skull fracturing.

Adaptation in design is particularly important when demonstrating emaciation, in this case due to starvation.

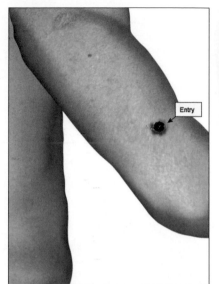
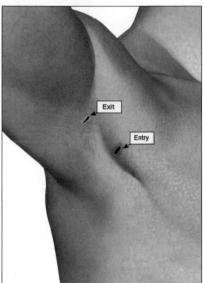
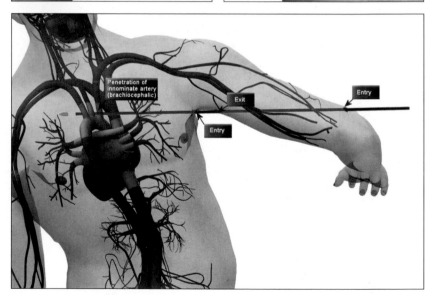

A series of images showing bullet entry and exit wounds in the outer right arm, armpit and chest wall. Derek used his medical expertise to line up all the injury pathways and create a body map showing the tilt in the victim's upper body, indicating an attempt to take evasive action on hearing the bullet fired.

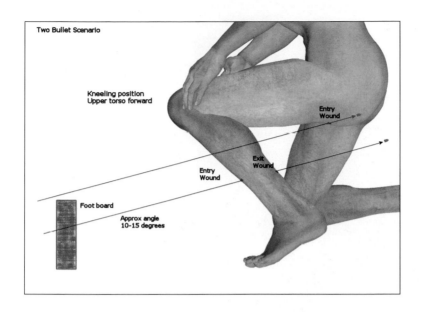

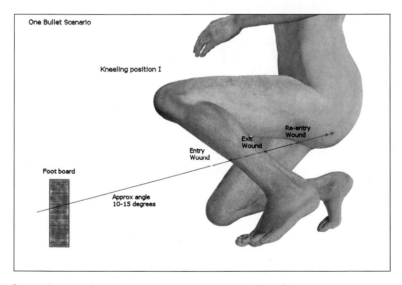

Comparing complex scenarios aids jury comprehension of the wounding process. Here, a man claimed to have been shot twice by an armed-response team. The armed-response team claimed a single shot. In 2D, the jury can assess the evidence through the observation of two wounding scenarios.

Celebrating Derek's 30th year at Guy's with Dr Iain West (right). Iain introduced Pauline to her first crime scene . . . and the world to the concept of injury replication for public viewing. His National Injuries Database has achieved worldwide acclaim as a specialist resource for injury comparison.

A shared sense of humour goes a long way in forensic medicine.

CHAPTER 11

DEATH BY DROWNING

I started performing drowning analysis during my years at the Gordon Museum, and from almost the outset of my transfer to the forensic department it became a very regular part of my job. Working close to the Thames, I saw a regular influx of deaths due to drowning, varying from accidents to suicide. Occasionally we would receive a body which had been dumped following a murder. Drowning investigation was, without doubt, not only a routine occurrence, but a field in which I rapidly became both adept and highly experienced.

At the time of writing, drowning has been found to be the third leading worldwide cause of unintentional death related to injury, with an estimated total of 360,000 deaths annually. It has been established — and I know, of course, from my own experience — that it is more commonly associated with males. In fact, men have twice the mortality rate of women. The explanation for this is that men tend to be far more likely than women to take risks around water, such as swimming when they are alone or having a boating accident. Men are also more likely to engage in drinking alcohol prior to swimming. As a major risk factor to children, drowning is estimated to be one of the top five causes of death of those between 1 and 14 years of age.

On a worldwide scale, occupational hazards are always strong risk factors, including commercial fishing and fishing in a small boat, for the purpose of subsistence. It perhaps goes without saying that those more in danger of drowning include people living near open water, including ditches, dykes and ponds, irrigation channels and swimming pools, with children particularly at risk.

In disasters related to flooding, drownings account for 75 per cent of deaths. In recent years, another scenario has also become commonly associated with drowning: asylum seekers travelling by sea, often in overcrowded and unsafe vessels. An overload of passengers can result in the capsizing of a vessel and the drowning of its occupants.

Drowning is, therefore, considered a major public health issue right across the globe, regardless of economic environment or region. The statistics are high, at over 90 per cent for unintentional drowning in low- or middle-income countries. The rates are highest in African regions, where they reach levels 15 to 20 times higher than those of the UK.

Data collection is not entirely reliable, however. Official figures do not always include intentional drowning deaths, as in suicide. The World Health Organization does not include, in any of their worldwide statistics, drownings related to flood or water transport. The WHO admits that the data compiled from high-income countries is under-represented by as much as 50 per cent, and that its statistics for non-fatal drowning events are unreliable, due to there not always being documentation of these.

There are very few scientists performing drowning analysis in the UK today. The number is now considerably fewer than when I started performing it, and even then I could count only half a dozen scientists specializing in the field in the whole of the UK.

A drowning investigation usually starts with samples taken by the pathologist at the post-mortem. When there is a suspicion of drowning, the police will be directed to me, by way of my specialist forensic provider, whose laboratories I use in my investigation. The organs of the deceased may be frozen in the interim but, once they have been conveyed to the laboratory, I will normally attend within five to ten working days and have my final results within just over 24 hours of commencing work on their case.

The process of drowning analysis is one in which I need to conduct a detailed scientific investigation on specific human organs, in which I will be looking to establish the presence of diatoms, otherwise known as algae. These are microscopic single-celled plants which live in bodies of water. They rely on light for their growth and vary in size from 5 to 500 microns, a micron being a measurement of length and thickness. To date, the number of species identified has been phenomenal – over 100,000. Diatoms can be found in salt water, freshwater, brackish water (where salt and freshwater meet) and also in soil. They can even be found on damp environmental surfaces, including rocks, trees, etc. They rely on the sun for energy and are more often found in well-lit surface layers of water.

Beneath their unique silica cell wall, known as a frustule, diatoms have complex structures. Not only do they vary considerably in size and shape, but their forms can exhibit unique patterns, ranging from squiggles to stripes and dots to triangles. This variation will depend on the valve type in their outer frustule. They are usually a shade of green, due to their chlorophyll content, chlorophyll being a pigment found in plants and microorganisms which rely on the sun for photosynthesis, the process utilized in their respective environments in order to sustain life.

Diatoms are stunning to view under magnification. Like snowflakes, there is minimal chance of predicting the exact type or combination found in any sample. Some occur more frequently than others. There are a range of factors which can impact which varieties are found, ranging from pH level (acidity and alkalinity) to the temperature of the water. The amount of available light will also affect the varieties, as will the level of toxicity from any chemicals or pollutants present in the water at the time.

Occasionally, a drowned individual might ingest silt from the bottom of a lake or a river and, in that event, I may well find dead silica exoskeletons from diatoms which have fallen to the bottom of that body of water and become a part of the sediment there. Even today, diatom exoskeletons can be found in deserts, on mountaintops and at the locations of dinosaur digs.

You could be forgiven for thinking that whether or not an individual has drowned would be an open-and-shut case, depending on whether water was ingested into their lungs or not. In fact, this is not actually the case. It is not common knowledge that there are two components to drowning: Type I Drowning, known as Dry Drowning; and Type II, known as Common or Wet Drowning.

Type I, Dry Drowning, is the lesser known. It results from the shock the body undergoes when very cold water hits the back of the throat. As this occurs, there can be an immediate spasm of the airway, or larynx, causing it to close up. This is the body's way of protecting the lungs from the inhalation of water. However, in so doing, it prevents the breathing process from continuing.

Another complication is that, at the same instant as the cold water hits the back of the throat and the airway closes, the brain triggers a nerve called the vagus nerve. This nerve connects the brain and the heart, and causes an immediate cessation of the heartbeat, a process known as vagal inhibition. So, with the cessation of the vital biological processes of heartbeat and continuous breathing, within a matter of seconds sudden death will occur. In such a scenario there is insufficient time for any water to be drawn into the lungs. So, in this case, in Dry Drowning, no diatoms will be found, as without ingestion of water there will be no diatomaceous material drawn into the lungs.

Type II, Common or Wet Drowning, the commonly understood process of drowning, is the opposite. In this scenario, if a person is submerged in water as they draw their last few breaths, the continued breathing process forces any inhaled water deeper into the lobes of the lungs. The increased pressure from the water will burst the air sacs, known as alveoli, and the diatoms present in the water will enter the bloodstream. In the meantime, the heart continues to beat until death occurs, which takes place after all the available oxygen has been used up. The diatoms that have entered the bloodstream will circulate around the entire body through the blood circulatory system, and in this way, before death occurs, diatoms can reach most, if not all, the organs in the body, and even the further reaches of the bone marrow. If pollen is present, or silt has been ingested from the bottom of the body of water, this will also enter the airways and lungs. At post-mortem, pathologists may also find evidence of weeds, and sometimes even tiny fish can be found in the airways.

It may not be a pleasant thought, but you may well be eating diatoms yourself, as they can be found on salad items, as well as on fruit and vegetables grown in a wet or muddy field. This raises the question whether this invalidates the drowning analysis results. Won't diatoms be present in every person's system, due to eating these foods? The answer is that diatoms cannot travel through the gut wall, so they cannot enter the bloodstream from the stomach or alimentary canal. If they are eaten, they will enter and exit the body in the normal way: basically, from stomach to intestines to toilet bowl. So it is a valid conclusion that diatoms will only be found in a person's organs as a result of Wet Drowning. As the scientist performing the investigation, I see the presence of diatoms as an indication that the deceased was alive and breathing when they entered the water and that the diatom-containing water circulated around their body until their heartbeat stopped.

Undoubtedly the most unusual drowning case I ever encountered proved just how small an amount of water could cause death by drowning. It took place long before the more stringent laws on drinking and driving were enforced, at a time when you could still legally drive if you had not consumed more than three units of alcohol and could walk in a straight line if apprehended.

One winter's night, in howling wind and torrential rain, two men were making their way home in a northerly direction along the M3 by car, both of them totally inebriated and virtually incapable. Despite this, somehow the driver managed to keep the car on the road, though, at one point during the journey, he pulled over to the hard shoulder for his passenger to relieve his bladder. He sat in the car while his friend wandered off … and never returned. At some point the driver gave up waiting, drove away and, on finally reaching home, went straight to bed. His friend failed to return home and in the morning his family alerted the police.

When the police arrived at the driver's home, he had forgotten his friend was still missing. He could recall only vague memories of the previous evening when questioned, but was, at least, able to indicate the site at which he had left him. This led to the discovery of his body, not very far from where the driver had stopped to let him out. From the position of the body, it was estimated that he had stopped at the top of a bank to urinate, lost his balance in his drunken state and rolled down the bank, perhaps even passing out before he fell. His body was now at the bottom of the bank in a flooded field, face-down in only two inches of water, showing all the outward appearances of a Wet Drowning.

As well as processing the man's organs for diatoms, I took a sample of the water in which he had been found. There were many diatoms present in the water, and therefore it could have been assumed that more than a few would be detected in the body. As it happened, though, not one diatom was present in his organs. Neither was there any pathological finding to account for his death. Although it was completely at odds with all expectation, the pathologist was forced to conclude that, based upon the collective findings, which indicated no other pathology, his death had been due to Dry Drowning.

Drowning does not only indicate accidental death such as this case, but can also have an association with crime. For instance, an urban canal can be a popular site for drug-related crimes, prostitution and so on, and occasional unexplained drownings can occur in such bodies of water.

These aren't always what they seem. One late summer's day, for example, a member of the public spotted a body-shaped package wrapped in black plastic and trussed with rope floating down the Thames at Kingston, Surrey. The police were called and immediately mobilized their diving team, who dragged it out of the water. It was conveyed to the local mortuary and Kevin was called out to perform a post-mortem. The package was duly unwrapped, whereupon it was discovered that it was a full skeleton, minus its head. This might have indicated a horrific murder involving decapitation, had it not been for the fact that it very quickly became evident that the skeleton was not of human origin and was, in fact, made of plastic.

As news of the investigation broke and was broadcast locally, along with a request for anyone with any knowledge about the incident to come forward, a group of red-faced Kingston University students presented themselves to the police. They owned up to having come up with a prank for student 'Rag Week': floating the university's teaching aid down the Thames in the hope of fooling the police into thinking they had a murder on their hands.

This had, no doubt, been a hilarious idea in the planning stages, and was of course highly successful. However, in practice it wasn't that smart. There was the not so very small matter of the extensive costs involved: those of the professional manpower mobilized to deal with the recovery of the 'body', including the police diving team, plus the pathologist's call-out fee. Then there was the additional cost to the British public, whose journeys along the major connecting road networks in the area had ground to a halt while recovery of the 'body' took place.

It isn't hard to imagine the warnings given to each new influx of students at the university following the incident, or the legendary status it must have acquired.

My preferred method for performing drowning analysis is as follows. I will describe it in layman's terms.

In a spotless lab, I will first chop up the human organs.

I have always had my own preferences in relation to the organs used for the detection of diatoms. I like to work with at least two organs, one of which will preferably be the lung, as undoubtedly this will be the organ most closely associated with diatom intake. In order to achieve valid results, it is vital to prevent any form of cross-contamination, and therefore I will request the major airway to be tied off before the lungs are removed from the body, which prevents any escape of water – and consequently diatoms. It also has the advantage of decreasing the potential for cross-contamination with any other organs which are likely to be cut up on the same table. A favoured organ, for me, is usually one of the kidneys, and I prefer to receive this still in its capsule. This allows me to remove the uncut kidney myself, in sterile laboratory conditions, again minimizing the potential for cross-contamination. A lobe of liver is always useful too.

If there has been a lengthy period of decomposition, these organs may all be compromised, and I will then ask for a femur instead. Even a large leg bone needs to be received uncut, if possible. I can then saw through it myself and recover sufficient bone marrow from an as yet unexposed and uncontaminated site. Bone marrow is not ideal for this type of investigation, as I am likely to spend a great deal of time scraping it from its deepest recesses – an awkward and very time-consuming process – so it is a last resort.

In earlier times at Guy's, I would request a sample of brain. It might be the only option if a body was in an advanced stage of decomposition. As the brain is already a very soft organ and, in a decomposed state, extremely mushy, this might seem an unusual choice; but the advantage is that it has remained safely contained in the uncontaminated closed environment of the skull. The brain, however, is such a fatty organ that it is never ideal for drowning analysis, the reason being that the process I use to determine whether or not diatoms are present requires the use of acid to destroy all living matter, and, as you may remember from John Haigh's use of an acid bath for the disposal of a body, acid will not easily break down fat, even the soft fat of brain tissue. So I would have to spend a great deal of time skimming fat off the top of a brain during the rendering-down process. I therefore largely abandoned this practice in the 1980s, opting for bone marrow instead.

Chopping the organs, be they lung, kidney, liver or bone marrow, increases the surface area that will be exposed to infiltration or penetration by the acid, which considerably advances the time spent on the destruction of tissue during my overall investigation. I use extremely corrosive, toxic acids to destroy the tissue of the organs, and these require great care in handling. Aside from the dense fumes they create, they have the potential to burn a hole through any organic matter, and that just happens to include my arm. There are strict Health & Safety regulations relating to drowning analysis, but I also need to be on my game. This includes elevating my levels of observation and keeping my wits about me at all times, as there is no place in drowning analysis in the laboratory for mistakes or accidents.

All the work is conducted using a purpose-built fume cupboard. This is an enclosed cupboard area in which I am shielded by glass. I perform the various tasks by inserting my arms into the interior of this cupboard space, after having first donned heavy-duty gloves, safety goggles, a protective white laboratory coat and a heavy apron. The fume cupboard, as its name implies, deals with any fumes created by extracting them. The work I perform has to be conducted at a very slow and meticulous pace; even without vigorous movement, adding acids will create dramatic frothing and billowing, which is a potential hazard.

Over the heat of a Bunsen burner I boil the organic material in nitric acid, which starts the tissue-destruction process. This can take two to three hours and sometimes longer, and I am unable to leave this process unattended. Boiling nitric acid is designed to render the tissue down to such an advanced state of destruction that it is no longer visible to the naked eye.

Once the tissue is no longer visible, I add sulphuric acid, another toxic chemical. The combination of acids elicits yet another burst of billowing toxic fumes.

Both acids are highly potent, especially when it comes to the removal of carbon. When I am destroying lung tissue, in particular, there comes a time when a ring of black carbon might form around the edge of the beaker containing the acids and fast-dissolving tissue. This indicates the presence of carbon in the sample. The lungs of heavy smokers, or industrial and inner-city workers, can take far longer to destroy, as this carbon can be present at phenomenal levels. It is the result of inhaling the carbon contained in cigarettes, or exhaust fumes, industrial pollution or just general pollution in the air itself.

I encounter an interesting phenomenon in this tissue destruction: no matter which organs of the body have been rendered down, by the point at which they have finally dissolved it doesn't matter what their original colour was; whether pale pink (lung) or purplish brown (liver and kidney), the remaining liquid is always straw-coloured. There is usually approximately 100–200ml in total, and I leave this fluid to settle overnight. The next morning I will lift away any fat which has solidified on the top and the remaining heavier matter will have sunk to the bottom of the beaker. I then decant the remaining liquid into several test tubes. These I place into a centrifuge, where they are spun at great speed in order to further draw down, or sink to the bottom, any remaining particulate matter. Both of the toxic chemicals I use are of a consistency thicker than water, and I will continually stop the process so that I can wash the sample through with distilled water, ridding it of the last of the remaining nitric and sulphuric acids. It is essential that I use distilled water rather than tap water, which could contain diatoms and skew the results. This is a real possibility if the tap water, despite the standard filtration process, is sourced from a rural setting.

I pour off the chemicals, with each rinse, into a specialist recyclable bottle, separating them from the normal waste disposal system, since they are such corrosive acids. The final sample will now potentially contain diatoms and possibly even silt. Whatever particulate matter now remains – generally approximately 10ml – is what I am most interested in for the final part of my investigation.

With the aid of a syringe, I now push the 10ml sample through the very fine mesh of a fine-grade filtration paper made of acetate. The mesh comes into its own because of the tiny grids on it. These enable me to estimate the number of diatoms remaining. These can range from very few to hundreds or even thousands.

I remove the filtration paper and mount it on a glass slide, which I then dry on a hotplate. This removes all the water from the filter paper and, once it is dry, I drip a few drops of mounting fluid onto it. Mounting fluid has the advantage of having the same refractive index as the acetate paper; in other words, the filter paper turns completely clear, leaving only the definition of any particulate matter remaining. Therefore, under a microscope, I can observe the exact nature of the remaining sample and see purely any particulate matter which has survived the boiling-down process. In fact, as my procedure destroys all living processes, any living diatoms will be killed off, leaving only their shells. I will therefore find myself observing the dead exoskeletons of any diatoms remaining; that is, if diatoms are actually present. Using the tiny grids of the millipore filter, I can now finally ascertain whether – and approximately how many – diatom silica exoskeletons are present and confirm or deny a Wet Drowning.

The presence of diatoms in a Wet Drowning which has taken place in an outdoor location is in itself proof that the person was alive, and their heart pumping blood to their organs, when they drowned. However, if the drowning incident was in an indoor location, such as a bath, there is much less likelihood of finding diatoms. The filtration process urban tap water undergoes generally renders it free of diatoms. There are, however, exceptions to this rule, as mentioned earlier, when the water has been obtained from a source such as a well, and where the drowning has occurred in a very rural area.

On one occasion I was asked to perform drowning analysis on a body found in a lake. I was expecting to find diatoms; however, the lake was stagnant. Without oxygen being present in the water, no diatoms were present in the organs of the deceased.

No matter what the situation, finding that there are no diatoms generally proves that the victim has not drowned from water inhalation. I am unable to prove a Dry Drowning scenario using the diatom analysis process. As no diatoms will have been ingested, the results will be exactly the same as if the victim had not drowned at all. Fortunately, though, there are several other observational signs of drowning which can prove strong indicators for the investigating pathologist. For instance, investigation of the scene at which the deceased has been found will include taking a site sample of the water in that vicinity. This will act as a means of proving the presence of diatoms in the water in which the body has been discovered. Witness testimony will also be of significant benefit where, for instance, the deceased was seen close to a body of water at the time the pathologist estimates their death to have occurred.

Other potential evidence of drowning can be found on dissection of the body at post-mortem. It may be discovered that the victim's major air passage is tightly closed, proving a Dry Drowning scenario. This reaction is, in fact, more commonly associated with people affected by drugs or alcohol. In a victim of Wet Drowning, at the post-mortem the pathologist may find the lungs to be heavy and waterlogged. In life, the interior of the lungs is always lubricated by a surfactant – a wetting agent – which can bubble up and is commonly seen around the mouth and nose of a victim of Wet Drowning. Prior to performing my drowning analysis, however, I will have very little, if any, awareness of findings indicating drowning, unless the pathologist has specifically passed this information on to me. In any case, it will have absolutely no bearing on my scientific process, which is being conducted specifically for the purpose of independent scientific corroboration. The final word in drowning analysis always rests with the pathologist. My own results will be taken into consideration, but, ultimately, it is the pathologist's professional conclusions that determine the final cause of death.

You may be surprised to learn that the validity of drowning investigation has been open to question for decades, leading to great debate in the forensic scientific community. Experiments conducted over the years have occasionally produced mixed results. To me, these indicate only that, somewhere in the process, there must have been cross-contamination.

I have performed my own, very strictly observed, control test using the organs of twenty-five cadavers. I obtained samples of tissue passed on by our pathologists from their mortuaries in the Southwark and Kingston-upon-Thames regions. Each of the samples was taken from the body of a deceased person who, in life, had had a close association with the Thames. None of these samples showed diatoms or any evidence of drowning. This enabled me to form the strong conclusion that diatoms were not present in the organs just by way of living near, or conducting recreational pursuits on, a large body of water. Having said this, there is a need to take the contextual circumstances of each case into consideration, for instance, the location in which the body has been found and the composition of the water present, in order to be scientifically accurate.

The bodies of victims coming out of the Thames told their own story. It was not uncommon to find that someone intent on suicide would first tie their hands to prevent themselves from swimming. Such cases might also be found with pockets full of stones from the riverbank to weigh themselves down. Once in a while, a body would be discovered with additional injuries. Our forensic pathologists had to establish whether the injuries had been sustained before or after immersion. For example, the deceased might show signs of having been beaten up before being pushed, or dumped, in the river. One victim showed a comparatively deep cut across his back and had sustained severe head injuries. The pathologist's conclusion was that his body had been repeatedly hit by the hull of a boat after submersion in the water. Another showed a spiral pattern on the upper back which, based upon the shape of the injury, indicated that it had been acquired from the repeated rotational action of a boat's propeller.

An unusual drowning case was to tap into my knowledge of the horrific lung disease asbestosis. For some time I had been performing histology for Dr Grant, who also acted in an advisory capacity on cases which were under review by the Industrial Claims Tribunal. They would review cases where an individual had worked closely with asbestos in an industrial setting and had unfortunately developed asbestosis. The disease was generally characterized by a particularly pernicious type of cancer known as mesothelioma. This would develop over time, cause debilitating symptoms and shorten the life of the sufferer. The Industrial Tribunal Hearing would often grant the complainants – usually the deceased's family – a significant pay-out, if the company was held liable for their deceased relative having contracted the illness on their premises in the course of the work they carried out.

Asbestos was a mined commodity which was used extensively at one time. This was largely due to the fact that it had great versatility: from making car brake shoes and pads to use as lagging for pipes, and in the production of corrugated roofing and fireproofing. It could be used domestically or industrially, in factories and ships, and was quite a common feature in older housing and in the insulation of steam pipes. It was eventually realized that it was hazardous to human health due to the strong possibility that its microscopic fibres were being inhaled by workers and causing damage to the lining of their lungs. In 1965 the national press revealed that there was no safe type of asbestos, and no safe exposure level (Hodge, Jones and Allen, 23 February 2018, referring to an article published on the front page of the *Sunday Times* on 31 October 1965). Countless people had, by then, found their health affected by it, and there was a sudden explosion of companies which were impacted.

From a scientific perspective, asbestos is composed of silicate minerals which, under magnification, resemble long thin fibrous crystals in a variety of colours. Once they are inside the body, the biological response is to bind up the fibrous crystals in proteins that are high in iron. Under magnification, the iron would show up as globules at the end of the long fibres, presenting in the shape of a dumb-bell, or drumstick. After performing histology on multiple deceased cases for Dr Grant, I was easily able to recognize these fibres. As a histologist, I also knew of the discovery of a stain which could be used to confirm such cases: Perls' Prussian Blue. This would turn the proteins present in the deceased's lung tissue a dark blue colour and make the fibres shine if exposed to polarized light. This was therefore my choice of stain in order to prove the presence of asbestos fibres, particularly as I understood the bio-refringent (shining) characteristics of asbestos.

So, when I received a case from Professor Mant in which a man had drowned in a body of water adjoining his company's industrial factory site, my histological knowledge of asbestosis was called upon. The factory was known to have worked with asbestos, and the water alongside the site was connected with the manufacturing process. On looking at a site sample of the water under polarized light, I managed to find shining asbestos fibres; I could also see the same shining fibres in the man's lung tissue. In fact, when I performed drowning analysis on his lungs, I recovered copious amounts of asbestos fibres from the remnants of the tissue sample.

Although this looked like an open-and-shut case of drowning, the conclusion was less straightforward. As the water alongside the factory had been used for industrial purposes, it was found to be highly polluted. The level of stagnation ruled out the existence of any life forms, and accordingly, even though the man was found to have clearly drowned in the water, no diatoms were discovered in his body.

As drowning analysis became an area in which I was an up-and-coming expert in the 1970s to 1980s, I became aware of a flaw associated with sample collection. I was very keen to eradicate this and reduce the chance of error, which had the potential to compromise scientific authenticity in this field of investigation.

To explain, the final process I choose to use involves pushing the collective matter of diatoms and silt, when present, through a millipore filter, whereby the grids on the filter enable me to count the number of diatoms present. I make it my practice to use the entire sample of liquid available; however, the recognised technique of which I had been advised was that only a sample of the available fluid, collected via the small end of a pipette, was necessary to determine a satisfactory outcome, not the entire amount. I had my reservations about this claim as, to my mind, it could miss vital evidence. Randomly choosing only a small area of the available liquid seemed scientifically inadequate. It had the potential to miss diatoms which might already be scarce in the first place. Expanding on this further, diatom-containing water begins to circulate around the bloodstream after a person has breathed water into their lungs as they take their last breaths. If the tissue used for drowning analysis comes not from the lungs but from a more remote organ such as a kidney or bone marrow, there is often less likelihood of diatoms being present. In fact, there might be so few as to be missed altogether. So, the standard practice was scientifically too arbitrary for me, and I felt it left way more to chance than was appropriate for an investigation which had legal implications. As it stood, it weakened the conclusiveness of the analytical results. I felt it was, in fact, negligent.

In view of my dissatisfaction, I took it upon myself to invent the millipore filtration method in drowning analysis which I have now been using for decades. By capturing all the available fluid from the organs and pushing it *all* through the filter, I was able to conclude that all diatomaceous material was present. However, it is not enough to change only your own practice, if you feel a scientifically negligent practice is being conducted across the board. So I tried to get the word out. A diatomology group had already been formed among my scientific colleagues in hospitals across the UK. We met regularly to disseminate knowledge and it was there that I discussed my new method, and the reasons behind it. I know of at least one diatomologist who took this method up as a result.

I am pleased to report that my millipore filtration system has never been proven to be flawed. The most I can be inconvenienced using this method is by finding a millipore filter clogged with silt, inhaled from the bottom of a body of water during the final stages of breathing. In lung tissue, I might also find that there is such a mass of diatoms present that I am left with a large round blob containing thousands of them, all heaped on top of one another. Neither of these findings is a disadvantage, of course. At least I know that any and all diatoms have been captured. Naturally, it has also worked the other way, whereby I have found as few as one or two diatoms – which might otherwise have been completely missed. The fact of the matter is that the technique has actually proven to be extremely reliable, and I continue to use it today, as one of the last remaining forensic diatomologists in the UK.

Long after I had left behind my laboratory days at Guy's, and diatomology as a specialism, I was approached by a professional colleague who had a proposition for me: would I like to offer a diatomology service, acting as a consultant for his newly evolving independent company? I have to admit that initially I did have my reservations, mainly because I had come a long way from being a purely laboratory-based scientist and felt a slight reluctance about returning to it. On the other hand, I knew there were very few remaining specialists in this field, and my decades of expertise would be invaluable.

In the end, I not only jumped on board, but became an enthusiastic advocate. I found myself quite in demand for drowning analysis, which came back easily to me, but also became involved in advising the police and forensic science trainees. This involved giving presentations and attending scientific events to publicize the service and give professional advice on best practice. It was a great advantage to be in at the outset, as the new laboratory was set up according to my specifications, and it has been rewarding to use my skills again for the advancement of police investigations into drowning. Not only have I found returning to this type of work stimulating, but also strangely therapeutic.

Personally, as a PA for a pathologist, I found that most of the unpleasant aspects of working in the mortuary tended to have an association with drowning. This was particularly evident at Southwark, in view of its proximity to the Thames and the number of bodies that arrived there due to drowning. I saw more bodies in a state of putrefaction in that mortuary than any other, and still have clear memories of those particular mornings, mainly because of their assault on my senses and, sometimes, emotions.

Taking dictation was never easy when I was engulfed in the somewhat sweet, though utterly repellent, odour of putrefaction. It was reminiscent of the smell of rotting meat that has been subjected to hot weather and the attractions of flies or maggots; though you would have to ramp up this olfactory connection 100 times to appreciate how intense, all-consuming and oppressive it could be. I would gladly have opted out of those mornings. One morning could feel like the passing of days. I had no idea how the pathologists coped, given that their task required careful and close observation, with time spent recording any signs of injury and the condition of the body, inside as well as out. I was at least able to maintain a certain distance, and in fairness they did place me as far away as possible in such instances.

Still, my concentration would slowly but surely ebb away, along with any good humour I had been feeling, and I would become increasingly fidgety and restless. Although I never had a full-blown panic attack, I believe I did come close to it. I would obsess about escaping, about inhaling clean, oxygenated air in huge gulps.

Being in the mortuary for this type of case was in fact one of the very few times I would question my involvement in an environment such as this. Gradually but insistently, the vile odour would work its way into my clothing, my hair, my skin … Somehow, breathing only served to reinforce it. It accompanied me all day, welded to my nasal passages. A hot shower might later eventually remove all external traces, but lunch was no escape – on those days, my favourite cheese-based sandwich would taste of decomposition.

There was far more to deal with in suicidal drowning. In such instances I had plenty of time to contemplate the suffering the person had undergone, possibly for a period of years, before they had taken that final step to end their life.

One Wednesday morning two drowning cases arrived. I braced myself for what was ahead, but couldn't prevent myself from becoming somewhat melancholic once I learned that one was due to suicide. The bodies took centre stage in the mortuary, alongside each other. There was no possibility of switching off from the sight, or of performing my job with my usual level of concentration. It took every ounce of determination to stay in my seat at the far end of the room. At the same time, I was perplexed to see a visible haze in the air, which seemed to grow denser as the time passed. A fog-like cloud seemed to hover over the two bodies. It was presumably generated by post-mortem emanations, or gases, from the bodies, though I had never before noticed anything like it.

On the train home that night I felt a sense of alienation from my fellow passengers. Their day would surely have been infinitely more pleasant than my own. Added to which, they weren't carrying the pungency of a mortuary home on their clothes. As I looked out of the train window, I was still seeing bloated flesh in pink, yellow and green.

As the evening wore on, I found myself ruminating on whether the mortuary was actually an appropriate place for me to work in. After all, I wasn't under any obligation to accompany the pathologist to it. It wasn't part of my job description. I could easily slip back into a more office-based role, no doubt with the pathologists' blessing. However, the moment passed. Such thoughts were largely unthinkable when I was feeling fresh and rested, and I recognized that drowning investigations were the exception, not the norm.

All the same, I can recall that, for some months afterwards, I would take in great lungfuls of air, almost as though my life depended on it, before entering the old mortuary. It seemed to have taken on epic proportions in my mind, becoming a darker, more forbidding place. It was important to make the most of every available opportunity to inhale fresh air, because I never knew what might be awaiting me inside.

CHAPTER 12

UNEARTHING HISTORY

With the work of five pathologists to manage and a typing speed in excess of 100wpm, I could clear between 50 and 100 post-mortem reports per day. Initially, at least, while I was settling in, there was little time to devote to tidying my new office space. So my library back-drop remained undisturbed for now, though at some point I knew I would have to address a few cluttered areas if I didn't want them to continually catch my eye as I worked. There was a push and pull between putting my own stamp on my territory and working at breakneck pace to remain on top of the constant influx of post-mortem dictation. I will admit that there was also a part of me that enjoyed leaving those areas undisturbed, maintaining them as they had been for decades. I didn't mind the fact that the dust had long since settled. It evoked a tangible sense of history, and a sense of contentment, every time I passed.

After approximately four months I found the time to make my office my own. That was when I found myself leafing slowly through a small pile of largely blank aged papers. I was several items in when I happened upon a banal brown folder. It appeared to have nothing in common with any of the stationery currently in use, but it was in pristine condition. Opening it, I found a sheet of thick yellow A4 paper, clearly an original document, accompanied by a black and white photo.

I wish now that I had opened the folder with more ceremony, given its contents. It wasn't so much the date on the document that alerted me to its antique nature, but the name of the person concerned. Instantly recognizable, it

Pauline in front of the library, where families congregated for paternity testing, and where two antique documents were buried in a pile of discarded paperwork.

sent a shiver down my spine. It was a murder report that I now held in my hands, and the victim was a very famous one. Her murderer was one of the most notorious figures ever to have walked the streets of London, a man who had committed a series of depraved attacks that had killed five, possibly more, women.

The black and white photograph showed the results of one of those attacks. I felt an immediate sense of pity for the victim, whose last moments would no doubt have been utterly terrifying, if not excruciatingly painful. There were unmissable marks of post-mortem stitching on her body – two lines running across her collarbones to meet at the centre of her chest, from where they travelled downwards to the base of her navel. Just above the navel, they veered off to one side, in apparent avoidance of cutting into this tough area. Some have considered this the hallmark of a surgeon, who will normally avoid cutting into this area of tissue. To me, it simply felt strange to be observing a photograph taken of a victim *after* the post-mortem had been performed; all the photographs I had ever seen in the department had been taken either at the scene of death or during the post-mortem. In a way, I was lucky; I knew that far more graphic photographs existed of the murderer's other victims, particularly his last.

The names of Catherine Eddowes and 'Jack the Ripper' are hardwired into the British psyche. Jack the Ripper is as synonymous with the Victorian era as Queen Victoria herself. Each consecutive generation becomes aware of his crimes through the multitude of books and documentaries, films and guided tours that repeatedly remind us of their still-unsolved status. The name 'Jack the Ripper' was acquired from a letter written in red ink, addressed to the press, and now thought to have been sent as a hoax. What we are aware of is that the murderer is considered to have been a lone predator, operating in the shadows. Despite 100 or so names being put forward, including that of Guy's Hospital's own physician-in-ordinary to Queen Victoria, Sir William Gull, the mystery remains unsolved.

I was now holding in my hands official proof of the date of Catherine Eddowes' death – 30 September 1888 – and reading the pathological findings of her post-mortem. The internet, of course, did not exist then, and therefore these details weren't freely available. Despite the eye-catching post-mortem stitching, I was left in no doubt of the brutality of the murder. I could see a cut throat and facial mutilation on the photograph. It was also evident that disembowelment had been involved.

Soon after, Professor Mant passed both the report and the photograph on to the curator of New Scotland Yard's Black Museum. It seemed a fitting place in which to retain them for posterity. It was also considerably safer than the corner of a bookcase, among a jumble of empty folders, where fate might have unwittingly consigned them to a bin.

If you looked hard enough, you could find all sorts of interesting objects hidden away or out of sight, on desktops, in cupboards or under benches. Some while before Pauline arrived in the department, I had been searching through one of our store cupboards when I came across two large black boxes I had never seen before. In them was a treasure trove of items dating back to the Second World War. I noticed that they seemed to be part of a collection, including photographs showing a young Professor Mant. Now head of our department, this very eminent professor was highly regarded by his peers and popular with the medical students, who packed out his lectures. Some time later we went to see his last ever lecture, and you couldn't get through the door; people were standing. But what I hadn't realized was that he had an intriguing professional involvement following the Second World War.

Prof, as we called him, had originally trained in Obstetrics & Gynaecology at St Mary's Hospital in London. In 1944 he had been called up and had joined the Royal Army Medical Corps. Promoted to major at the end of the war, he had been posted as officer-in-charge of the War Crimes Investigation Team's pathology section in north-western Europe. Placed in charge of the Special Medical Section of the British Army's War Crimes Group, in 1946 he found his initial responsibility was the exhumation of the bodies of Allied airmen and airborne personnel that had been found in cemeteries and unmarked graves. German personnel were either already in custody for these war crimes, or were soon expected to be. The full extent of Nazi war atrocities was just coming to light and Prof's activities included interviewing SS officers, as well as those known to have worked for them. The interviews included anyone implicated in conducting the human medical experiments that had taken place in several of the concentration camps. At this time Prof took over 100 witness statements from staff and inmates, which were later used at the War Crimes Trials. A number of mass graves were exhumed and Professor Mant personally conducted over 150 autopsies on these bodies. He later wrote his doctoral thesis on the subject.

When I discussed the photographs with him, he explained more about his earlier work, particularly the exhumations. I heard in detail about the discovery of the bodies and about the scarves issued to British pilots to wear around their necks. On them was printed a map of Europe which, if they were shot down, provided a means of helping them find their way back to safe territory. The pilots whose bodies were excavated had been executed by a gunshot to the head, rather than being taken to a camp, and their bodies hastily buried still wearing their scarves. These proved excellent evidence in establishing their identity as British. My own parents had told me about their experiences of the Second World War and of the air battles in which enemy planes had been shot down in front of them over the Thames estuary. I found listening to the stories of these Allied airmen, told to me by a figure of authority who had played a significant role in their exhumation and identification, to be a very sobering experience.

I also found records of Professor Mant's visits to various concentration camps, in particular Bergen-Belsen. Routine access to this kind of photograph wasn't available in the 1970s and this evidence of mass exterminations was shocking to me. There I was, looking at original photographs showing piles of emaciated bodies, exactly as they had been discovered when the camps were entered by the Allies at the end of the war. Seeing them while sitting alongside the pathologist who had actually been present at the scene brought home to me what I was viewing, and how unbelievable it was that it had happened only a few decades previously.

As well as unearthing history, of course we unearthed bodies. There is always a sense of expectation surrounding an exhumation. So much rests on the outcome. For the relatives of the deceased, their loved one is no longer missing and they can perform a proper burial. For the police, there is the satisfaction of knowing that they have given the relatives an answer and a mystery has been solved.

During my career I have attended a handful of exhumations. The first of these was an eye-opener. Dr Stephen Cordner and I had driven north from London to Oxfordshire. We were sitting in the police station, drinking a cup of coffee, when the atmosphere suddenly became electric. The police presence had inexplicably grown, and we watched with interest as everyone put forward their best bid for a place on the exhumation team that day.

The body we were about to exhume was that of an 18-year-old girl who had been missing for some time. A man had recently handed himself in at his local police station, presumably unable to live with his guilt. He had confessed that, having lured the girl to his home and killed her there, he had buried her on a neighbour's property in order to rid himself of any connection to the crime.

The property in question had been undergoing renovations, including the laying of a new garden path. This had enabled the defendant to use an adjoining rear footpath, which bordered several properties, to transfer the girl's body under cover of darkness and bury her beneath the newly laid path.

The exhumation therefore required the removal of a series of large paving blocks. Digging was then undertaken, with spades, to the required depth, in order to retrieve the deceased girl's remains. All this took some hours to complete.

The post-mortem examination took place that afternoon at Oxford mortuary. This has to be one of the oldest mortuaries in the country and it appeared not to have been treated to any kind of upgrade since its very first opening, decades earlier. It was dark and dingy, with a simple Anglepoise light above the mortuary table. The weather had been bright, clear and dry in the morning, but that afternoon it became typically unpredictable. I first became aware of this when my attention was drawn to the drip ... drip ... drip sound of water. It was rainwater running down the metal tubes of the lighting directly above the mortuary table, straight onto the area where Dr Cordner was working. This didn't seem to disturb him, and he concluded that the girl had died from strangulation. As the defendant had already admitted his guilt, he was given a life sentence for murder.

CHAPTER 13

BOMBINGS

The 1970s and 1980s saw an intense bombing campaign by the IRA on the British mainland. When bombs were detonated in two public houses in Guildford, Surrey, on 5 October 1974, five people were killed and dozens more injured. As our pathologists covered the Guildford area, in due course an influx of body parts came to me at Guy's. I was asked to ascertain if there was a way of pulling out any particulate matter from the flesh. It was hoped this would enable the police to understand more about the bomb's main components. Therefore it was my depressing task to go through all the body parts from the scene and sort through all the remaining human tissue, no matter how small.

In order to perform this task in an environment appropriate to such a huge undertaking, I relocated to the basement, where Guy's anatomy department had an embalming facility. I had decided to use their large boiler, which they themselves used for flesh removal purposes on occasion. It had already occurred to me that it would be necessary to soften down all the tissue, so that I could more easily extract any pieces of metal, glass, wood or plastic from the pulp I expected to be left with.

I first took a considerable amount of time to sew together a series of muslin bags, into which I put every last trace of flesh recovered from the scene. Then, over the next two days, I simmered every item over a very low heat. This enabled the flesh to fall easily away from the bone. Next, wearing rubber gloves, I sifted through everything by hand, pulling out all the larger non-human components. Every piece I found needed to be sorted and categorized. It was painstaking work, but at the end I was left with a very fine anatomical substance which I took up to the animal house, at the top of the medical school. I planned to use live X-ray to identify all the remaining non-human material. Donning a lead apron for protection, I used forceps to pull out all the relevant pieces while they were still visible on the screen.

I ended up with quite a useful collection of objects, including a piece of the battery casing and a cog from the clock that had acted as the timer. Everything of interest was delivered to the police's own laboratories for further study. The whole process had taken me approximately two weeks, but it was gratifying to know that I had been able to identify all the materials present.

I found requests of this nature unusual, but rewarding, due to the ingenuity and common sense required to achieve the desired results. I enjoyed working out the best way to do things, especially when they demanded dexterity and precise attention to detail. I was also acutely aware of the tragic and unforgettable circumstances leading up to this request, and to have contributed to solving this aspect of the investigation was, ultimately, gratifying.

* * *

Some time later, no doubt as a result of recent events, Dr Iain West began to take a greater interest in researching the effect of bomb blast debris and its depth of penetration into human flesh. Of course, you couldn't actually test this on anyone. However, it is well known in the medical profession that there are strong parallels between human flesh and the flesh of a pig. Allowing for the fact that the skin of a pig is notably tougher, the structure is anatomically quite close to that of human flesh, with a similar colour and texture. It was therefore natural that a dead pig came to mind as the ideal item for a scientific experiment. That was how I came to be involved in a rather secretive undertaking.

The initial stages took place in the closed environment of the government's Defence Science and Technology Laboratory at Porton Down, Salisbury. This was where a dead pig was 'blown up', using components similar to those used in a bomb. Once the carcass had been delivered to us at Guy's, my own part in the experiment began. Once again I decided to use the live X-ray machine in the medical school's animal house to determine the location of the pieces of debris. Iain was then able to study the bomb parts on X-ray, with a view to ascertaining their angle of distribution.

However, that wasn't the end of the story. We were now faced with a greater problem: how should we dispose of the carcass? We were stuck for ideas as to how we could get rid of it without drawing undue attention to ourselves, especially as it closely resembled a reasonably well-sized, rounded human body.

I remember our tea break that day, and the discussions about the possible methods we had at our disposal. I can remember personally suggesting that we could just cut it up into chops. Once all our more 'creative' ideas had been shared, I set about the task of actually pulling off the whole operation. The problem was that it was the height of summer and I had a very limited time before the pig would begin to decompose.

Fortunately, I had already perfected the art of looking as casual as possible when I was performing my job, which generally diverted attention from what I was doing. I also knew that if I wore my white lab coat, it would camouflage me in any hospital setting. The third part of my plan to blend in while transporting a 'dead body' around relied on the confusion of any visitors having to find their way around a huge London teaching hospital. Hopefully, they wouldn't be paying any attention to the somewhat bulky, shrouded corpse on top of my trolley. I wasn't sure which would be more alarming: the thought that the mysterious object might be a dead body, or that it was the body of a pig which showed signs of having been blown up.

I needed to find the largest plastic bag I could lay my hands on. However, on this particular day there were no black bags around and I had to settle for a less inconspicuous colour: psychedelic orange. This wasn't going to do my subterfuge any favours. But, with no other option, I wrapped it around the pig several times and loaded the body onto the largest trolley I could find. As casually as we could, my serology colleague Mike and I, in our white lab

coats, set off on the long journey to the engineering department's boiler room.

Seeking anonymity, we had decided to use the maze of
tunnels beneath the hospital's many buildings. We felt very
self-conscious and must have looked like a pair of shady
characters, but fortunately the concealed tunnel system
really came into its own that day. Without incident, we
finally reached the boiler room, home of our ultimate destination: the hospital incinerator.

We now thought we were in the clear, but the hardest
part of our operation was just about to start. As we arrived
at the area where the incinerator was housed, we were
faced by a suddenly very animated man, who was in
charge of operating the incinerator that afternoon. The
look on his face was a mixture of pure horror and
confusion, which made it very difficult to keep a straight
face. But I tried.

'Good afternoon. We're from the forensic department.'
Pointing at the large psychedelic bag, which you really
couldn't miss, I added, 'We've got to get rid of this.'

The man looked it over slowly with increasingly bulging
eyes. 'What is it?'

'It's a pig,' I said casually.

Immediately, he began to back off, arms waving. 'Oh no,
man! What have you got there? A *body*?! Oh no, man!'

Mike and I couldn't help chuckling, but I did my best to
be reassuring.

'Don't worry. It's fine. It's a fully grown pig, and all we've
got to do is dispose of it. We just want to tip it down the
chute into the incinerator, that's all.'

The incinerator operator was still gesticulating wildly. 'I don't want to get into trouble! Oh no, man!'

It was a few moments before we were able to calm him down and convince him that it *was* just the body of a pig, not a human body we were trying to dispose of in this way, for whatever nefarious reasons. Finally, he told us to go ahead.

We made our way up in the lift to the incinerator, where, between us, we somehow managed to hoist the heavy and awkward body into the chute. Finally, the pig slid away to its destruction.

When we thought about it afterwards, we had been incredibly lucky to 'destroy the evidence' so easily, without even unwrapping the body for inspection. We had managed to dispose of 'a body' in the hospital incinerator. It had all the hallmarks of the perfect crime … and we had just pulled it off.

CHAPTER 14

DEATH BY MISADVENTURE

It was some months after joining the department that I was introduced to a subject I had only ever heard of remotely before: death by misadventure. I knew it was occasionally given as a cause of death at an inquest, but had zero knowledge of what it meant in real terms. So, when it became evident that I had absolutely no idea what my colleagues were talking about, I was almost frogmarched by Kevin and Derek down the corridor to the little-used laboratory outside the infamous cutting room and given a seat beside a long deep bank of wooden cupboards. I began to prepare myself for whatever was about to be launched at me. The inclusion of Kevin in this educational moment led to a certain amount of trepidation. He had a particular habit of showing me photographs of murder/suicide scenes I wasn't always prepared for. What was he about to show me now? Would I find it rewarding, amusing … or terrifying?

My first view, once the cupboards were opened, was of a row of skulls. These apparently had nothing to do with why we were there, but as Kevin and Derek took them out I was shown injuries to the bone arising from various traumas.

Once all the skulls were out on the unused worktop, we turned to our real purpose for being there. It was explained to me that our pathologists regularly came into direct contact with suspicious deaths which were connected to some of the more unusual requirements for which central London, in particular, catered. On occasion, items had been brought directly from the scene of death to the department. Specifically, these cupboards.

The reason they had come into our possession was indicated by the word 'misadventure', 'mis' indicating failure, error, accident. Clearly these 'adventures' had resulted in an unexpected outcome: the person's demise. Kevin and Derek proved to be very able storytellers, and they were aided by props from the cupboard. They started with several gas masks, and their accompanying breathing apparatus.

Controlled self-asphyxiation is a far more commonly recognized sexual practice today than it was then. A few years ago, I was surprised to read two interviews in which it was mentioned. We're not talking specialist publications here, but the glossy pages of *OK!* magazine. What's more, the subject was casually thrown into the interview, in a clearly boastful way, by very high-profile British celebrities. The aspirational and untroubled tone of their descriptions led me to surmise that they had no idea of the failure rate. Though it can lead to a greater sexual high, there is no doubt in forensic circles that controlled self-asphyxiation carries the very real risk of inadvertent death, as the borderline unconscious state is reached and the ability to recommence oxygen intake is lost. Be it a gradually tightening noose or the deliberate reduction of oxygen via a gas mask, it is dicing with death every single time.

In addition to the gas masks, I was shown a homemade noose, the use of which had likewise resulted in death.

I was told that there were London clubs and brothels which catered for these particular sexual tastes, at least one of which offered a degree of safety by way of observation. Practised in the home, however, controlled self-asphyxiation might well lead to the mortuary. A case of this nature typically came to our pathologists' attention, I recall, every three months, occasionally more often. That's not an insignificant number when you consider that we covered only a few counties and an area of London, not its entirety. It's a tragedy when you contemplate the fact that death was unintentional.

While these items were related to deaths that were unplanned, work of a forensic nature will always include the reverse side of the coin: suicide. I won't be mentioning any specifics here, as it's a subject which is particularly hard to come to terms with, but suicides would arrive at the mortuary with regularity, and in the course of my work I was shown evidence, or given verbal accounts, of people using any and every talent they had in the planning and execution of their own demise.

However many times I heard about suicide, though, I never became desensitized to it. I found the idea utterly horrifying. On occasion, Kevin – in the hope of adding to my forensic education – would present me with a work-related photograph to test my observational skills, hoping that I would correctly identify features of note. These scenes would play on my mind, as they often involved suicide or accidental death. It was flattering to be asked to decipher direction of blood spatter, for instance, but, especially in the early days, I would return home with a headache after viewing these images.

I felt quite sickened, therefore, by the contents of those cupboards. Their association with planned and unplanned death was a lot to handle. In fact, I was relieved beyond measure to return to my desk.

I next saw those objects over a year later, when they were taken out again, no doubt for someone else's edification. This time they felt less threatening and seemed less incongruous. Their ability to shock me had obviously been neutralized in the time that had elapsed. Or, more accurately, I had become more immune to shocking materials.

CHAPTER 15

THE TRAUMA OF MASS DISASTERS

I was fascinated by my scientific work, but there were times when I had a few sleepless nights as a result of what I was involved in. It was impossible to hear a case history and not imagine the terror the victim had experienced, or the depressed resignation that had led to suicide. But the most harrowing situations in which I was directly involved were those connected to a mass disaster. When something of this nature occurred, it was necessary for everyone in the department to get involved, so that all available medical staff could immediately respond to the crisis.

My first experience of the major scale involved in the handling of a mass disaster came through the Clapham Junction rail crash. On 12 December 1988 a passenger train packed with commuters had approached the mainline station at Clapham, with its driver unaware that, up ahead, a train had stopped for a red light at a junction. At the same time, on an adjacent track, an empty train was approaching from the opposite direction. Unavoidably, the commuter train ploughed into the back of the first train at speed and, in the process, side-swiped the empty train. Thirty-five people lost their lives and almost 500 were badly injured.

Injury on such a scale impacts hugely on the emergency services and on nearby hospitals, all of whom are focused on keeping the injured alive. The bodies of the deceased were therefore transported straight to Westminster mortuary. This was the point from which an alert was conveyed to our department, requesting the mobilization of all available staff. Only our secretary at that time, Lorraine, remained behind to cover on-site communications and liaison. Everyone else left immediately for Westminster mortuary.

As we arrived, we noted that several of our pathologists were already gowned up and working. Even the coroner's officers got involved, as did the coroner himself, Dr Paul Knapman.

Ian Bradbrook, who worked in toxicology and paternity testing, and I were identified as being able to offer a valuable source of continuity, if we were willing to sort body parts. The destructive nature of the collision had produced a huge number of these, and a room needed to be found which was appropriate for reception of them. The cold room at the back of the mortuary was more routinely used for dealing with hazardous substances, and for the newly evolving cases of HIV, as well as for the victims of drowning. Its lower ambient temperature and specialist equipment, such as air extraction facilities, helped to mask any smells from the rest of the building and therefore it was effectively sealed off from the outside. This was where we based ourselves.

We didn't have to wait long before a stream of police officers and firemen delivered bags and bags of body parts to us. They built up so quickly that we lost all available space on the surface areas and eventually had no choice but to empty the bags carefully across the floor. Sifting through the contents by hand, we noted any specific features which might lead to further identification. First, we dealt with items that particularly stood out – for instance, legs and arms, which were a little bit easier to match – and we took them back into the mortuary, holding them up and calling out their defining features. Someone, typically a pathologist, would respond and call us over, so that we could deposit the item on their table. This was somewhat easier when the item was distinctive or unusual, for instance, an ankle with a cycle clip around it or an arm with a garter around the sleeve, or a foot in a patterned sock. In this way the identification process progressed, lessening the overload in the cold room.

Situations like this are very surreal. There is the shock of the incident itself, which has only just happened, and is in the heart of the capital city. You work in that city; you travel there every day alongside thousands of commuters similar to the ones whose body parts you are now sifting through. There are sights you have never seen before, certainly not on this scale. It is hard to get your head around it.

We were able to match a significant number of body parts that day, and work continued non-stop until about 9 p.m. Over the next few days the pattern was repeated over and over, until all possible parts had been accounted for.

When the pathology element of this major disaster ended, we learned that the police involved in the operation had been offered counselling. This was totally understandable. Sadly, for us there was no such support, even though, despite the fact we dealt with death in some form every day, this type of event affected us in exactly the same way as anyone less used to it. There was no professional outlet to help us come to terms with what we had seen.

I don't remember ever talking in any great depth about my work with my wife either, even in situations such as this. It was far easier to discuss things among colleagues the next day, over coffee, which provided relief, in its way. Another good way of offsetting the angst was an energetic game of squash. Often, though, getting through an experience like this meant raising the emotional aftermath in the pub with the pathologists over a few drinks.

We had all been involved. We all had harrowing dreams at night. But we all knew that, in our line of work, there was no choice but to continue with our jobs exactly as before.

Soon after, however, the police presented me with a badge of recognition in acknowledgement of my participation. I greatly appreciated this, and it helped me, personally, to find some form of closure.

Only eight months later, another disaster befell London. Late in the evening of 20 August 1989 a party boat on the Thames, the *Marchioness*, was making its way centre-stream towards Cannon Street bridge. It had originally been one of the 'little ships' that had sailed to Dunkirk in 1940 to rescue stranded servicemen. On board, a female merchant banker was celebrating her twenty-sixth birthday and many of the party were also in their twenties.

At 1.45 a.m. that morning, a dredger named the *Bowbelle* was also travelling centre-stream along the Thames. The boats collided, and the anchor of the *Bowbelle* began to slice through the side of the party boat, immediately capsizing it. The superstructure of the pleasure boat detached and quickly filled with water. Tragically, the continuous forward momentum of the dredger pushed the *Marchioness* still further underwater, and only 30 seconds after the collision the *Marchioness* was completely submerged. Twenty-four people lost their lives, most of whom had been on the upper deck at the time of the collision.

Our departmental staff were still reeling from the Clapham rail disaster. Sadly, we were going to have to perform a very similar role in this incident. Several of our pathologists were called out and departmental staff received an immediate call over to Westminster mortuary to assist. The task I was allocated was that of collecting and cataloguing any forms of identification found, including driving licences and items of jewellery. For this, I needed to examine the clothing of the deceased and note down everything I found. This included the contents of wallets and any drugs found in pockets. It took several days to sort through all the clothing, and was a very depressing task, given that there were so many victims, all of whom were so young. At the end of the day there was no possibility of switching off, not with the sights we had been witness to.

Understandably, the experience of handling two mass disasters in quick succession made me feel traumatized for some time, and I remember how long it was before the visions faded and my sleep pattern returned to normal.

CHAPTER 16

ARMED AND DANGEROUS

When life got stressful, the one thing Derek, Mike and I prioritized was playing squash. It wasn't purely a sport to us, more a way of life. At first I was only a beginner, but both Derek and Mike were happy to train me up. The game became the perfect foil to any work-related brooding, which was easily forgotten in a frenetic charge around a court after a tiny ball. There was no difficulty at work this game couldn't put into perspective.

This was just as well, as supporting staff mental health was an unheard-of concept in the mid-1980s. Bullying, though unwelcome and frowned upon, tended to be regarded as a matter for the victim alone to resolve. No advice would be offered or action taken. The fact that bullying is driven by lack of self-esteem wasn't commonly understood back then. So any situation of this nature would remain unacknowledged and unresolved.

Years had passed in which we had enjoyed a fantastic departmental camaraderie. We had become good friends as well as colleagues. Our rapport meant good times at work and outside, in any social setting. Yet when a few of our pathologists moved on, through retirement or promotion, very often to Australia, the best part of the camaraderie and humour went along with them. This greatly impacted the spirit of the department and, in time, resentments grew, mistrust marred the atmosphere and personal relationships became strained. As is so often the case, an icy atmosphere could instantly be lifted through the shock tactic of kindness and consideration, but the professional intervention that might have defused any stand-off was decades away from formal introduction into the workplace. Instead, we all adapted to the negative energy, rather than addressing it, which was such a shame and a lost opportunity.

Another concept that had yet to be introduced to the workplace was Health & Safety. In terms of physical safety, a glass cubicle at the entrance to the medical school indicated that space had been provided for a security officer, but no one was employed in that capacity. Nor was there a receptionist. Everyone, be they staff or visitor, was left to their own devices. As I found on my interview day, finding someone to assist you could take a while.

There was no perceived need for induction either, no guidance on behaviour, no formalization at all regarding physical safety in the environment. We were all still bending from the waist to lift heavy objects and taking on tasks that were outside our remit. Personal safety was down to vigilance and luck.

Having said all this, having no rules to abide by was heaven. It was quite enjoyable to be able to use your own judgement; to be master of your own domain. Perhaps we were also reassured by the close proximity of the Accident & Emergency department.

We were also lucky that the hospital's commitment to staff health was demonstrated through the provision of excellent swimming and sports facilities. Outside, the medical school roof was used for sunbathing, and we weren't averse to the idea of inhaling the hot fumes as the tarmac melted. It only detracted slightly from our enjoyment, as we spent lunchtimes toasting ourselves a deep brown. In fact, I wrote off this assault on my lungs as a good way to burn off the more unpleasant smells of the mortuary!

In the mortuary, protective clothing for me, as the PA, was never a cause for concern. I stood or sat at a safe distance from the body and was never splashed by any bodily fluids. However, one day Westminster mortuary's superintendent, Peter Bevan, for whom I had a lot of affection, valiantly, if a little hesitantly, put forward the suggestion that I 'might like' to wear protective plastic foot covers over my shoes. He couldn't bring himself to meet my gaze, probably because he knew how important my appearance was to me. At 21 I was daily showcasing any fashion trend which called for short skirts and high heels, and I was conscious that my clothing choices had, so far, been appreciated by everyone, as the department was largely comprised of men, as was the mortuary. So this unexpected suggestion of covering my precious stilettos rendered me speechless, and more than a little alarmed.

I mean, seriously, the idea was appalling! Did he think I would willingly dent my 'street cred' in this way? I suffered for that look. Twice daily, I spent 40 minutes managing a pair of heels across what felt like half of London, risking blisters and a twisted ankle, and stoically struggling to avoid the uneven paving slabs that were cunningly spaced to have gaps at precisely the average stiletto-walker's stride as I crossed London Bridge.

Potentially more lethal to my gait were the solid metal grates, 2 feet wide, that spanned the entire width of the bridge. Literally wrong-footing me, a grate would regularly attach itself to my heel. Not to be deterred by this leaden weight, especially as I had no way of removing it myself, I would gamely limp on for a few paces, dragging it noisily along with me in the hope that continual movement would somehow dislodge it. But as I learned, even heaving it upwards with a near-impossible kick into the air wouldn't shake it off. When this didn't work I would adopt the 'This isn't really happening' approach that I had used in the skirt situation. Finally, when the excruciating sound of dragging metal on stone became too loud to ignore, I would have to stop and acknowledge the crowd of commuters these antics had attracted. I would look around me and see people colliding as they decided whether this spectacle was worth pausing for. With the screeching resistance of the grate, the attempts at air kicks and the hobbling lurches forward, it was a scene which, I now realize, resembled a remarkably nuanced study of the Hunchback of Notre Dame. Perhaps the crowd was wondering where the cameras were.

Fortunately, half a dozen of London Bridge's male commuters never failed to rush valiantly to my aid, thankfully unconcerned by their association with the embarrassing person making this exhibition of themselves. While they freed my foot, female bystanders would smirk from the sidelines. It's understandable. There must have been a certain satisfaction in seeing the young woman in the attention-seeking miniskirt and heels getting her comeuppance.

But imagine, after all this, being asked to *cover* my footwear! Surely speed-walking in stilettos was an accomplishment on which I should be congratulated. Why, then, would I ever elect to cover my shoes with these unflattering blue plastic circles of shame?

I did secretly sympathize with Peter's attempt to gently and considerately enforce some Health & Safety rules in relation to my presence, especially given that everyone else followed them in his domain. But plastic foot covers were never going to last more than a second before being punctured by a heel ... which would be my go-to excuse if ever I needed one. Furthermore, I still considered myself a visitor to the mortuary and there was no requirement for me to wear anything other than whatever clothes I had chosen for that day. I couldn't see any harm in wearing bright colours and keeping the skirts short and the heels high, other than occasionally causing a bit of a distraction. In this otherwise sombre environment, a splash of colour and an air of normality seemed welcome.

So I couldn't bring myself to comply, and although Peter raised the subject one more time I noticed Iain immediately shut it down with a discreet but firm shake of his head.

* * *

There was, though, one incident that did give me pause for thought concerning the issue of protective clothing. It took place when Stephen Cordner was close to finishing a long list of post-mortems one morning. All the mortuary staff had already abandoned ship and changed back into their civvies. Stephen was working on his last case and had apparently reached a point where he needed to take samples for toxicology, the process that would check for the presence of drugs and alcohol. With no one else around to help and his shouts going unanswered, he called me over from my seat in the corner, hurriedly handed me a narrow-necked bottle and asked me to kindly hold it steady.

With no inkling of what was to come, I took the tube and helpfully held it out.

Standing in front of me, Stephen assessed the distance between us, then gestured for me to stand further back … and further back … until I was pivoting, my arm held outwards at full stretch.

Turning swiftly away, he then turned back towards me with a metal weighing-bowl. A cold, swaying, greyish-pink, chunky liquid swished to and fro inside: the contents of someone's last meal, direct from their stomach.

As Stephen raised the bowl into the air, I took in what he had in mind. With abject horror, I watched as he swiftly tipped it downwards in the direction of my bare hand. Time stood still. I had never been so focused in my life. I waited for the cold trickle – or cascade – of what constituted vomit over my hand.

Unbelievably, Stephen's aim was impeccable: not even the tiniest droplet escaped the tube. I would have applauded, but I was rather busy. As I began to breathe normally again, I made a conscious decision *never* to agree to 'help out' in the mortuary before first establishing *exactly* what I was getting myself into.

The mortuary may have been off-limits to the public, but the medical school, at that time, allowed full public accessibility. Anyone could wander through the corridors. The constantly open laboratory doors gave easier staff access to the labs, though laboratory processes that had medico-legal connotations remained largely open to view. Theft was prevented by caution and luck rather than locked doors. How we didn't regard any of this as an issue for concern is a mystery. To us, reaching our offices in the morning, or returning from the squash court at lunchtime, an open door was a homely, welcoming sight. Years of unacknowledged, literal open-door policy thus continued.

The most challenging aspect of this laxity could have been the issue of public access and the regular on-site attendance of members of the public for paternity testing. These people were unknown to us, were not particularly well monitored on-site and were in dispute with former partners, as mentioned earlier. On the whole they were anxious, and many were aggrieved about a needle being inserted into their arm as a way of settling a legal issue with monetary connotations. In short, at any given moment things could really kick off, were they to meet their former partner in a corridor. We had no security, no recourse, and, should things turn nasty, we were all at risk.

* * *

How deeply ironic it was, then, that our department was home to a stash of weapons. We're talking rifles and automatic weapons here, not 'just' your average handgun, though there was an impressive collection of those, too. Every weapon had been acquired from the scene of a crime or suicide. That in itself was fairly shocking to me, given the number of weapons present. More alarming still, almost every weapon was accompanied by whatever quantity of live ammunition had also been found at the scene. And perhaps just to add a touch more jeopardy, a proportion of the live ammunition was kept in the locker *with the guns*!

This didn't seem to be of overwhelming concern at the time. Admittedly, the gun locker – your average tall, narrow, grey cabinet – was padlocked and rarely opened. Nevertheless, when it was, the guns were taken out and examined over a period of perhaps a couple of hours, largely to introduce the latest unsuspecting novice to the department's impressive collection.

On the day it was realized that I had not yet become party to the unveiling of this treasure trove, I couldn't keep up with Derek or Kevin as they virtually ran down the corridor, vibrating with nervous energy, delighted at having found a new audience for their expertise. Locking the office door conspiratorially behind us, they unlocked the cabinet with eager hands and embarked on a detailed and knowledgeable description of each weapon. There were two Berettas, a Mauser, a Luger, and a military service revolver .45. There was even a homemade pistol. At the other end of the scale, there was a Lee-Enfield bolt-action magazine-fed repeating .303 rifle. At some stage, a sawn-off shotgun and a .22 hunting rifle had also been acquired. Perhaps the most shocking item – to me, anyway – was a British military submachine Sten gun, with its silencer, plus, of course, its ammunition. This had originally been used by the Special Boat Service as they parachuted into France at the end of the Second World War.

Derek and Kevin were the proverbial 'boys with their toys' and I instinctively knew I was supposed to be as excited as they were about the collection. The guns themselves were in outstanding condition, I had to agree. What didn't occur to me at the time – in our departmental environment of openness and trust – was that the security applied to the guns was *somewhat lacking*! Although there was an implicit understanding of the need to maintain secrecy, apparently the locking of the office door at the time they were on display was deemed sufficient.

This changed when Iain West, then our newly incumbent head pathologist, and himself a dedicated member of a gun club, came to be shown our cache. His immediate response was: '*Christ!* They shouldn't be here!' and arrangements were swiftly made to find a more secure location. Tipping off a contact at the Metropolitan Police, Iain got to proudly show off his inherited weaponry to one of the ballistics team, before our prized collection took up residence with them in, it is certain, a far safer environment than our department had provided.

CHAPTER 17

TOO YOUNG TO DIE

A suspicious death would create a significant police presence in the mortuary, ranging from the most senior
down to those who were about to witness their first
post-mortem examination. Once or twice I had cause to
leave the main part of the mortuary to make a telephone
call at the request of the pathologist. Suddenly I would find
myself joined by a junior officer, evidently unused to the
sights and smells of the mortuary, who would almost
collapse into the first available seat, pale and sweating. I was
surprised the first time it happened, and even more so when
these officers showed concern for me. They apparently
thought that I was making a quick exit because I was unable
to cope, which meant they were dumbstruck when they
heard that I was there to work. Some even pressed the
point, making sure that I really was in the mortuary by
choice. Passing a few minutes in casual conversation
allowed sufficient time for them to recover. Perhaps my
lack of concern rubbed off on them as, by the time I was
ready to go back in, they invariably joined me.

I remember one occasion, though, for its ominous atmosphere. I had never experienced anything like it, not least the

number of officers present. Iain and I had returned to Guy's from Westminster that morning to learn that he was wanted back in the mortuary straight after lunch. As we re-entered the mortuary, about a dozen officers were present, the atmosphere between them strained and tense. There was no conversation. Everyone's eyes were downcast and I soon learned that the top echelons of the relevant police force were present. They were standing in a line, but as soon as we arrived they began to encircle a body on the floor, laid out on a white sheet.

Iain West immediately took charge, which came as a relief, and while the most senior officer related the details of the case to him, I had a moment to appraise what I was seeing. I realized that I knew a bit about the incident that had led to the body being there. It was all over the news headlines. The deceased was a young Mayfair prostitute, a girl in her mid-twenties, and the cause of death was a single gunshot injury to the head.

Unfortunately, this was the second unwitting victim of an abductor who, it appeared, had a certain *modus operandi*. The first victim had climbed into a car driven by a man of approximately 30 years of age. He had driven away from the Mayfair area and immediately locked the car doors. When the woman had tried to escape, he had threatened to shoot her. She was later found alive on the edge of the M25.

The second victim had been witnessed also leaving Mayfair in a man's car and it appeared that a similar scenario may have played out, except that this time the victim had been fatally shot at close range. Her body had been dumped in a similar location alongside the M25.

It wasn't surprising that the police were brooding and monosyllabic. There was a sense the gunman would strike again, and they would be in the political line of fire, should that happen. Prostitutes had been warned about the likely presence of a murderer in the vicinity. In fact, it was the top news story and dotted all around the capital on placards. For women in an occupation which required them to override their gut instinct and take risks, even with their lives, it must have been a terrifying time.

Iain's findings were to be of paramount importance, given his expertise in gunshot injury. He was able to identify the calibre of gun used and the range from which it had been fired. Given the powder burns on the exterior skin, the woman had clearly been shot at very close range. The depth and angle at which the bullet had penetrated provided further evidence of her position in the car. Elsewhere, technicians were simultaneously analysing her clothing, looking for traces of fibres which might have been transferred from the interior of the abductor's car, or from his own clothing, or anything which could provide crucial corroborative evidence, should a potential suspect be identified.

Within a few days we heard that the police had apprehended the girl's killer. How they managed this, we did not hear. However, it was a very fortunate outcome for all concerned, not least because the suspect had stated his wish to go down in history as a famous serial killer. Thankfully, his plans had been thwarted.

*　　*　　*

I found that the bleakest days in the mortuary were connected to the body of a child or young adult. Whatever the circumstances of their death, it was always a struggle to witness that much smaller body in a mortuary setting. An adult or elderly person had at least had the opportunity to live their life to the full, and as they wished. The body of a child could also indicate that death had been due to unnatural causes, which was doubly difficult to contemplate.

One of the worst experiences – actually, a real low point for me – was when two young children's bodies were in the mortuary on the same day. I remember the morning's case having uncommon parallels with the later abduction and murder of a similarly young child, Jamie Bulger. The child in this case was only 5 years of age and had been led away from his home environment by older boys, who had killed him on waste land. The afternoon's case was a boy of 13. Although there were no suspicious circumstances, looking at him I still felt incredible sadness. An older adult would have lived a full life, one in which you could imagine they had been loved by, and devoted to, family and friends. When someone had died young, I couldn't help imagining the trauma of their death and the distress of their family.

That particular day a feeling of sadness and loss began to filter through me. I had to drag myself back to the present and steel myself for a period of sustained emotional detachment as the internal investigations were performed on the small bodies. But the melancholy that descended was unavoidable, and by the time I reached home that night a cloud of depression had settled, sucking the colour from the world around me. A good night's sleep helped, but when I woke the next morning my mind was instantly back in the mortuary, picturing the two bodies and reimagining the circumstances of their demise and the impact on their family.

This was new territory, from which I couldn't easily return. I just had to try to deal with things in my own way. I hadn't mentioned the events of the day at home; neither did I ever mention them at work, not even to Derek. We were all busy with our own tasks and it just never occurred to me that I might need support. Today there would be the chance to talk it through with a professional and move on. At the time, I loved my job, I had no intention of appearing unable to cope with it and I knew I didn't have to confront cases of this nature very often. These thoughts, however, did very little to alleviate my lower energy levels, generally depressed mood and the overwhelming feeling of sadness that engulfed me for a while.

There was another side to this incident. I had long seen myself as emotionally resilient. I had the confidence of youth and I had been used to this environment for some time. I was convinced I took it all in my stride. Suddenly I was side-swiped into realizing that I wasn't as emotionally untouchable as I'd thought. This was somewhat reassuring, as it meant I was still emotionally engaged, and it was healthy to allow my emotional self to emerge from the studied professional detachment I had adopted in order to work in the mortuary every day. Recognizing this went a long way towards getting past the circumstances that had brought me up short.

This was another time when I questioned my continued dedication to mortuary attendance with the pathologist. Of course, it brought home the fact that it actually did take dedication; in fact, it required considerable emotional strength. It was the point at which I fully acknowledged that I had those qualities.

It may surprise you to learn that the case that shocked me the most, though, wasn't generated by murder, or suicide. It related to something I had never heard referred to at work, or seen any evidence of in the mortuary. When I heard the pathologist's cause of death, I was left literally speechless for several minutes. What's more, that case is a cautionary tale for women everywhere.

The morning had started with Kevin breezing straight in to see me as per usual, and immediately handing me a photograph. I recognized the beginnings of a question and answer session, something I enjoyed as long as the images weren't too confrontational. On this particular day I found myself looking at a black and white photograph of a young woman lying on her bed in a face-down position, her head tilted slightly to one side. She appeared attractive and healthy. The only oddity was that she was lying on, rather than in, her bed.

She had been discovered by her family, who had been unable to rouse her for work and raised the alarm. She had apparently been very active and sporty, with no known medical conditions. As I gazed at her photograph I began to feel increasingly uneasy. There were parallels between us: her age, 22, was identical to mine; she, too, was dedicated to sport. It was unnerving. Kevin had found no physical or pathological features whatsoever to account for her sudden death, which appeared to have taken place when she was asleep.

I took in everything I was seeing in the photograph and admitted that I could see no evidence of foul play. At that point Kevin told me the cause of death he had given: toxic shock syndrome.

For those unfamiliar with the term, this is the major area of concern associated with the internal use of sanitary tampons. Warnings given on the instruction sheets in boxes of tampons are designed to impress upon the user the necessity to change them regularly in order to prevent bacterial infection. This can occur if a foreign object remains inside the body over an extended period of time. Due to the internalized nature of the process, the infection can very quickly advance, to the point where toxins enter the bloodstream, which is medically known as acute septicaemia, or blood poisoning. It is fatal if not treated immediately, in hospital, as an emergency.

I was thunderstruck by this cause of death. It was alarming to discover that someone so fit and in such vibrant health had been killed by what – up until that point – had been just a distant warning, expounded on a bit of standard packaging available anywhere. Read, understood, acknowledged, yes, but just a warning, surely? Not something which could claim a young, fit and healthy life?

That young woman's death was – and is – a lesson to women of any menstrual age, underlining the importance of taking such warnings seriously and acting with the greatest caution.

CHAPTER 18

MERGERS & ACQUISITIONS

I loved the variety of my scientific work and couldn't wait to get to work every day, but there were occasional downsides. The less worrying variety was being asked if someone could borrow my arm to take my blood. More of a concern was being asked to take part in some type of medical experiment.

The 'honour' of being a guinea pig might have fallen to me because of my apparent gung-ho, try-anything attitude. But I also like to think it was an acknowledgement of my scientific status.

I wasn't, in fact, the only guinea pig in our department. There were occasions when a pathologist and I would conduct an experiment which would help us reach a better point of understanding, or which would give us a sounder scientific conclusion.

When a very young boy in a clinical case – by which I mean living rather than deceased – acquired a series of long, striped, abrasive, red marks on his cheeks, it looked like a foregone conclusion that it was a case of child abuse. The marks were so highly visible that the parents immediately fell under suspicion of having caused them. The child himself was too young to articulate any of the circumstances leading up to the injuries. The parents both continued to strongly deny having harmed their child. However, the fact was that there was no other way of accounting for the marks, so eventually they were charged with abuse.

Iain West began to have his own suspicions as to how the marks might have been caused. He asked me if I could procure an item which was very easy to buy on the local high street. Next, he conducted an experiment to see if it was possible to reproduce the marks using the item.

The skin of the inner forearm tends to be softer and more delicate than the skin on the top of the arm. Therefore, using a standard Bic disposable safety razor, Iain scraped up and down both his inner forearms. The result was a set of parallel scrape injuries identical to those found on the face of the young boy.

The conclusion? Having witnessed his father shaving in the mornings, the little boy had just been trying to copy Daddy.

Heists and drug deals among gang members going horribly wrong isn't a scenario confined to fiction or the film industry. One afternoon we discussed a multiple shooting which appeared to fit exactly this scenario. Four gang members had allegedly been sitting in their car when an argument had broken out. One of the men had found the other three turning on him, accusing him of trying to double-cross them, after which they apparently bound his wrists tightly with duct tape. Although he claimed that at first he could not escape from his bindings, eventually he did struggle free. A further altercation resulted in the shooting of the three other gang members and, when questioned by the police, the man claimed he had been acting in self-defence.

To a medical observer, his version of events didn't quite add up. Iain and I discussed the police photographs he had brought back to the department, which showed a man with extremely hairy arms. If he had been bound tightly several times around the wrists, as he claimed, we would have expected to see redness or marks of some sort, but there were none. Given the sticky nature of duct tape, we also expected evidence of at least some hair loss, as the glue on the duct tape would have wrenched the hairs out when he pulled the tape off.

We decided to perform an experiment to figure out whether it was possible for him to have removed the duct tape without producing any hair loss or skin reddening. A quick survey was conducted among those present in the office to see who had the hairiest arms. No doubt it was to everyone's relief that it was my own which, everyone enthusiastically agreed, were the hairiest. Therefore I had no option but to allow my wrists to be bound together with duct tape and then to try to wriggle out of the bindings, preferably without leaving any tell-tale marks or losing any hair.

What had at first seemed like a good idea lost all its appeal as the hairs closest to the adhesive tape were ripped from their roots. In all, we measured a loss of 5cm in width of hair on each wrist, not to mention the reddening associated with it. It was some time before the skin on my wrists healed. On the other hand, we had successfully proven the suspect's account was false. This raised sufficient doubt about his claim of having shot the other three gang members in an act of self-defence and pointed to an attempt to keep all the loot for himself.

Our photographs were passed on to the investigating police force and went some way towards proving, at the subsequent trial, that the man had murdered the other gang members.

In the mid-1980s work became a bit of a refuge for me. Circumstances at home had led to a crisis in my personal life and my marriage was on the rocks. Within a few months my wife and I separated. I was concerned about the impact on my children, and it was much harder to concentrate at work with the continual conflict at home.

Few people knew about my situation. At work at the time it didn't feel appropriate to talk about such things and, in any case, I considered it my private business. So, apart from Pauline, whom I trusted and discussed my situation with over tea breaks, my colleagues in the department, and in the wider medical school, had no idea. I don't even remember telling any of the pathologists at the time, even though I was sure of their support. The department felt like a battlefield in those days and there was no way I was going to risk confiding in anyone. I couldn't foresee an end to the bad atmosphere and all I felt I could do was carry on with my job the best I could and keep the situation to myself. You feel bad enough that your marriage has failed, without having to broadcast it.

* * *

Naturally, the department's ignorance of Derek's domestic situation made things particularly hard for him, as the pressures arising from his fractured home life were no longer being offset by a supportive working environment. Added to which, our department was losing its heart and soul. A lack of trust had arisen, divisions were playing out, and you could sense the underhand dealings and duplicity in the air. In the background, for some time, political alliances had been crystallizing. Groundwork was being prepared, agreements reached.

Personally, I had achieved fulfilment at the highest level, was performing my role to the peak of its potential, and had achieved all I had ever wanted. Yet this was all countered by the dread of returning every afternoon to an office with a hostile atmosphere. What a paradox.

Despite the fact that Derek and I had gradually become something of a confidant to each other, I knew that such a toxic atmosphere was detrimental to my overall well-being and personal happiness. Leaving was a very difficult decision to take, given how devoted I was to my job and how hard it was to 'leave Derek to it' in such a hostile environment, but I took that decision.

Perhaps predictably, as I left my job on a Friday afternoon in late September, the person who had had their eye on it for a couple of years rapidly transferred across to fill my metaphorically still-warm seat at 9 a.m. the following Monday. I had given my best years to that job, and had received huge personal reward from doing so, but the time had come when I felt it was necessary for my own well-being to move on, however difficult that proved to be.

* * *

By now separated, and with two children under ten, I was allowed to leave work mid-afternoon, which gave me just enough time to race home and arrive at the school gates. But leaving work at 3.00pm every day to drive 13 miles into Kent – in London traffic – was not a feasible long-term solution. I continued to juggle work, the afternoon school runs and the life of a single parent for some months, until the arrangement eventually gave way to a more workable solution for all of us. But that meant that my children, whom I had so looked forward to seeing at the end of the day, were no longer returning to my home during the week. Suddenly I was returning to an empty house at night.

With the children gone, I was suddenly free to do whatever I wanted. This meant I would either go to the gym or sit at home watching TV with a bottle of martini. The other, healthier, option was a game of squash with one of my contacts, one of whom was Pauline. We would meet up somewhere in London and have a quick drink afterwards before going our separate ways, but not before I had updated her on my situation, and she had given me some moral support. The jokes and laughter were taking on a more serious tone.

Leaving the forensic world after six years wasn't easy and I wouldn't be honest if I didn't say that I missed it with a passion. However, as fate would have it, this wasn't the end of my association with it. Fast-forwarding a little over a decade, I would return to the forensic world in a different guise, one which was so original, and so perfect, it's fair to say I could never have imagined it for myself. At this stage, though, neither Derek nor I had the remotest idea of ever working together again. Added to which, if you had told us then that we would be in business together as husband and wife ... well, I don't think either of us would have believed you.

Throughout my time at Guy's, there had always been someone known to me through my social circle in whom I had a romantic interest, or was going out with. Several months before I left, Derek had even arranged a blind date for me with one of his contacts. We had hit it off immediately, but, after a series of dates over a period of three or four months, during which we wined and dined our way through London's trendiest cocktail bars and restaurants, much as I felt a strong attachment to him, I sensed there might be no longevity in the relationship and reluctantly ended it.

Now, as Derek and I spent our working days apart from each other across London, when we did meet up we both discovered the real person behind the professional exterior. We began to see each other differently and to realize just how much we liked each other, and that the opportunities to get to know each other more deeply couldn't come quickly enough.

It's an incredible moment when you realize that someone truly 'gets' you. Despite our different life experiences, Derek and I found a commonality in our outlook on life. We were beginning to finish each other's sentences and were feeling an attraction we hadn't been aware of before. We both felt valued, safe and appreciated when we were together. This shift in a relationship which had started as friendship five or six years previously was an unanticipated turn of events. Neither of us would have predicted it, but we had fallen in love.

I can pinpoint the exact moment I realized I was in love with Derek. I was temping in London and he had arranged a week's holiday with his children in Greece. While he was away I missed him like crazy. He had been completely sure of his own mind for some time; however, as a young single woman, with the commonly held expectation of marrying a single man, I naturally had been feeling that I had so much more at stake than him, in the long run, and had been unwilling to commit to a relationship. The separation did the trick. When he returned, I was ready for us to take our relationship to the next level and look for a place we could move into together.

However, recognizing I was in love with Derek wasn't without its complications. I instinctively felt there would be a need to brace myself for a storm of the public criticism that tends to descend on a single person who is about to take on a formerly married one. It takes strength to stand firm in the face of nay-sayers. The same was true of Derek's situation: his formerly positive view of marriage did nothing to lessen the stigma of his separation and divorce, and everyone has their own opinion about a marriage breakdown, however misinformed or misguided.

At the same time, I hadn't envisioned the possibility that I might fall in love with someone who came with a ready-made family. I had never thought of joining a family rather than creating my own. In the event, Ross and Gemma were easy to love and we bonded very quickly, creating an exciting and loving environment for them in the time we all spent together at weekends.

Transforming from a singleton into a girlfriend with two stepchildren might have been a bit of a curveball, but I coped. However, the permutations of this new set-up were still felt at times. It wasn't something that came from within; it was the general sense of disapproval that came from society. There was a general inference that this couldn't be a serious love match, not with a 10-year age gap. Derek found that people felt that, as a divorcé, he didn't have the right to find happiness with someone younger. Meanwhile, people were telling me that it was inappropriate, as a younger woman, to be spending time with someone else's children. Without variation, the condemnation came from those who were ignorant of the circumstances and/or had suddenly developed a puffed-up sense of sanctimony. Ironically, those who evidently felt the deepest sense of outrage were the men – married men, I might add – who had been the most creepily solicitous towards me when I was single!

It could have been a struggle to master the inevitable challenges of integrating ourselves into a part-time, ready-made family unit, but we made it work. In time, Derek and I moved in together, and just over two years later we married – on a blazing hot day at the end of March 1990. Returning from our honeymoon in the Cotswolds, we were accompanied by virtually every type of British weather, from sweltering heat to snowstorms and back to the blazing sunshine of our utterly dependable corner of the south-east coast. Unbeknown to us at the time, we also brought back a newly developing life.

In the meantime, Ross and Gemma, now 14 and 11 respectively, joined us at weekends for long days at the beach and explorations of the woods and countryside surrounding us. Ross was quick to appraise the local antique and bric-à-brac shops, discovering an entrepreneurial talent for buying and selling. Spending pocket money on Second World War memorabilia in one shop, he would immediately walk around the corner to sell it at profit to the next. Gemma would happily settle down in front of any romantic film or musical to paint and draw.

On New Year's Eve 1990 our son Rowan was born. His immediate response to a musical beat, as he found his feet, hinted at the future drummer within. September 1993 saw the arrival of our last child, Amber. She regularly pitted herself against her daredevil slightly older brother, to become just as adventurous. Our family was complete.

CHAPTER 19

HEART ATTACK

Throughout the whole of my technical career at Guy's, staining pieces of tissue for histological analysis was a routine task for me. Once I had cut the piece of tissue to a certain size, I would mount it in a thin block of wax, which would then be sliced on a microtome in order to produce a fine sliver. Once I had subjected this sliver – officially known as a 'section' – to the relevant staining technique, any pathology present would show up according to the range of dyes used to determine it.

In forensic medicine there was always the 'holy grail' of finding a staining technique to improve the chances of finding early myocardial infarction, otherwise known as a heart attack. Early myocardial infarction wasn't always readily detectable to the naked eye, as very little sign of its presence was exhibited in the heart itself. During a heart attack the blood vessels will become blocked, though the heart continues to pump and its muscle fibres continue to work. Eventually, however, all the available oxygen in the individual heart cells will have been spent and, as a result, they will die. The problem for the pathologist is that, during their post-mortem examination, the changes in the cells are not always visible to the naked eye. In some cases the heart tissue may appear slightly bruised, but sometimes – if the heart has stopped beating rapidly, for instance – the tissue is far less likely to show any visible damage to the muscle fibres. This lessens the possibility of unequivocally giving heart attack as a cause of death. Even as a histologist, if a routine staining technique is used, these changes to the heart might not even be evident under the microscope.

My research in this area began with a free sample of a new dye, Rhodanile Blue Sulphate, which was sent to me by a scientific stockist. When I read up on it I learned that it acted on tissue in a state of reduction, i.e. deterioration, or, in layman's terms, tissue in which oxygen is being depleted. I hit on the idea of trialling its use when staining a piece of heart tissue in a case of suspected heart attack. What I actually noticed was that it highlighted, in a different colour from the healthy surrounding tissue, individual muscle fibres affected by the lack of oxygen. These turned a much darker purplish-blue than the more oxygenated, healthy heart tissue.

My new technique worked so well that it caught the attention of Dr Dick (Richard) Shepherd, one of the pathologists with whom I worked at Guy's. He is now very well known for his television series *Autopsy: The Last Hours of* … He became a very active supporter of my research and began to collect samples of tissue specifically for me to experiment on. We also worked together on clarifying the results, and eventually wrote a paper on the stain and my scientific findings, which Dick asked me to present with him that year, 1991, at the American Society of Forensic Sciences in New Orleans.

Dick Shepherd (left) seems to be winning this round of banter, as Derek makes his point and Westminster Mortuary Superintendent Peter Bevan (centre) looks on, amused.

My research was, overall, so well received that many of the pathologists present requested a handout to pass on to their own technicians. However, one British pathologist wasn't so enthusiastic, and expressed surprise that I was able to present a paper, as I was 'only' a biomedical scientist, not a doctor. This, of course, flew in the face of the decades of knowledge and scientific expertise involved in creating such a valuable asset to the pathology community.

Prior to my research, and my subsequent presentation at the conference, I had never required more than a basic scientific qualification – my full technical certificate (FTC). Now, seeing the rather short-sighted reception with which I was met by this detractor, Dick put to me the suggestion that I would 'have more clout' if I were to gain a higher qualification. His own wife, Jen, had just gained an Open University degree which had taken her from nursing to work as a general practitioner, and this was the direction in which he pointed me. He knew only too well how much credibility a scientific degree would confer, and how much more validation it would give to my findings as a scientist.

Thanks to Dick's advice I flew home with a new agenda. Only a few months later I was sitting on my usual commuter train into London Bridge with huge study books from the Open University on my lap. This was the start of a six-year study period aimed at obtaining a Batchelor of Science with Honours degree. Train journeys had previously offered me an opportunity for sleep, after starting out at the crack of dawn. This was now abandoned, as I studied instead during my 90-minute commute into London each day. I would study again on the journey home, after a full day's work. It wasn't easy when I was tired, but I had fully committed myself to the weekly 15-hour study time-frame required, and knew I had to reshape the course of my working day, including my lunch breaks. A less welcome element of this was missing out on many of our boozy departmental lunches. However, I was keen to adhere to my set agenda in order to keep up and not lose any valuable study time, and not let it encroach on my home life, if possible.

After the requisite six years I gained my degree, and it changed my life almost immediately. Through the work I had conducted I had by now become a recognized injury pattern expert, and the Royal Photographic Society honoured this by conferring the title of 'graduate imaging scientist' on me, quickly followed by another honour:

'associate' of the Royal Photographic Society. Dr Iain West had helped here, by giving the Society a glowing review of my achievements, including all the contributions I had made to the forensic department at Guy's over my many years there, and my crucial contributions to the National Injuries Database.

CHAPTER 20

NATIONAL INJURIES DATABASE

D r Iain West was the mastermind behind two ideas that were to impact forensic medicine – and police investigation – far beyond his time. His concepts are still in operation today, both playing a major role in the investigation and presentation of injury. Both were ideas I would have a major part in taking forward.

It was in the early 1990s, before our office work became increasingly computerized, that our departmental head had his first brainwave. It began with the idea of creating an imaging data source, which could be used for teaching purposes. It would be designed so that anyone involved in forensic pathology could use the data, including doctors and trainees – basically, anyone who needed to study injury.

The concept soon took on more complexity, with the intention that it would be used specifically to record – and link – injury data. We knew that we ideally needed a search engine to recognize specific findings of wounding at post-mortem and to bring to light any consistency in these features. Consistency could potentially indicate the *modus operandi* of a serial killer. An added bonus would be the gathering of statistics from this data source, including analytical crime data.

As our laboratory manager at the time, I took on the responsibility of designing and writing the entire coding for our program. Within a few more months we had acquired a dedicated full-time administrator for the database, Sonya Baylis. Together, Sonya and I worked on refining and optimizing the newly entitled Forensic Medicine Database.

Initially, it was run purely for our own casework within our department at Guy's, as had been the intention. That work had been accumulated by our half-dozen senior pathologists who, once a murder trial had finished, would pass on their hard copies of all the documentation. We would painstakingly add these details to the database, including witness statements and reports, as well as electronic data such as video footage or photographic records of the scene of crime and of the post-mortem itself. Eventually we further refined the search capability to include specific descriptions of injury and their location on the body. Basically, any field which could be subjected to categorization was included, optimizing the results.

Dr West managed to convince the Home Office to fund our project and, shortly after, two other forensic departments, based in the north and west of the UK, requested the installation of their own satellite database. These were also funded by the Home Office, and Sonya and I set them up. We were joined in this venture by Keith McGovern, our expert in computer technology. So, what had started out as our own bespoke database grew to have the potential of becoming a specialist source of information for the entire

UK, via just the one searchable system. If it proved to be successful, we planned on information-sharing on a national level.

With the marked increase in information flow we initially received from our pathology sources, we agreed that additional help was needed to input the vast amounts of data to our database. We began to take on gap-year students for a one-year work experience placement, or newly qualified postgraduates, who took a dedicated internship with us. It was a fast-growing venture, with three student internships taking place at a time, allowing us to optimize the increase in searchable information now flooding in from external pathologist sources, who were now contributing their casework to our data. Inputting all this was a painstaking process, as each source of information had to be scanned in, including every photograph in some very large photographic albums, and this was alongside the ongoing work both Sonya and I had. But it meant we were able to acquire a huge amount of data from various scenes of crime and from post-mortems, from where we could access all the external and internal injuries. For the mid-1990s this construct was way ahead of its time.

As I built the system, I was able to reflect on the importance of certain features I felt ought to be included. As it was imperative to build in the capability to extend the comparison program so that we could assess as many cases as possible, I optimized it to compare up to four cases simultaneously. I was mindful of the fact that, prior to the advent of computerization, tracing information was nowhere near as effective, especially if a suspect were to relocate outside the county in which the crime had been perpetrated. If someone remained at large, undetected, in a new part of the country, often the only way to pick up on a repeated pattern of injury was through an information-sharing opportunity with another force. It tended to be only when new information came to light as part of broader press coverage that a force might discover a link between the murderer they had been chasing and a pattern emerging elsewhere in the country. This had always been a source of frustration. Now, with the introduction of a searchable system to compare up to four cases of wounding alongside each other, there was ultimately the potential to spot parallels in injury type and distribution across the whole of the UK and so identify any emerging serial killer.

As a team, we began to perform routine searches on our database to compare any similarities we found between cases and scientifically analyse the results. In the meantime, our pathologists had taken up the original way of utilizing the system: teaching medical students about wounding. There were unforeseen educational benefits for me, too. I was now studying such a huge variety of wounds and complex skin patterning every day of my working life that my exposure to patterned injury was dramatically boosted and my expertise in injury types broadened.

Sonya and I began to disseminate information about the database by giving lectures to our police clients on a national scale, and there was an immediate buzz of interest. Everyone appeared to have designs on it, aware of its value in respect of their own professional interests. This led to us hitting the tour circuit, travelling all over the country to present talks to police forces. We covered not only the database facility itself, but also my specialisms in weapon and wound overlay and a new field I had recently begun to pioneer: injury body mapping, this being Iain West's second inspirational concept.

More will follow on this subject, but in the meantime, as recognition of the database increased, discussions began to centre on the benefit of relocating it to a police-centric facility. At the time – the end of 1999 – our Guy's department had been impacted by university budget cuts and our pathologists were talking of branching out independently. Consequently, both the department and our premises were, sadly, on the point of closure.

The database was relocated to the National Crime Faculty at Bramshill in Hampshire and became known as the National Injuries Database, the name by which it is known today. As Sonya and I were both still very much involved in work on the database, we also relocated to Hampshire. I had just turned 50 and decided to set myself up as a part-time external consultant in an office at home. Sonya, on the other hand, chose to become an on-site full-time member of staff and commuted every day from Southend to Bramshill.

My new circumstances enabled me to work on referrals from the Injuries Database alongside my own independent casework in weapon and wound overlay. I would also continue to build on my injury body-mapping services from my office at home.

In time, the National Crime Faculty relocated once more, this time to Wyboston Lakes in Bedfordshire, from where it is run today under the auspices of the same agency, now known as the National Crime Agency. The National Injuries Database is now recognized as a unique source of support and advice in the investigation of serious crime, on both a national and international scale. I continue to work as an external consultant, primarily giving professional advice and providing evidence in cases referred to me for weapon and wound overlay.

CHAPTER 21

PATTERNED INJURY EXPERT

I t was my role as the forensic department's photographer that was the catalyst for my gradual emergence as an expert in injury patterning, and how it can be identified through the biological reaction of skin to impact by a weapon. Initially, I was called out to the mortuary to photograph injuries where death had occurred in unusual circumstances, if the pathologist wanted to retain a photographic record of their findings. I vividly remember two cases in particular: one related to photographing the injuries suffered by a base jumper whose parachute had failed to open after he had dived from the top of one of London's tallest hotels. The other involved the murder of two homeless people who had been sleeping in a shop doorway and had, inexplicably, been stabbed by a passerby.

One of my earliest cases of superimposition to establish identity involved a badly decomposed body found in the grounds of Blenheim Palace, Oxfordshire. It was that of a young woman. She appeared to have been strangled with an item of her own clothing. There were clear signs of animal predation, her bones being scattered around the site at the time her body was discovered. With no reports of any local missing persons, her identity had remained unknown. Police were able to assess her clothing, though, and establish that she was a Norwegian national. A check of police records identified her as a missing person last seen hitch-hiking around the UK.

To facilitate a formal identification of the body, Professor Mant asked me to superimpose a negative image of the woman's skull onto a black and white photograph, taken of her in life. As soon as I viewed the jaw, there was sufficient asymmetry to confirm a totally unique match, the uneven features lining up precisely with those in the photograph. This allowed us to confirm positive identification to the young woman's relatives. Her disappearance had, until then, been inexplicable, but now they knew the body was their daughter's they were, at last, able to obtain some form of closure.

My earliest superimposition techniques would involve matching a negative transparent image of a deceased person with a photograph beneath, of their facial features when living. I would invariably do this by comparison of the angles, such as the jaw or cheekbones. Any matches in bone structure were then highlighted. I would make assessments between the height of a forehead and the width of a jaw, and if there was any facial asymmetry, or irregularity of the features, this would become particularly noticeable. It was far easier to spot a match when there were evident areas of unique asymmetry. However, if visible on a photograph, very often it was teeth that provided the best clues.

This might sound like a simplistic practice, but it achieved a surprisingly good level of authentication. In the 1970s, I performed it in a dedicated space in a small dark room. I always found it gratifying to perform. However, in the early days it was a very slow and laborious process, involving hours of repeat photography, an array of variously sized photographs and negatives, and the use of a photographic enlarger and chemical developers. Working in the dark could be a disadvantage, too, and large parts of the day would disappear before I was in a position to re-emerge. Even more frustratingly, I might get very close to a match, but even a slight error in alignment would mean having to go back to the drawing-board to start the process all over again. Conclusive proof was only possible if there was a 100 per cent match between both photographic mediums, giving the level of accuracy that was considered valid proof in a court of law.

One day, I hit upon the idea of using closed-circuit TV. This allowed me to mix the two images together using a mixing desk, significantly boosting the speed at which I could work. I performed the superimposition with the use of two video cameras, one of which focused on the skull, the other on an image of the deceased, and was able to successfully capture a combination of the two images as an overlay. This was a method I used several times before the advent of the computer age.

However, once I had a computer this type of work came into its own. Initially, this procedure had been performed purely for identification purposes. However, I began to realize that it could be applied to injuries on skin and a suspected weapon.

* * *

During the years at Guy's I was provided with countless opportunities to observe patterned injury. The pathologists would arrive and hand me their photographs of injury and wait while I formed my own observations and theories before we discussed the case. Such routine exposure meant I became quite skilled at observing the features of injury and recognizing the types of weapon responsible for causing them. I was soon able to spot a relevant pattern and pick up on a detail which might, to the untrained eye, appear to be insignificant. Often, even the smallest, faintest feature can prove to be the link you are seeking.

My knowledge of injury was founded on understanding the reactions of human skin to any sudden force or impact. The most significant changes occur below the surface, deep within the skin's underlying structures. I would learn the most about these both from Iain and from our new head of department, Dr Nat Cary, who took over from him when he retired in 1998. It was Nat who took the time to explain the more deep-seated mechanisms of bruising from the pathologist's perspective, adding expertise and depth of understanding to my increasing exposure to this field of investigation.

The circumstances that give rise to injury beneath the skin are not well known outside forensic circles, which can lead to a certain amount of assumption and therefore confusion. A non-medical investigator can easily mistake certain elements which arise in connection with bruising. This then becomes a matter of conflict in both the findings themselves and the subsequent possibility of giving conflicting evidence in court. Further complicating the issue is the fact that some features of intradermal bruising can, at times, contain elements which seem at odds with expectation.

As anyone who has been unfortunate enough to have knocked themselves on a hard surface will know, when an object strikes the outer skin with any degree of force, bruising is produced. However, the complication arises when you realize that bruising is not singularly classified. There can be variations in skin itself – for instance, thickness and suppleness – and variations in it across the body. For instance, there will be differences according to whether bone lies beneath it or not. However, the most commonly misunderstood process is how deep bruising occurs. After an object hits the skin with sufficient force, the small blood vessels in the lower regions of the skin break, and blood can track along through the deepest layers of the skin, causing deep bruising.

Another type of injury which confuses is that of crush abrasion. In this instance the surface of the skin becomes abraded, or chafed. This is not actually classified as bruising. However, it becomes of interest to me when, due to its surface nature, there might be the possibility of patterning at this level of the skin.

Most of my work is conducted on marks on the upper layers of skin: the intradermal layers. Bruising here will occur when an object hits the skin in a very precise, fast and straightforward on–off motion. If there happen to be any protruding parts on the object, these will displace the very fine blood vessels – the capillaries – in the upper layers of the skin, just below the surface. Each of these capillaries is of the same diameter as a human hair. When there is considerable impact, the blood inside these tiny vessels has nowhere to go, and so is displaced in a forceful, outwards trajectory. With the pressure of this displaced blood suddenly hitting the surrounding tissue, the small capillaries within that tissue also burst. In this way they invariably take on the shape of the outer margin of the object used to strike them. If the skin has been struck at an angle, the outer edge may be very clearly defined. If it has been struck from directly above, the entire outer perimeter of the object may well be incorporated into the pattern left behind.

Let us now suppose that the object that has struck the skin happens to be the tread of a shoe. Trainers, in particular, tend to have a series of grooves and indentations in their sole. If the strike was a stamping motion, any of these patterns are likely to show up, and there may well be areas of increased definition and complexity. However, there are many variables here, including skin type, the force of the strike and the angle of delivery, especially if it involves a curved surface. Sometimes I can observe incredible detail; at other times virtually none.

As a rule, though, when an object which is patterned hits the skin, when the blood is displaced outwards it will flow forcefully into any grooves where parts of the pattern have not made contact with the skin. Blood might also accumulate along the edge of the injury. Whatever the case, the resulting pattern will have very decisive characteristics, and quite possibly mirror the item that has caused them.

You are probably already aware of the process of blanching – obtaining a paler, whiter area when you press your thumb down firmly onto a fleshy part of your hand and quickly release it. In healthy, living tissue, as soon as the pressure has been released the blanched skin will return to its normal colour as blood returns to the area. In the case of intradermal bruising, however, blood cannot, as a rule, return to the area, as the impact will have disrupted and damaged the blood vessels in the innermost layers of the skin. If, at this point, the victim's heart stops as the result of the attack, the intradermal bruising will remain in place and not fade. However, in a living victim, the body's natural repair processes will commence almost immediately, and within a matter of days the bruising will have faded.

There have been occasions where patterned marks of injury have been missed or overlooked and, as a result, a fresh pair of eyes such as my own can sometimes turn up new evidence. Nowadays I am able to use software to look specifically for patterns, zooming in very closely to look at the skin in considerably magnified detail. If I spot something I consider to be relevant, I am prepared to invest a considerable amount of time in examining it closely. Computerization has revolutionized the entire process. I am even able to prepare an animated video presentation in which I demonstrate a weapon fading in and out over a patterned injury.

Weapon and wound analysis usually involves viewing a series of photographs of the suspected weapon, although sometimes I receive the weapon itself. There is one crucial element to the photography: whatever weapon is under review, it will ideally need a centimetre scale – or rule – alongside it when photographed. This simple device can mean the difference between a straightforward weapon and wound matching process, and the compromising of vital evidence, due to an inability to prove the true size of the injury or, indeed, weapon.

The omission of a proper scale on police photographs of injury occurs more often than is useful. The difficulty is that, if a scale is missing, it is often too late to request a second series of photographs. By then, the marks on the skin may have become fainter. They may even have disappeared completely by the time I receive the images. It is then down to me to try and establish some form of comparison by which to measure the marks.

I have found a measure of success in using the photograph of a body part for this purpose. It's surprising how often an ear can be useful – as long as it is actually in the photograph of the injury itself with a centimetre scale alongside it. I will then lay the one image of the ear over the other. When they are correctly aligned, I will have a scaled photograph of the ear. I will cut and paste the new scale above the layer showing the injury, keeping the matched layers of the ears intact. I will then fade down the additional photograph of the ear, which will give me a multi-layered, but scaled, image of the original photograph of the ear, with the scope of providing a scaled overlay. But if a centimetre scale is photographed alongside the injury at the outset it saves all this time and effort, as well as avoids any risk of the loss of potential evidence.

How do I match a suspected weapon to an injury? I will use the example of a trainer sole to illustrate this, as these tend to contain a lot of detail. Overall, I am looking for matching characteristics. Initially, I will make a visual assessment, looking for distinct lines or swirl patterns. First, I check the skin of the victim, then I look at the suspected weapon itself. The distinctive patterns and shapes on a trainer mean that, occasionally, I can find correlations not only between the pattern on the sole, but also the stitching at the top or side. When I observe the edges of all the patterns I see, I am looking for any raised areas and assessing the nature of any indentations on the weapon.

Objects other than the sole of a shoe can leave patterns ranging from the extraordinarily large to the seriously minute. For example, I have been asked to look at the criss-cross patterning of the grille of a car. At other times I have been looking at the detail found on a patterned ring, worn on a hand suspected of delivering a punch.

The naked eye alone is insufficient to spot any similarities, but another factor which can obscure any pattern is when dark bruising has resulted from injury. More difficulty will arise when there have been two or three blows to the same area, as is often the case. I can spot a 'double-strike' and will adapt an overlay to incorporate several areas of patterning if necessary.

When I find what I suspect to be a positive match of weapon to wound, I construct an animation, starting with the base layer of the injury. Over this I place the layer of the photographed suspected weapon. I then create a short program showing a gradual fade-in/fade-out of the top layer – the weapon – to demonstrate any and all relevant correlations between weapon and wound.

However, as much as an animated superimposition can be an asset to the prosecution by revealing the characteristics that match, a mismatch will throw light on the tenuousness of that link. If I cannot see a sufficient degree to use for comparison, I can produce a negative report, though it is rare for a negative result to be taken further, as there needs to be sufficiently conclusive evidence.

I have found that the type of case that leads to the most complications is that of slapping by a hand, which is mostly applicable to cases of suspected child abuse. Many cases of slapping come to my attention, but it is one of the most difficult scenarios in which to find positive proof.

A case which highlighted this was one where the marks present on a child's face appeared to demonstrate a row of identifiable finger impressions. Almost the whole length of every finger of a hand, including the rounded tips, was visible on the skin at the time the photograph was taken. Three people were in the frame for having made these finger marks: the child's mother, her boyfriend and an older sibling of the child. The mother claimed not to have been present at the time and said she suspected her boyfriend of having caused the injury. The hands of all three suspects were photographed and passed to me for overlay comparison. I found clear differences between the hand sizes of all three parties. Of the most striking significance was the hand size of the woman's boyfriend who, at over 6 feet in height, had large hands which spanned a greater area than the patterned injury on the child's body. The sibling's hands were significantly smaller. The mother's hands presented as somewhere midway between the two. In this instance I could prove, using overlay, that her hands were the greatest match, as was clearly evident in the shape and size of each finger outline on the child's skin, though this was the only claim I could realistically make.

It is extremely difficult to prove that hands have been used as weapons. This is due to the nature of skin itself, which is a movable surface, as you will see if you rub your thumb over the skin of your hand or arm. The act of hitting the skin of a victim – hitting a movable surface, using a hand, which is also a movable surface – creates a situation where, as they come into contact, any resulting outlines have already stretched out of shape to some degree. This is evident in the amorphous patterns I often see, which are very difficult to assign to the hand of any specific individual without some additional type of immovable 'marker' or pattern, such as a ring. A ring generally leaves a mark of its own. Another inconsistency is the fact that everyone has skin which is as individual and unique as they are.

In the case outlined above, although I could not submit any conclusive proof, when the mother was shown my evidence ruling out the sibling and her boyfriend, she admitted having injured the child herself by slapping it hard enough to cause a recognizable handprint. The fact that my evidence had prompted a confession was a positive conclusion to my evidence in this investigation.

Another of my cases related to a finding by a social worker. To the eye of a professional with training in observing injuries to children, a mark on a very young toddler closely resembled a cigarette burn. The parents were brought in for interview by the police, but both protested their innocence. Then the child's grandmother became involved. Rallying to the parents' defence, she recalled having seen her young grandson fall over onto a toy when in her care.

My task was to review a series of photographs of the child's toys, in case I found one which seemed to account for the injury. I noticed that one of them incorporated an array of plastic knobs and dials with round protruding elements, one of which was an exact match, in size and shape, with the child's injury.

During the police interviews with the parents it had been discovered that the toddler had been suffering from eczema. Suddenly the pieces fell into place. In toppling onto the toy the child had damaged the surface of his skin, accidentally exacerbating his pre-existing condition, which had subsequently flared up around the site of injury. As a result of my overlay comparison, the inquiry was dropped.

When a person is found dead with some form of covering placed over their face, police suspicions are often directed at those best known to them. A case of this nature was referred to us: a woman had been found stabbed to death in her kitchen, with her face covered by a towel. It was suspected that it had been placed there by her murderer.

Outside, in the garden, her husband had been knocked unconscious, he said, by an intruder. He was claiming disability allowance, as his only means of getting about was a wheelchair. When the police searched the property they discovered that the video-recorder and television had been stacked up, indicating an attempted robbery. Presumably things had got out of hand and the items had been abandoned in the perpetrator's rush to get away.

The husband was taken to hospital for an assessment of his injuries. He was accompanied by a very enterprising policeman who photographed the injuries. I say 'enterprising', because not only did he record the evidence, but he had the presence of mind to use a scale.

When I viewed the photographs, I noticed a distinctive patterned mark on one of the man's palms: a long-limbed inverted V-shape which pointed towards the web of his thumb and index finger. There were also a couple of half-centimetre circular marks evident on his palm. One of the knives found at the scene showed distinct sunken rivets on its handle, and when I looked at them under magnification and compared them with the circular marks on the husband's palm I found the spacing perfectly matched. The evidence now pointed to the man having held the handle of the knife in a very tight grip at some point.

When this evidence was put to him he confessed that he and his wife had had an altercation in the kitchen. He claimed that during their argument he had hit down very hard on the flat blade of the knife in order to stop her from picking it up from the kitchen surface. This seemed to explain the V-shape reflecting the blade of the knife in his thumb-web. However, the marks of the rivets in his palm indicated that he had gripped the handle of the knife with significant force. It was therefore evident that he had used the knife to repeatedly stab his wife.

There were additional interesting features in this case. The man had been claiming to be less mobile than he was. His apparent attempt to fake a burglary also indicated intent to cover up a crime. Finally, of course, in an act of guilt by association, he had covered his wife's face with the towel. On the strength of all the evidence, he was convicted of her murder.

Another overlay referral concerned a female victim who was very much alive and well. However, the case required some troubleshooting, due to the length of time that had elapsed before I was given the photographs.

The woman in question was accusing a man of causing her Actual Bodily Harm. The accused was a chiropractor who, for sexual kicks, used a typical old-fashioned head-master's cane. It was made of bamboo and had a large hooked end which resembled an elongated candy cane.

Having seized the cane, the police provided me with photographs showing a series of wide curved marks across the woman's buttocks – patterned injuries which, at the time of being photographed, were reddened with inflamm-ation. This certainly looked like an open and shut case of matching weapon to injury … except that there was no scale to provide definitive proof of injury size.

This complicated things, but there was a problem of greater proportions. Even though the woman was alive and willing to have her injuries rephotographed, several weeks had now passed and her injuries were in an advanced stage of healing. This had rendered them so much less visible to the naked eye that taking any new photographs for overlay purposes would be out of the question. There had been such a loss of detail that the results would undoubtedly be inconclusive.

I re-examined the original views once more, hoping – rather than expecting – to spot some markers I could use to determine actual size. As I viewed the skin I noticed the presence of several small moles on the buttocks. If you are looking for injuries, moles are not a feature you will necessarily be tuned in to, but in this instance they were exactly the type of marker I required.

I requested a new set of photographs, with the woman standing in exactly the same plane, but this time focusing the camera on her moles. A centimetre scale was placed in position alongside them.

I superimposed one of these new photographs over an original photograph of the injuries. As soon as all the moles were correctly aligned, I knew that the original injuries were correctly sized.

The overlay that followed demonstrated an excellent match to the handle of the bamboo cane, and my evidence was accepted in court. The defendant was given a custodial sentence.

Even after many years of working closely with the concept of deliberate wounding, there are occasions when the sheer brute force exerted by a perpetrator on a victim can leave you feeling shocked and enraged. The following case was, sadly, one of them.

The simple act of advertising a Gameboy in a local shop very nearly cost a woman her life. A young man responded to the advertisement. He made an appointment to see her and entered her home on the pretext of viewing the item, but after a while he indicated that he had changed his mind and left the house.

A few hours later that afternoon, the woman, who was in her thirties, answered a knock on her front door. As she opened it the same man pushed his way roughly into her house. He continued to push her back through her hall and into the kitchen, where he punched her in the face, knocking her completely off balance. She slumped onto her tiled floor, her nose bleeding heavily. Shockingly, the man then stamped on her neck with such force that it caused her to black out. When she regained consciousness she found that both the man and the Gameboy had disappeared.

The assailant may have run off with an item of significant value, but he had left behind an item of significant value: forensic evidence. Although the victim was unable to give any further information about him, insofar as he was totally unknown to her, the police found a bloody imprint of the sole of his trainer on the tiled floor. It was an easily identifiable, common brand of trainer, and the approximate shoe size was also apparent. In view of the level of violence shown, it was felt that the police should continue with their investigation and the evidence was passed to me for weapon and wound overlay.

The attack had been shocking enough without the stamp to the neck when the woman was already immobilized on the floor. What was of significance, though, was that the stamp had been so forceful that the woman's neck also bore an imprint of the trainer.

In that imprint I found there to be a set of clearly defined bright red intradermal patterned marks, consisting of a series of circles, lines and loops. The amount of detail was intense, the patterns signifying a stamp of such violence that it was apparent that the woman had only narrowly escaped a more life-threatening injury. The force had, on impact, created an amount of distortion to the skin of the neck. As a result the patterned injury I was viewing was stretched in the direction in which the foot had been travelling when the blow had been delivered.

For my overlay I studied the curved surface of the stamped bruise, with its slightly elongated shape. I didn't have a trainer with a patterned sole to match to the injury, no suspect having yet been apprehended. But there were sufficient patterned markers within the bruise to provide me with considerable evidence, should a suitable trainer be found. But while this was an excellent outcome in terms of forensic evidence, even were the correct shoe to be recovered, without a suspect there was no one to link to it.

The breakthrough came only a few months later. A young man was arrested for breaking and entering a property through a window and, on entering, he had left a perfect shoe imprint on the window ledge. In fact, it was so well defined that the police were able to check their records and match it to the earlier case and to my overlay. DNA analysis of the robber's trainers also proved significant, there being blood still present in the grooves of the tread. This had been transferred from the victim's nosebleed. With my weapon and wound overlay of the shoe tread pattern on his previous victim's neck, and the evidence of the DNA on his trainer sole, the burglar was imprisoned for theft and serious assault.

CHAPTER 22

DEFINITION OF A WEAPON

It is never easy to contemplate the vicious and intentional wounding of another human being. What's more, if my overlay work has taught me anything, it is that almost any object can be used as a weapon.

Most leave an identifiable mark, and matching weapons to injuries forms a major part of my workload. As well as referrals of forensic cases (a deceased victim), referrals also come from clinical cases (with a living victim), as not everyone will have died as a result of their injuries. Violent attack is always an alarming subject, however, and I can still find it disturbing to think about as I begin independently assessing an injury.

Shoes and trainers tend to be the most common items referred to me with the suspicion that they have been used as a weapon, but there are more extreme cases. I was once asked to perform a scoping (checking the viability) of a fence post as a weapon.

I have also been asked to perform weapon and wound overlay on a range of household items, often items used to burn. A hairdryer nozzle was identifiable from a round grill burn pattern. Household irons leave very straightforward burn marks which, in one case, consisted of a large triangular pattern broken intermittently by regular, tiny, circular steam holes. Added to this list are hot cooking apparatus, such as spatulas, which again tend to feature a clearly identifiable spaced pattern of burned columns along-side straight areas of spared skin, with surrounding burned edges.

Sadly, I find that quite commonly burn injuries have been inflicted on children. One burn mark suggested that a child's arm had been pushed onto a hotplate. I have also matched injuries to implements ranging from a heated frying pan to a griddle pan, the latter with its obvious pattern of striped columns. Even the bowl, or rounded base, of a hot spoon has been used to burn a child.

A fork, meanwhile, will leave a set of regularly spaced abrasions, due to the piercing of the skin by its sharp edges. If it has been dragged across the skin, it might leave a series of regularly spaced parallel lines where the tines have made contact.

There have been more than a few occasions when I have identified the scraping of a serrated knife on skin. Often this has been the result of scraping with a bread knife, which delivers a series of regularly spaced lines. Such lines can be fairly easy to rule in or out, depending on the width of the knife's serrations when matched to the patterned injury on the skin.

A house can provide a variety of weapons. In one instance a chair was swung and caused identifiable injury to a child due to the particular weave pattern along its edge. Other cases of child injury have included strikes on skin using a baby chair and a child's car seat, as well as strikes from a toy. In another household case, a fireguard – ironically, intended to protect – was used as a weapon. I have been asked to scope plastic mops and a household brush consisting of multiple strands of bristle. The latter was used, along with a range of additional weapons, in one of the many incidents of so-called 'honour' killing.

My experience of household tools that have been used as weapons includes wrenches, screwdrivers and hammers. In one injury I was able to decipher the clear outline of the jaws of a wrench. Depending on the force used, these implements might also leave the incriminating shape of any protruding elements, for instance a bolt or screw, which is a valuable aid to alignment when overlaid on the patterned injury to skin resulting from it.

A golf club tends to be a recurring weapon. The cases that have come to my attention have generally shown deep bruising to the skin. However, a golf club can also cause the fracturing of bone, and I have been able to match the shape and size of a fracture in a skull to an identifiable part of the golf club alleged to have caused it.

In another case I was asked to perform an overlay on an industrial-sized tin-opener, which had caused the death of the person whose skull had been fractured by it. Again, its size and shape were reflected in the resulting fracture.

If an attacker has been wearing an item of jewellery, this can prove to be advantageous in the weapon and wound overlay process. As mentioned earlier, the patterns of a ring may produce distinctive patterns on skin. Bracelets and neck chains have quite recognizable shapes, too, and belts and buckles are relatively easy to identify when they have been used to whip the skin.

Early in the millennium there seemed to be a sudden spike in referrals connected with an identical weapon: a dumbbell. One of these involved a young female victim whose naked body had been discovered, partially covered with leaves, in a Welsh wood. Close by, the police had found a circular dumbbell weight.

When I examined the photographs I saw nothing of particular note until I began to study the injuries under high resolution. Then I saw a tiny laceration just above one of the eyebrows. Under intense magnification it was revealed to be a series of parallel vertical lines. Such an unusual pattern promised to be a critical discovery, should a weapon with a similar configuration be found.

I examined the dumbbell weight and made a close observation of its respective features and shapes. On its very edge I found a series of parallel lines which I knew to be manufacturing tool marks. What was more, those lines were unique to the grinding machine that had made them.

As soon as I superimposed the photograph of the dumbbell weight, and these lines in particular, onto the parallel lines of the injury, it became apparent that there was a perfect fit. However, this turned out not to be the only proof. When DNA testing was carried out on the dumbbell weight, evidence was found to link it to this specific attack. Together, both sets of evidence secured a life sentence for the girl's murderer.

* * *

Another case came my way when the police passed it on for review by our team at the National Injuries Database, even though it had already been concluded that the death was due to a fall.

The deceased was a diabetic pensioner, whose bank cards had subsequently been used by the suspect in custody to withdraw money, so he had already been charged with theft. Now, however, it was decided that the case merited further investigation.

We learned that the deceased had regularly walked to his local off-licence for provisions, and it was thought that the suspect had noticed this and followed him home with the intention of robbing him. When his body was discovered he appeared to have sustained head injuries, as well as fractures to his ribs, and had loose change scattered on the ground around him.

My colleagues and I reviewed the post-mortem photographs and noted several deep lacerations on the scalp. These showed well-defined angular parallel spaces, beneath which were serious skull fractures. Similar-shaped patterned injuries were evident on both his right cheek and his back. As I viewed them I had a distinct recollection of a case on which I had performed an overlay only a few months before. These patterns were almost identical. In the previous case the deceased had received multiple blows to the head and I had been able to trace the patterns to a dumbbell bar, in particular the screw threads on which the weights were attached. I therefore felt there was good reason to re-use the image of the dumbbell bar from that case and perform an initial scoping exercise in respect of the present investigation. I at least wanted to make sure I was thinking along the right lines. Any likeness, or discrepancy, between the implement used in each case would no doubt become immediately obvious.

In fact, as soon as I scoped the injuries on the pensioner against the photograph of the dumbbell bar from my previous investigation, the resemblance was clear.

Accordingly, we broached the idea of a dumbbell being in the frame. Dr Peter Jerreat, another Guy's-associated pathologist I had known for many years, agreed, and the suggestion was passed on to the police. With this new knowledge in mind, we all attended the mortuary as Peter performed a second post-mortem on the pensioner's body. Despite the passage of time between the first post-mortem and the second, the series of linear injuries to the scalp, plus the skull fracturing beneath, and the patterned injury to the back were still very clear. In fact, the quality of the injuries that remained was sufficient to confirm them as identical to the injuries seen in the deceased from my previous case.

The suspect was re-arrested and his home searched. A dumbbell bar was found, and when DNA analysis was performed on it, it was possible to ascertain that it was directly linked to the fatal attack on the pensioner. Along with my weapon and wound overlay evidence, the suspect was subsequently charged with murder.

In my line of work, parts of vehicles also feature from time to time. They can range from the small – a car cigarette lighter which, of course, leaves a tell-tale round burned indentation – to the large – a drive belt, which, when used as a whip, causes striations of a particular thickness and width. Then there are the occasional referrals that involve the allegation of a person being run over by a car. In one such instance the metal radiator grille at the front of the car had left a tell-tale mesh pattern of intradermal bruising on the victim's back.

More unusual overlay requests have included scoping a ridged pattern on an area of concrete. In a clinical case, the insertion of a small hacksaw blade into a victim's anal orifice resulted in an overlay showing the blade to have left micro-incisions in the skin. I have even produced a positive match to the base of a beer bottle which had been used to hit a man on the head. In this case the manufacturer's ridges in the glass base matched the ridges evident in the injury. Surprisingly, he survived the attack.

When there was a sudden increase in injuries from a dumbbell, I found matches not only to the weight on either end, but, more often, to the bar itself. Both resulted in death.

In other unusual cases, I have been able to match a dog chain used as a whip, and also to identify rope patterns, and electrical flex, in cases of strangulation. I had one case where a cosh had been wrapped in tape and I was able to show a correlation between the overlaps in the spacing of each wind of the tape and the marks on the victim's skin. During my career I have also used image enhancement techniques very successfully to establish a perpetrator's birthmark from CCTV footage, and to prove innocence in an allegation of exposure.

There are more extreme cases. I was once asked to examine an imprinted mark on a victim's face against any of the shapes identifiable on a JCB digger.

CHAPTER 23

CATCHING ROCHDALE'S RIPPER

One of the most memorable cases in which I was involved was filmed as part of BBC2's documentary series *Trail of Guilt* in August 2002. It was an extremely high-profile case, at the centre of which was such a sadistic murder that even the most hardened detectives were shocked by it. 'Close to Home: Catching Rochdale's Ripper' investigated the murder and introduced the experts who had worked to solve the case. My own contribution had been matching a patterned injury on the victim to the weapon used by the murderer, and my evidence would prove to be one of the most crucial links to the killer.

The residents of Rochdale, Lancashire, had lived through a period of terror in the summer of 2000, when several women in the town had fallen victim to an assailant. One had been tortured and another had died as a result of her injuries. I was asked to examine the evidence related to one of these attacks: the seemingly senseless murder of a retired schoolteacher.

One summer evening, Mrs Eileen Jawczak, aged 65, had been socializing with friends in her local pub. She lived only yards away, but on the walk home she was brutally attacked, being badly beaten, sexually assaulted and strangled with a pair of tights. Ordinarily, a pair of tights might provide DNA evidence, given that an attacker would grip them tightly in his hands to use as a ligature and potentially transfer sweat from his hands to them. However, in this instance the tights, the body and the scene were all so heavily contaminated with blood that DNA profiling was rendered impossible.

Not many days later, another attack took place within a mile of the murder scene. This time the victim was a girl of 19, who was raped and beaten, stabbed with a knife and left for dead. The ferocity of the attack shook the investigating detectives. What's more, they were coming under increasing pressure to reassure the residents of Rochdale that everything possible was being done to catch the perpetrator. However, progress was slow, as no DNA had yet been identified. In the meantime the perpetrator had acquired a name which alluded to the sheer ferocity of his attacks and linked him with both Peter Sutcliffe, the 'Yorkshire Ripper', the notorious serial killer of the 1970s whose own crimes had been committed not many miles further north, and the original 'Jack the Ripper' a century before him.

One lunchtime two forensic scientists on the same police force were having a chat about the nature of their separate investigations when they simultaneously became aware of the apparent similarities between them. Both victims had been threatened, both had been cut with a sharp implement and both left for dead. So copious was the blood seeping from the injuries inflicted on one girl with a broken bottle that when a passerby came across her he at first thought she was wearing a red dress. The most compelling evidence was that both victims had been advised by the perpetrator: 'Don't look at me!' and in one case the attacker had told his victim: 'I've done worse!'

Michael Hardacre was a local criminal aged 24, who had previously been convicted for robberies and burglaries, though not, so far, suspected of sex offences. However, the police had found a bloodied handprint on a railing at the scene of one of the attacks, and, obtaining DNA evidence from Hardacre, they were able to charge him with the two rapes. They felt sure he was also the killer of Eileen Jawczak, but there was nothing to link him to that crime.

The senior investigating officer was clearly frustrated at having reached a dead end when he was certain he had in custody a very violent murderer who would, if released, kill again. He had already spent a considerable time going over the photographic evidence from the murder scene and the post-mortem photographs, but felt compelled to do so once more. As he did so, his attention was suddenly drawn to an anomaly no one had noticed previously: almost impercepti-ble cuts had been made into the eyeballs of Mrs Jawczak. The senior investigating officer was instantly reminded of the words of the rapist: 'Don't look at me!'

These cuts were significant: if Hardacre had made them, it proved he had used a sharp object to do so. That put him in the frame for all the blade-related attacks.

At this point in his investigation the SIO forwarded the photographic evidence to our National Injuries Database team. We were in the process of relocating to Bramshill, but we collectively addressed the particulars of this case. What I spotted was an area on the left cheek of Mrs Jawczak which showed all the signs of being a footwear mark. In fact, I thought it was very likely to have been made by a trainer.

Interestingly, Michael Hardacre had attempted to prevent any connection between his footwear and the murder scene by delivering his Nike trainers in a plastic bag to a neighbour, giving a plausible reason for asking them to look after them for him. In the meantime his cousin, concerned about the escalation in violence towards these victims, began to have suspicions about him. Acting on instinct, he secretly called on the neighbour to collect the footwear. Furtively handing the bag in to the local police, he tipped them off that the trainers were the evidence for which they had been looking.

Once I had sight of Hardacre's trainers I performed a weapon and wound overlay. Mrs Jawczak's face showed a distinctive bar-shaped pattern and, on the trainer soles, I was able to find an area which correlated, giving the police their crucial link between murderer and victim. In the meantime a separate investigation by forensic scientists revealed that coloured fibres from Hardacre's fleece jacket matched those found inside the mouth of Mrs Jawczak.

Michael Hardacre's crimes already included robbery, indecent assault, rape and grievous bodily harm. Now, with these sets of forensic evidence, he was sentenced to 146 years for murder.

CHAPTER 24

IRREFUTABLE EVIDENCE

There have been many interesting cases over the course of my career in which weapon and wound overlay on patterned injury has had considerable relevance to the outcome of an investigation.

One unusual case involved the cover of a DVD. The DVD itself was neither expensive nor collectable. The issue was that its owner had photographed its cover, intending to sell it on eBay, and, only days later, been discovered dead. It was therefore considered highly suspicious when the DVD case turned up in the home of the prime suspect. I was asked to review it and found that the external box casing had an area where the plastic moulding had become quite stippled. When I made an overlay comparison of this stippling with the original photograph uploaded to eBay, I found there to be a unique match. This feature implicated the man who currently possessed it and proved his involvement in the murder.

There have been many such curious cases, but there are two that have undoubtedly been most influential on my career. Solving them involved a combination of lateral thinking, dogged determination and, in one case, the ability to remain calm and unyielding under pressure.

The first began with a very unusual request: the examination of a piece of wallpaper, on which had been left a
bloody handprint. This was a particularly brutal murder,
with suspects already in police custody. It had arisen from
an altercation on Easter Sunday 2004. That day, two brothers in their thirties were in a public house when they
happened to bump into the man who had been their former
stepfather. It was not a happy reunion for any party, not
least because the brothers' mother had told them her former
partner had once tried to strangle her. Two days later, when
his lifeless body was discovered in his flat, the brothers were
immediately arrested as suspects.

The bloody murder scene, and the injuries to the victim's
body, suggested he had been beaten ferociously and stamped
on. Bloodstained handprints were discovered on a banister
and on the walls. One of them was traceable to the mother.
However, there was to be a yet more disturbing find when
the police began a search of the kitchen. In the fridge, at the
bottom of an opened can of beer, was one of the deceased's
eyeballs. Worse still, the pathologist's conclusion was that it
had been gouged out while the victim was still alive.

A deformity to one of the brother's hands led police to
recognize that one of the bloody handprints on the wall
might belong to him. This was the evidence I was asked to
examine, with a view to performing weapon and wound
overlay to find any signs of a match.

When the officer arrived, he brought with him the roll of
wallpaper and passed it to me for a visual analysis. When I
unrolled it, the realization hit me that this would not be an
open-and-shut case. The wallpaper had already been

subjected to blood testing analysis by the police's own forensic science laboratories. Extremely crumpled, soft in texture and dirty in appearance, it had the feel and texture of an old dishcloth, and the handprint on it was now barely visible. I instinctively knew that it would be almost impossible to give any decisive input in relation to it.

I also knew, however, that the deceased had been stamped on, and it occurred to me that there might be additional evidence that had been taken from the scene. I therefore asked if I could examine the photographic albums showing the deceased's body and a series of shoes which had been taken from the suspect's home.

Looking through the photographs of injury first, I found some interesting ring-like intradermal bruising on the victim's back. There were three or four evenly spaced ringed marks and, to my eyes, the definition was excellent. The police already knew about the bruising, and had, in fact, already employed the services of their own scientific footwear expert to investigate them. Footwear experts are generally referred marks of footwear patterning discovered on inanimate objects at a scene, such as flooring, clothing, furniture and so on. Where my services differ, due to being a forensic *medical* scientist, is that 90 per cent of the time I am assessing footwear marks to skin. The other 10 per cent is usually observation of patterning found in relation to bone, most often the skull.

However, in this case, the injuries had already been written off by the footwear expert. This was due to his conclusion that the sole of the footwear was the wrong size to match the block of bruising he had seen. However, examining the injury photographs, I found a significant number of patterned injuries with characteristics that appeared, to me, like marks from the sole of a trainer. So I asked the officer to leave the photographs of the suspect's trainers with me, along with the images of the soles of all the trainers recovered from the scene. I also retained a complete set of injury photographs, which I planned to analyse in greater detail. Fortunately, the officer had had the presence of mind not only to deliver the roll of wallpaper itself, but also the whole range of photographs of the suspect's footwear. This rapidly moved on my part in the investigation.

I was able to rule out all but one of the pairs of trainers: the Nike trainers. This seemed, visually, to be the most likely to have caused one very distinct injury in particular. It was located on the skin of the deceased's back, where I had found the series of ring-like intradermal bruising. I therefore created an overlay using the patterned injury as a base image and placing over it the layer showing the patterned area I had found on the heel of the trainer. As I worked to line up the scaled injury and trainer sole, it was almost immediately apparent that I had a match.

When I rang the referring officer, he was thrilled by my success, though baffled by it. The police's own footwear specialist had written a statement confirming his opinion of there being no apparent link to the suspect's footwear. Two professional sources, both skilled in the study of footwear, disagreed.

The police chose to go with my evidence, so the police footwear specialist found himself representing the defence in the impending murder trial. I was confident that I had found a match, but the discrepancy in our views led me to take extra care to ensure that I had a watertight case. I knew this would be a crucial area for cross-examination by defending counsel.

I went back to the original photographs of the trainer and studied the injury's circular patterns again in minute detail. It was at this point that I became aware I had possibly unearthed a piece of evidence which could provide a breakthrough. A miniature abrasion – the tiniest of nicks – was just visible on the deceased's skin, within one of the ring-like loops on which my findings hinged. If I could find a link between this tiny abrasion and the suspect's trainer, it would prove irrefutable evidence that this specific trainer had been responsible for this specific injury. To my mind, this would prove to be invaluable evidence, regardless of any discrepancy in footwear sizing.

When I looked at the sole of the trainer under higher magnification, I couldn't believe my eyes. Just visible – and still trapped within the grooves of the relevant circular area on the tread pattern – was the tiniest of stones. Almost holding my breath, I moved the image of the sole of the trainer, with the tiny pebble in its tread pattern, over the swirled injury with its tiny abrasion. Once I had the image of the pebble directly in place over the abrasion, there was no longer any guesswork involved: it was a perfect match, the pebble's identical position to the abrasion therefore making it unique.

There was now no question in my mind that the accused's Nike trainer had made the patterned injury on the deceased.

This specific trainer, in my expert opinion, was now categorically linked to the crime. To me, this finding was non-negotiable; the presence of the pebble in the tread was too unique to that specific shoe. I couldn't imagine this one being argued away, even by the most dedicated defence barrister. Whatever challenge I might face in court – which was likely to be considerable, given the conflict in evidence of two footwear experts – I now felt totally unshakeable in my opinion.

But I was still troubled by the police footwear specialist's conclusions. He had established that the trainers responsible for the patterned injuries were size 5. But the shoe size of the defendant was 7.5. This, of course, would undoubtedly be a hard fact to argue away, given that it involved a difference of two and a half shoe sizes – too great a difference to write off as a manufacturing size issue. This preyed on my mind. Checking on trainer sizing in more intimate detail was going to be of fundamental importance here. I needed to take the time to conduct further research.

Contacting the manufacturer of the Nike trainers, I spoke to a senior source within the company. I learned that they used, as standard, a mould for their footwear treads which covered the manufacture of all the soles of their trainers from … size 5 up to size 8. This was a crucial discovery, and just the corroborative evidence I needed.

Next came the murder trial. I cannot overstate how tricky I knew the situation to be. Naturally, the defence was gunning for this so-called expert who had announced irrefutable evidence of a connection with their defendant's footwear, when the police's own footwear specialist had ruled it out. Even more challenging to us both was the fact that we had been pitted against each other in court. I was a prime target for what could be a spectacular showdown.

As expected, I was given the 'third degree' by a defence barrister clearly keen to discredit both me and my findings. However, I was in no doubt of the veracity of the evidence I was upholding.

Given the large number of patterned bruises found on the murder victim, it was not entirely surprising when it eventually came to light that, as specialists coming from entirely different angles, the footwear expert and I had been focusing on *different* areas of injury. I discovered that he had been looking at a solid bruise resembling the curvature of the heel of a shoe, but with no patterning by which to specifically define it. As I had been focusing my own observations on the fine intradermal bruising pattern of the rings, I had been able to find the matching pattern, which correlated with the sole of the trainer.

There was very little scope to argue against such unique evidence, and the defendant was, as expected, found guilty and given a life sentence for murder.

The other influential, and highly challenging, case involved an allegation of murder. A dog-walker had discovered the naked body of a young girl at the edge of a copse. It was established that she had been badly beaten, raped and strangled with her own bra strap. When the case came to me I studied the post-mortem photographs, but was unable to find any features of particular note. Certainly, from the mortuary photographs, there seemed to be no marks on her body with the characteristics I would associate with a particular type of weapon, as far as I could tell.

A major drawback was that the photographs had been taken in the mortuary after the body had been washed by the technician. Washing of the body cleans the injuries and allows the pathologist to make a more accurate inspection of them. It is part of the initial process followed at post-mortem. However, from a scientific perspective, the presence of water will reflect any flash used in the photography that follows. In this case the victim's still-wet skin had caused significant flash flare in every one of the photographs available. There was no possibility of observing specific features, let alone patterning, and unfortunately the worst flash flare was on the photographs of the woman's face. In a case of strangulation this was a major disadvantage, because my examination necessarily focused on the face and neck. With so little visibility, I could identify nothing at all; if any patterned injury had been present it had been totally obscured. It was frustrating to know that the photographic record of injury for a murder case had been severely compromised through lack of understanding about this technical issue. I could see no way to contribute my particular skills to the investigation, and was forced to break this unwelcome news to the senior investigating officer on the case.

Not long afterwards, I was working late one evening when I took a call from the same SIO. He told me he was certain that the police had the correct suspect in custody; however, without any evidence, they were unable to charge him. I later learned the suspect was the woman's former boyfriend. He had previously been charged with stabbing a former female partner repeatedly when she spurned his advances, so the SIO was deeply troubled about the fact he might get away with a barbaric murder and far worse crime this time. He implored me to take one last look at the photographs.

Having already spent a considerable time poring over the post-mortem photographs to no avail, I turned to the only other source I now had in my possession: the photographs taken at the scene. They had been taken before any washing of the body, so there was no possibility of flash flare, and even an apparently insignificant mark might mean the possibility of providing a partial match to a weapon. So I started to scrutinize these photographs. As I studied them, one particular detail stood out. Its significance would change the whole course of events.

The outdoor aspect of a crime of this nature renders the body open to the elements: dampness, wind-carried pollen and pieces of the surrounding foliage. Tiny pieces of twig, grass, dirt and so on can obscure injury, or even have the appearance of an injury. Washing of the body will rinse away such objects, which is why I will generally only require images taken at the post-mortem. Cleaner injuries give clearer detail.

In this instance the body had been dumped among plants. I was therefore viewing a quantity of plant material around the injuries. As the cause of death was strangulation, I looked particularly closely at the woman's head and neck. What I found was a mark on her cheek resembling the side view of a bucket: a line indicating the base, and two side components which ran away from it to an equal degree, parallel on either side. It sparked a memory of seeing a similar pattern somewhere before: crucially, a bucket-shaped block on the heel of an outdoor shoe seized from the home of the suspect.

However, I now had a problem of a different kind: no scales would be present on any of the photographs, because scene photography is not taken with scales. I therefore had no scientific proof of the size of the bucket-shaped injury. Were I to produce a weapon and wound overlay at this stage, I would run the risk of being challenged in court that I had made the evidence fit myself. The patterned injury wasn't sufficient proof in itself.

Despite this possible setback, the SIO was thrilled when I passed on the news of my discovery. He now had at least a potential connection between the victim and the man they presently had in custody. I was frustrated, however, by not being able to provide sufficiently conclusive evidence. I somehow needed a way of measuring the injury.

The next day I set about studying the photographs of the crime scene all over again. First, I noted the position in which the woman's body had been found: lying face-down, with her head turned to the left. I noted that her blouse had been stuffed into her mouth and her bra tied very tightly to constrict her neck. As I looked over her neck in closer detail, my eyes took in an item located at the back of the neck on her left. There, glinting in the light, was a silver chain with a hollow, angled heart-shaped pendant on it. Both chain and pendant were situated on the top of her bra, which happened to be bunched upwards. This was a pivotal finding, as the bunched-up bra raised the pendant and chain to the exact same height as her cheek. It also helped that the chain was lying in a straight line. It was not lost on me that the odds of a neck chain ending up on the outside of a ligature, rather than caught up inside it, were seriously slim. In fact, this was incredibly providential, as it was lying in a perfect position for me to conduct an overlay. Both the pendant and the chain were in the same plane as the bucket-shaped injury I had found, level with each other. I knew that if I could acquire the same necklace and have it photographed with a scale alongside it I could use the chain to scale the original bucket-shaped mark. This would give me the required precision I needed regarding measurement.

When I rang the police to find out whether they still had the chain in their possession, I was apprehensive. So much was riding on this. Further anxious minutes passed, so I was relieved when they confirmed they still possessed it, and I immediately requested a series of photographs of the chain and pendant, with the vital scale alongside the jewellery.

Once I had the scaled photographs in my possession I began my overlay by supersizing an image of the chain and heart-shaped pendant. I enlarged the photograph until it filled my computer screen, making the next stage considerably easier. Next, I used my graphics pen to painstakingly 'cut' away the edges and interior of each link of the chain layer. It perhaps goes without saying that this was a time-consuming and complex business because of the many rounded shapes involved.

With the new image of the chain I superimposed the

chain links onto the scene photograph of the neck of the victim. I then resized the links until they perfectly matched those of the chain in the original scene photograph. Now that there was a clear correlation between them, I had the scale required for attempting a match between the bucket-shaped block on the heel of the shoe and the bucket-shaped mark on the face.

I now needed to take possession of the outdoor shoes of the suspect and become better acquainted with the heel tread. When I asked for access to them I was rewarded with a visit by a detective who delivered a whole range of separately bagged footwear to me, all taken from the home of the prime suspect. There was, however, only one set of footwear which had any real significance. I scanned their treads myself, with a centimetre scale alongside, and was then ready to attempt a weapon and wound overlay.

For this, I used an original photograph of the injury to the woman's cheek and added the layer showing the scaled pendant and chain. I opted for one of the heel treads of the suspect's shoes for the next layer of my overlay, as both soles contained identical blocks on their heels. Then the scaled shoe was placed over the injury. It was obvious, as soon as I moved the layer of the heel tread into position over the bucket-shaped mark on the skin, that there was a very distinctive match between the patterns, in both size and shape. In fact, the pattern of the shoe tread was so unusual – one I had never seen before and have never seen since, despite performing many hundreds of overlays – that it proved a hard point to argue against and a perfect match of weapon to injury.

As it turned out, my own evidence was not the only constructive find. Along with the accused's footwear, the police had seized his clothing, and passed some items on to an expert in palynology ('pall-in-ology'), the specialist field in which comparison is made between pollen and plant life, relevant to the geographical area and climate in which a body is found. It can be used to provide evidence that a victim or perpetrator, and their clothing, have a link to a specific geographical location. Analysis was therefore performed on the jeans and trousers of the ex-boyfriend of the deceased, and it was ascertained that the bottoms of his trousers contained traces of plant spores from the location in which his deceased girlfriend's body was found. There were also identical botanical traces applicable to the outdoor shoes I had been working on.

With our combined corroborative scientific evidence, the man was convicted of the murder of his former girlfriend and sentenced to life imprisonment.

As a footnote to this case, I made use of my platform as a forensic imaging consultant at conferences, on training courses and in any appropriate business scenario to notify as many photographic professionals as possible about the importance of using a scale in post-mortem photography. I also made a point of warning about the potentially disastrous loss of evidence if skin was photographed when wet, and of the fundamental importance of avoiding flash flare.

Due to the number of times I have discovered instances of patterned injury being missed, for whatever reason, I always recommend taking photos of *any* marks on skin.

Infrared light and specialist lighting such as UV, laser, etc., can better highlight the characteristics of an injury. Even weeks after an incident, patterned marking can be detected under such lighting conditions, and you never know when they might turn out to be useful to someone like myself.

In my line of work it is a fact that any object which leaves a shaped pattern on skin can be subjected to weapon and wound overlay, if there is a suspected weapon available to provide a comparison. One of my more surprising cases actually started out as a secretive-sounding meeting with a detective constable in child protection services who, unusually, asked me to meet her at a London café. It turned out that she had a request of a highly sensitive nature.

It was the mid-2000s, and a teenage girl had accused her father of entering her bedroom at night to interfere with both herself and her younger sibling. Particularly wanting to protect her younger sister, she told her mother, who didn't believe her. Wanting to prove she was telling the truth, she had the foresight to set up a video camera using an infrared setting and leave it running all night. In due course, footage was captured of someone entering the bedroom in the middle of the night. The sisters shared bunk beds in a small room, though, so only the calves and one arm of the person were visible.

I was asked by the detective whether I could add any scientific weight to confirming the identity of the alleged perpetrator. I had never been presented with a request of this nature previously, but it quickly became clear to me, on watching the footage, that the veins on the backs of both arm and calves became highly visible on an infrared setting. The patterning would be distinctive enough to warrant an investigation by photographic overlay.

I ideally would have liked good-quality still photographs of the suspect's arm and calves, taken under infrared conditions, to use as a measure of comparison. Standard photographs of his calves, taken in the custody suite, showed insufficient vein detail, so I asked for these to be rephotographed under infrared conditions. However, permission was refused by the suspect – as was his right – and I therefore felt it necessary to rule out vein superimposition on the calves.

However, I was in luck, as the standard photography already taken of the suspect's arm did show very distinctive vein patterning, and I chose to use one of these photographs as my base image. Next, I created a new layer, used a graphics pen to map/trace the veins, and copied this layer onto an infrared still image taken from the girl's camera footage of the arm. I rotated and adjusted this layer into place on the veins shown on the arm, and once the layers were lined up I found there to be a complete match.

I could have left my evidence there, but I knew the world-renowned anthropologist and anatomist, Dame Professor Sue Black, from my days at Guy's, and I felt it would be advantageous to seek her opinion. I asked whether she could perform her own experiment, tracing the vein patterning on the arm using a different colour from my own. She sent back an identical image, which I added to my own overlay as a further layer, before saving a composite image of our respective findings on the suspect's arm veins.

I next called Nick Marsh, senior photographic expert with the Metropolitan Police Force, with whom I had worked on several cases during my days at Guy's. Nick offered to take a series of controls for me and proceeded to ask as many of his colleagues as possible for a photograph of their arm. He subjected these to standard photography and infrared, to provide a source for comparison of vein patterning. It was immediately apparent that each person's patterning was unique to them.

I now had a composite image showing two layers of carefully traced vein patterns, along with a set of control images from a respected police photographic source. All had been taken independently. Scientifically, we felt they made a very watertight case.

I submitted our collective evidence to the child protection services and in due course the case went to trial. Waiting to go into the courtroom, I was rather surprised to see one of the barristers stride out of court towards me and announce that my evidence would not be required; the case had been dropped on a technicality.

I was shocked to learn, some weeks later, that the child protection officer who had brought the case to me had been so disillusioned by this outcome that she had resigned her post to take up a job as an air hostess. However, better news reached me when Sue Black confirmed that, as a result of this particular case, she would be conducting further in-depth research into vein patterning, as it would provide a useful source of identification for cases such as this. She was already aware of security companies using vein pattern matching in identification of their staff.

Dame Professor Sue Black has gone on to advance vein pattern recognition as a professional field of forensic scientific enquiry. It must be of some consolation, also, that the girl who had the ingenuity to set up infrared photography to capture these images started a chain reaction which has led to conclusive legal rulings, based on the overwhelming evidence that an individual's vein patterning is apparently as unique to them as their own DNA.

CHAPTER 25

INJURY BODY MAPPING

E arly in 2000 my working life completely changed direction. Until now I had been travelling up to London from the Kent coast every day, which took up a lot of hours, was tiring and meant I did not see as much of my family as I would have liked; added to which, the forensic department at Guy's was reconfiguring. The pathologists were becoming independent and forming their own pathology group in an eventual move away from London to Oxfordshire. This happened to coincide well with an offer for early retirement and redundancy made by the medical school to anyone who might be considering this within the next 10 years. This appealed to me, so I decided to accept. But at 50, rather than giving up work, I embarked on a split of my professional time. While I initially continued to work part time in the forensic department as it closed down, I also set up my own business.

Two years later I was juggling several roles, but I had the best of both worlds. Not only did I work as a consultant for the National Injuries Database, staying in Hampshire for two days a week, but the remainder of my week was spent working from home, running an increasingly successful freelance business which drew on my expertise as a forensic imaging consultant. By now, I was single-handedly producing injury body mapping for murder trials across the whole country.

At this time my links with the pathology team at Guy's became especially valuable. Nat Cary, in particular, gave me unwavering support and encouragement. Dick had initially been instrumental in pointing me in a direction which opened doors professionally, and Nat now took a keen interest in the development and success of my new business venture. Although I was starting out, effectively, alone, it was with the full backing and loyalty of my former Guy's colleagues, for which I was extremely grateful. As a result, my independent professional life quickly took off.

I was very well known within medico-legal circles for my weapon and wound overlay imaging expertise, but many calls were now requesting my forensic injury body mapping services. Police forces across the entire country had rapidly learned about the work I was pioneering, and it was becoming the innovation most synonymous with my name. It had all started during the Seventies and Eighties, when there was an explosion of interest in emigration to the Middle East. Hospitals sprang up around the burgeoning oilfield industry and vacancies were advertised with excellent on-site accommodation, sports and social facilities. Doctors, nurses and medical secretaries, among others, were attracted by the promise of hotter weather, new friends with similar interests and aspirations, and a significantly increased financial reward for their services. The only downsides were the vast distance involved in relocating halfway across the globe, away from family and friends, and giving up alcohol, or at least honouring the restrictions on alcohol consumption, which, if flouted in an Arabic country, could result in severe punishment.

It was therefore not uncommon, in our circles, to know of someone who had gladly left behind the British winter to live and work in the Middle East. But in the course of our Guy's-based work we became aware of two cases where British nurses' new lives abroad had ended in tragedy.

The first of these occurred in May 1979, when a British nurse, Helen Smith, was found to have died in suspicious circumstances in Saudi Arabia. Her father, a former policeman, spent years personally investigating her death and attended our offices for advice. To him, it was never satisfactorily resolved. He felt that key questions remained unanswered and that the forensic evidence, in particular, seemed to indicate a potential murder and its cover-up.

But it was the second of these cases that would have far-reaching consequences for us. On a practical level, it altered the processes involved in preparing for a murder trial; in legal terms, it changed what was deemed acceptable to show as forensic medical evidence to the public.

On the evening of 11 December 1996, in a hospital in Dhahran, in the eastern province of Saudi Arabia, an area with strong associations with the oil industry, an early Christmas party was held by three nurses in one of their rooms. However, one of them, an Australian nurse, Yvonne Gilford, failed to report for work the following morning and a search was conducted. She was found in her room, having sustained 13 stab wounds and died from asphyxiation by a pillow. It was established that the two British nurses who had joined her the previous evening, Deborah Parry and Lucille McLauchlan, had been the last two people to see her alive, and they were subsequently accused of her murder. Apparently, a dispute had arisen concerning their interpersonal relationships. It was also discovered that the two British nurses appeared to have withdrawn $1,000 using the deceased nurse's bank card after the established time of her death.

Under questioning, both nurses confessed to the crime. However, later they attempted to withdraw their confessions, claiming coercion through sleep deprivation, intimidation and the threat of sexual violence. They also claimed to have been promised deportation, rather than prosecution, if they confessed to the crime. Under Saudi law, Deborah Parry, in fact, stood to be executed and Lucille McLauchlan to receive 500 lashes, plus 8 years' imprisonment. The murder trial that followed focused heavily on their signed confessions. However, no witnesses were present in court and no cross-examinations took place. Nor was there any reference to forensic evidence which might have been found at the scene or afterwards at post-mortem.

When the story reached the attention of the British press the profile of the case was significantly raised, though coverage was heavily biased against the nurses, due to their signed confessions. In time, the media focus culminated in an intervention by Tony Blair, then Prime Minister, who personally appealed to King Fahd for clemency during a state visit. The nurses' sentences were subsequently commuted to time already served, and Deborah Parry's sentence lessened from execution to life imprisonment. As part of the arrangement effected by Tony Blair, the nurses were deported back to the UK.

Deborah Parry maintained her innocence for years afterwards and requested an exhumation of Gilford's body in the hope that new forensic techniques might clear her name, but permission was refused. In the intervening years Lucille McLauchlan died unexpectedly from a brain haemorrhage.

An interesting footnote to the case is that two years previous to this crime, in the same hospital complex, a nurse had died in very similar circumstances. However, any connection was summarily dismissed.

My part in this investigation arose due to the strained international relations, which had not gone unnoticed by the BBC. They made preparations to cover the case in their topical investigative series *Horizon*, and the producers engaged Iain West to give his opinion as an independent forensic pathologist. Iain was strictly opposed to showing the public the real photographs of injury, as they would make extremely harrowing viewing for the viewing public, let alone the victim's family. In addition, he considered the idea of showing the body of a high-profile murder victim, along with its multiple injuries, in a pre-watershed viewing timeslot, on national television, extremely inappropriate. A solution had to be sought which would give the public an understanding of the injuries sustained while avoiding the showing of disturbing and graphic photographs.

Iain discussed it with me – as the go-to person for any unusual request – and we came up with the idea of creating some kind of visual aid with which we could impart the nature of the deceased nurse's injuries, including their locations on her body. This was, for its time, a highly original idea.

Accordingly, I started to experiment with a new paint software program, creating a series of images which represented the injuries graphically. They had to be observable with relative ease on thousands of British television screens, including those where children might still be watching. I produced graphics indicating the length and shape of each stab wound and, although they bore absolutely no resemblance to what Pauline and I produce today, we felt they had sanitized the injuries sufficiently to be shown.

This new method of injury representation came to the attention of the many British detectives who were watching that night and it wasn't long before enquiries began to filter through to our forensic department, asking whether I could produce body mapping for their own murder cases. The police clearly recognized the value of these graphics in the setting of a murder trial, in illustrating the facts while shielding the jury from the shocking reality. Detectives had already shared with me the oppressive reactions occasionally suffered by jury members when confronted with photographs of injury. A courtroom is, by its very nature, a fairly intense setting for the average member of the public, and, until now, having been required to witness distressing photographs, the police were well aware that there could be unwanted consequences. I have been told of jury members being taken ill or fainting, or even running out of the courtroom. In this environment there is no convenient way to prepare a jury for real photographs of injury, or of the body of a wounded deceased victim in a mortuary setting. Such images can be disturbing even to hardened detectives. Even I, myself, have been shocked at the worst of them, on occasion, despite the hundreds of injuries I have viewed over the course of my career. Juries are comprised of a complete cross-section of the general public, who are not, as a rule, medically aware. Depending on the case, viewing injury may, though, be a key part of the legal process they are required to go through in order to form their personal opinion of it. With these sanitized and representative images of injury, a jury member could begin the process of serving, whatever their previous experience of death.

It is also a prerequisite that jury members concentrate for a given period of time, as vital information is passed on to them. It can be very exacting for them to maintain focus, and introducing medical terms into this environment can be perplexing. It is also counter-productive if distress is inflicted through images to which they are subjected. If a jury member were to mentally shut down as a means of withdrawal from what they are being told or shown, there would be no benefit to anyone. The sole purpose of a jury's attendance is to evaluate, with an open mind, the details of the case, so as to form an independent, informed verdict. So the detectives to whom I spoke knew that showing far less traumatizing graphical representations of injury to the jury would be a major step forward in the legal process.

My first attempt at this style of injury presentation, although basic, had now evolved into something far more sophisticated. At Guy's the pathologists had been using it to illustrate their post-mortem findings in court. Now, as word spread, calls were coming in from senior detectives across the country. A handful of paralegal case officers in the Crown Prosecution Service also began to routinely request body mapping for the murder trials they were arranging. My workload consequently soared.

Prior to the arrival of body mapping in the courtroom, pathologists might present their findings with a small, simple, pre-printed line-drawn body outline and show injuries by means of a series of crosses, or other marks. This was a standard way of denoting location, size and length, and used by pathologist and medic alike. Whatever it achieved in accuracy and assistance, though, it was still a very basic format which hadn't moved on through the decades. The lifelike portrayal of injury I could now produce took out any guesswork. Complex information could be presented in a way which was easily understood. The anatomical knowledge of the jury member no longer mattered. Even their first language was immaterial. A picture crosses the communication barrier; virtually everyone can understand it.

At the same time, my job, as the forensic graphic artist, was to ensure accuracy in what was being presented. Here, my extensive background in forensic medicine and anatomy enabled me to ensure my graphics were an exact replica of the injuries I could see on the post-mortem photographs. However difficult an injury was to replicate, I found a way of graphically representing it. Reassuringly, our police clients reported that regardless of how gruesome, or eye-catching, my graphics were, adverse effects related to viewing such images had diminished almost to the point of being negligible.

As body mapping became more established in its own right, demand for it extended to include almost the entire national police force. At the same time, it occurred to me that there were bound to be ways in which to develop it as a specialism. A distinct advantage, I felt, would be to add graphical features to show the weapon pathway through the body of a victim. External images could be complemented by an internal view of an injury, increasing the jury's understanding of the injury process. Therefore I began to develop 'internal body maps', ranging from penetrating knife wounds to underlying bruising to the more complex trajectories of gunshot injuries. I extended these to include graphical representations of wounding to major organs, such as the heart, lungs or liver, and cuts to major blood vessels. A simple arrow, or even an image of the suspected weapon, was integrated as a graphical means of conveying the depth of injury and the effect, inside the body, of this penetration. The overall purpose was to show the link between external wounding and internal consequence: how the victim had died as a result of their injuries.

The internal workings of the human body had to be clearly demonstrated, if the images were to meet the requirements of its viewer, while on the other hand complex information had to be conveyed. But it seemed to work. Body mapping soon became the crucial add-on everyone wanted for almost every murder trial.

CHAPTER 26

PROFESSIONAL RECONNECTION

As Derek's body-mapping services were expanding to take in police forces across the country, I was working as a senior PA, first in London, then closer to home, facilitating more quality time with our younger children. After a sudden restructuring process in the large pharmaceutical company for whom I was temping rendered me jobless, I took on shorthand assignments for local senior businesspeople, though as the summer of 2003 drew to a close I was considering my next options.

One afternoon Derek was talking about his workload and speaking wistfully of the client database he no longer had the time to set up. This immediately piqued my interest and within minutes I had received a whistle-stop tour of a software program and was creating the database for him. I was also given *carte blanche* to build in whatever design features I wished as the face of his company.

Derek had known for some time of his need for assistance, but it had never actually occurred to either of us that we should join forces. I had felt under pressure to bring in a regular wage to accommodate any fluctuations in the cash flow of his small business. Therefore, to me, work was something I did away from home. Also, with a backlog of cases accumulating, what Derek really required was not only a business administrator, but also a graphic designer, one with the ability to handle detailed photographs of injury and understand a pathologist's post-mortem report.

As our working days together progressed, though, it began to dawn on us that, as I had already taken on so many responsibilities in his business, he had no need to look elsewhere. His business partner was, in fact, far closer to home than either of us had realized. True, I had never considered working as a graphic artist before, though I did have the necessary artistic eye. Yet here I was, with years of experience of the mortuary, and accustomed to photographs showing violent injury. Initially I did have to brace myself when viewing such photographs again. Clearly, I had 'normalized' in the years following my departure from forensic medicine. However, in time, I was replicating bruising, stab wounds, defence injuries involving deep gashes and missing parts of fingers and thumbs. The photographs of injury could be horrifying, but, after those first few seconds of emotional adjustment to such sickening sights of intentional injury, the artist in me would take over.

During that first week of being shown how to replicate the more simplistic injuries, such as light bruising, I found I had produced a series of body maps ready for demonstration to the jury in an upcoming murder trial. It was only some time later that it dawned on me: I had just had re-entered the world of forensic medicine ... this time as a forensic graphic designer.

*   *   *

With Pauline producing graphics alongside me, our output almost instantly doubled. It was a relief to know I had a business partner to take the pressure off me, but other benefits were also immediately apparent. In our line of work we translate a pathologist's report into images which need to show the highest level of accuracy and relevance and reflect often complex medical terminology. This requires an analytical mind, backed up with good anatomical knowledge. In Pauline, not only did I have *a* business partner, I had the *perfect* business partner.

It had come as a surprise to us both, but once we were working together I had difficulty remembering how I had ever managed alone. We couldn't think why we hadn't thought of this solution sooner, particularly as we both possessed the required know-how. Between us, we had spent hundreds of hours observing external and internal wounding. In view of this, we had very little cause ever to scratch our heads when it came to replicating injury. We could both pinpoint specific internal organs from a photograph and identify rib and hairline skull fractures. Crucially, we could also read a pathologist's report; in particular, identifying which were the most relevant injuries directly associated with the cause of death.

Working together also had its advantages when it came to troubleshooting; if either of us needed advice, the other always had a solution. There were times when no photographs existed of a particular injury, particularly those that were of a clinical (living) nature, whether they had already healed or perhaps been surgically altered. Despite this, we were able to produce graphics due to our understanding of the terminology alone. Occasionally, photographs obscured normally easily identifiable features, if they had been taken too close to the body. But, due to the time we had spent viewing bodies in the mortuary, we were able to distinguish between a knee and an elbow, or a rounded leg or upper arm. Our medical knowledge therefore gave us a huge advantage.

In the same way, we could adapt our skills when it came to interpreting wounds which surgical intervention had obscured. A surgeon might cut through a stab wound in an attempt to save a victim's life, for example, and we could replicate the original injury prior to this intervention based on our knowledge of wound shape and, again, medical description.

It was with great satisfaction that we found our work well received, as credible evidence, by pathologists, barristers and judges alike.

CHAPTER 27

BODY MAPPING IN THE MURDER TRIAL

I n body mapping's earliest incarnation as a visual aid for the jury it was prepared as a set of 2D images for printing on glossy paper. However, I kept a very close eye on the way graphical software was evolving in the public domain. My idea was that body mapping would be a progressive concept, keeping up with computerization. This meant integrating improvements in software as soon as they became available. One way I did this was championing 3D graphics as the way forward. As a format it had the possibility of illustrating any type of injury. Using a single three-dimensional image of a rotational computerized body, all wounds could be painted and contained in just the one 3D image of a rotating body, rather than having to prepare a whole series of images to cover every angle and location of injury. The fact that this 3D body rotated on a screen allowed every injury to be shown in a continuous rotation, forming a complete presentation in itself. In this way 3D work had the advantage of being easier for the barrister to use, as they turned the body through a full 360 degrees, using the mouse or cursors of a computer.

Next, Pauline and I invested in Hollywood film industry-based software, which was built bespoke to our specific requirements. We now found ourselves able to create graphics that could show every major internal anatomical system. The systems could be turned on and off to demonstrate either one at a time or a combination, according to relevance. If I wanted, for instance, to create a graphic showing a stab wound to the chest, I could now show the angle of the stab wound track going into the body, nicking the rib cage on its way through (layer showing bone), and entering and exiting a lung (layer showing the respiratory organs), before finally coming to rest in the heart (layer showing the cardiovascular system). In a case of head injury I could demonstrate the external laceration, or tear in the skin, and show the skull fracturing beneath it, as well as detailing the bruising and haemorrhage to the brain. A considerable amount of medical information was now viewable in just the one rotational image.

In a short time our software became synonymous with our brand, and we, in turn, found limitless ways of demonstrating any type of injury.

You may have seen this software in action. It subliminally came to the public's attention in the cutting-edge – for its time, the year 2000 – science-fiction horror thriller *Hollow Man*. 'Hollow', in this case, refers to invisibility (not to be confused with the 2020 thriller *The Invisible Man*). The film follows a group of scientists working on a process designed to achieve invisibility in humans. An early scene is particularly arresting. A huge (animatronic) gorilla, which cannot yet be seen, is injected with a concoction designed to return its body to visibility. At first, all we can see are electrodes, apparently attached to thin air. Then the gorilla's skeleton takes form, followed by its major internal organs and an erratically beating heart. This overpowering sight is gradually joined by the gorilla's multitudinous network of blood vessels, followed by its skin, or, in this case, fur. Once each anatomical system has reappeared, the entire body of the gorilla is visible. It is a very powerful introduction to a violent and bloodthirsty, but incredibly thrilling, film. Without giving too much away, the scientists go on to replicate the process in a human. What is most outstanding is the quality of the visual effects. They were way ahead of their time, and are just as astounding today.

Using this software, with images of computer-generated human bodies of slightly differing shapes and sizes, we have the capability to prepare each case according to its forensic medical requirements. For the viewer, as the body rotates, the outer layer of the body – with its external injuries – fades to reveal the injuries beneath. These injuries, incidentally, are all drawn painstakingly by us, by hand. One layer at a time, you will see the relevant layers of anatomy fade until you have reached the deeper levels of injury, down to the bone. So, in the case of a head injury, for instance, the scalp wound will be the first image seen, fading to the bony skull beneath, revealing any fracturing, then fading again to the bruising or haemorrhage in the brain beneath. This is not only anatomically correct, and therefore educational in its own right, but it also links the internal wounding process in the body so that anyone can understand the connection between these injuries. With the case of a bullet trajectory through the body, an entry hole on the skin will fade to demonstrate severance of a major blood vessel in the circulatory system, demonstrating how severe blood loss from that vessel has resulted in death. If a sharp injury has penetrated a major organ, you will see an internal view of the body with cuts in whichever organs have been penetrated by the weapon. Whatever type of injury is depicted onscreen, the first and final image you will see is the gradual replacement of the skin, as the body rotates to its original frontal view.

This three-dimensional format is especially valuable for demonstrating multiple injuries. It is also possible to convey the severity of an attack, which, if particularly frenzied, will perhaps show as a group of injuries in the same area, indicating that the deceased was probably already incapacitated when these occurred, and therefore unable to fight back. Whatever form the injuries take, the fading rotational three-dimensional body map is useful for revealing both the severity of an attack and the injury distribution around and inside the body.

This form of body mapping is instantaneous and elegant. It is continuously engaging in a way a series of images on photographic paper is not. There is definitely still a place for two-dimensional imaging, if there are very few injuries. However, the advantages of the three-dimensional format are clear: engaging a jury's full attention and making their job of understanding penetrating layers of injury simpler.

One area of injury body mapping we have not so far mentioned is that applicable to the child protection case. Such cases may require the viewing of brain scans and

X-rays; our body mapping will often show old and new fractures, in addition to the abrasions and bruising. There might be brain haemorrhage and *contre coup* injury – injury understood to arise from shaking. Often we need to include haemorrhage to the optic nerves behind the eyes. It is important that these processes are all understood by the jury so they can make a responsible decision as to whether the harm was intentional.

Lastly, we also produce presentations to include all the available information, but with the complete versatility of a non-linear format. In this way everything can be accessed, from the scene to any bindings used, photographs and video footage taken, weapon and wound overlays prepared, and body mapping drawn up, in both forms (2D and 3D), at the click of a mouse.

In the future, data capacity is likely to continue to expand exponentially, and graphical technology will possibly change beyond all recognition. We are even now witnessing the life-size body scan which highlights historic injury, and perhaps this expensive, though engaging, form will become the norm for courtroom presentation. It is our opinion that, in time, artificial intelligence will likely take over the preparation and courtroom presentation of this evidence. However, in current times it is surely reassuring to know that any evidence has been established – and presented to the court – with a commitment to the highest level of accuracy by all parties involved. This holds true whether you are leading counsel, a senior investigating detective, the pathologist or a defence barrister. It is especially relevant if you are a member of the victim's family or the accused.

Whatever decision is reached by the jury, everything hinges on the evidence – and this is the aspirational ethos that drives us both professionally.

CHAPTER 28

BODY MAPPING IN WOUNDING SCENARIOS

At first sight, what I was viewing seemed to constitute a relatively straightforward case for body mapping. I had been sent a pathologist's report with a set of accompanying police photographs. They showed a taxi driver who had been shot dead while driving a right-hand-drive taxi. The incident had occurred in broad daylight in a northern town centre, with several witnesses present. However, when I came to show the bullet trajectory through the body, things took a slightly different turn from the one I was expecting.

The entry wound appeared to show the bullet entering at the back of the victim's right elbow. However, once inside the body, it had not taken a direct route across the chest, as anticipated, but had instead travelled upwards from the elbow, towards the shoulder. It had exited the arm just beneath the right armpit and entered the chest wall at the same height. From there, it passed across the chest to enter the right lung. When it exited the right lung it entered the root of an artery known as the brachio-cephalic, at the point where it joined the aorta (the main heart vessel). The length of the internal bullet pathway was 25cm and, having travelled across almost the entire chest, the bullet finally passed into the upper lobe of the left lung, where it came to rest. As a result of so many internal injuries, the victim suffered massive blood loss and died.

For the murder trial I needed to show all the sites of injury – not only those on the surface of the body, but the internal sites of entry and exit as well – to enable the jury to comprehend how this shooting had led to the victim bleeding to death. I began to move my chosen computer-generated body, or avatar, into the stance of a seated driver, though without any reference to a car, so that I showed just the body in a seated position. I knew that, ideally, it needed to be shown from behind, as the trajectory of the bullet would be better seen from this angle, as it had entered the body from the right. I planned to use an arrow to indicate its pathway across the chest after it had exited the arm.

However, despite the detailed reporting of the pathologist in reference to each injury, I realized I had a bit of a problem on my hands. When it came to the point where I needed to line up all the external entry and exit wounds on the outer skin layer of the avatar, I realized that the wounds were completely out of alignment with each other. Therefore the assumption that the taxi driver had been in an upright seated position when shot could not be correct. The angle of entry of the bullet into the back of the elbow and its subsequent upward trajectory indicated a shot from ground level or lower. This was not only implausible; it did not comply with the witness testimony, which referred to an apparent two shots having been fired from ground level.

I set to work on creating a three-dimensional avatar, so that I could move the body around to ascertain the correct position of bullet entry. I then added in our internal software, which, back then, was a fairly new addition to our repertoire. Studying the various internal photographs provided by the police, I took note of the entry and exit wounds to the lungs. Next, I located the photograph showing the damage to the brachio-cephalic artery, which was evident from the photograph of the heart itself. As I tried to work out the position from which the deceased had been shot, I realized that the arm needed to be raised. In fact, it needed to be positioned much higher before the internal bullet track would align with the external injuries to the arm and the chest wall. As the right arm of the avatar reached a certain height, I concluded that the taxi driver had been sitting with his elbow resting on the top of his open car window.

However, I now had another problem: the internal entry and exit wounds of the lungs and at the junction of the brachio-cephalic artery still did not line up. I had to move the avatar's body to align the internal wounds. It was as I began to bend the upper body over, to the left, that full alignment of all the injuries took place. I could now deduce that not only was the victim's arm raised at the time of the initial bullet entry, but he had been leaning to the left at the time of wounding.

Based on this forensic injury body mapping, the conclusion could be drawn that the taxi driver had heard the first of the two witnessed gunshots, which missed, and, taking evasive action, had tilted himself away from the window and towards the interior of the car.

I was thus able to provide a very clear scenario and produce an image showing his dive to the left and his bent arm. Being able to interpret the wounding described in the pathologist's report had been essential. I was fortunately able to indicate to the jury how the taxi driver had been attempting to shield himself as the second bullet had penetrated his body in a horizontal trajectory, travelling from right to left, before fatally severing a major artery.

It is always gratifying to know I have established the sequence of events for the benefit of a jury, or highlighted disparities between accounts. In fact, I consider this a very important part of my job. In the following case there were two versions of events: that of the defendant and that of the pathologist. I designed two contrasting scenarios that conveyed the two points of view involved and showed the disparities between them.

I was asked to portray a particularly unusual scenario, when a man was seen waving a pistol in the air in a public place, apparently intent on using it, which prompted the dispatch of the local police armed response team. As soon as he witnessed their arrival, the potential gunman clambered to the top of some nearby scaffolding. This had been erected around the doorway of a church which was being renovated. A stand-off took place and, given the man's increasingly erratic behaviour, the armed response team fired a shot, with the intention of disabling him and placing him under police control.

This might have been the end of the story, except for one curious fact: the man sustained two bullet entry wounds, indicating that either he had been shot by more than one member of the armed response team, or one member of the team had shot him twice. In either scenario, there could arguably be an accusation of excessive use of force. As it was, the man lodged an official complaint.

One of the entry wounds was in his left lower leg and the other was in his left buttock. The injury to the lower leg indicated the bullet had travelled straight through the leg, entering the front of his shin and exiting the calf, at the back. The injury to the left buttock indicated that the bullet had entered the front of the left leg, high up, and then come to rest in the muscle at the rounded crease towards the back of the buttock.

The man's claim was that the first bullet had penetrated the wooden foot board atop the scaffolding, behind which he had been standing, travelled through the front of his left shin, exited his calf and continued onwards, beyond the immediate area. No trace of the bullet casing had been found, so the conclusion would be that it had disappeared into the surrounding area. The man also surmised that the second shot had been fired at his leg, but had missed, instead passing straight into his buttock and lodging there.

The member of the armed response team who had fired maintained that he had fired only one bullet. His claim was that the gun had been aimed at the man's lower leg, with the intention of temporarily disabling him. According to this single-shot theory, the bullet had passed through the left lower leg and travelled straight back to enter the buttock. The only way it could have done this was if the suspect had been crouching.

The pathologist asked if I could provide body mapping to indicate both scenarios.

The issue was that if there were proof that two bullets had been fired, the resulting investigation would be likely to involve a public inquiry, with potential consequences no one would welcome. After all, the man had not actually discharged the pistol he had been waving, and the shot, or shots, from the armed response team had not been fired in self-defence.

On viewing the body mapping I had produced, the man offered to tell the truth about the circumstances in which he had been wounded. He admitted that his accusation of being shot twice was a fabrication and that his own gun was fake.

In medico-legal circles, you do hear all sorts of claims. There is one that crops up from time to time, usually in the course of investigating a domestic dispute. It is usually associated with a woman being accused of fatally stabbing her husband or partner. Claiming self-defence, she will make the allegation that the stabbing was unavoidable, because the deceased 'walked onto the knife'. It is hard to envisage someone willingly subjecting themselves to a sharp and potentially lethal blade, but at one point this was such a common plea from defence witnesses that I chose to prepare a two-scenario animation as a form of visual aid for the jury. An animated scenario can be enlightening and, after all, there is a major issue to consider with this claim: if the deceased partner did, in fact, walk onto the knife, the suspect should be accused of manslaughter, whereas if he was deliberately stabbed in the course of a heated argument it would be a case of murder.

A prime example was the case for which I made the animation. A woman had been arguing with her husband, a man considerably taller than herself, when, she claimed, he had attacked her with a knife. She went on to say that she had been able to wrestle it from his hand and had held it up quite high in the air, intending to warn him away from her. In spite of this, she claimed, he had chosen to move towards her. Given his forward momentum, he had walked onto the knife.

Under questioning, she was asked to describe the position in which she had held the knife, using a ruler to indicate the angle. She demonstrated the knife being held outwards at her shoulder height, at a completely horizontal, level angle. The fatal injury her husband had sustained was a single deep entry wound to his chest, and it was situated quite high. So this seemed to tally with her evidence.

Enter the pathologist, with the news that the internal evidence indicated a very different scenario. While the stab wound was located in the upper chest, the weapon had travelled steeply *downwards*, at an angle of approximately 45 degrees, and in a left to right direction. The blade of the knife had struck the heart, dividing the root of the aorta (the main artery in the body) at the top, and had passed into the right chamber of the heart before finally entering the right lung, where the wound track ended.

The woman's claim of self-defence, and putting no energy into the stabbing, was firmly debunked by this post-mortem evidence. The internal wound track confirmed that the weapon had been wielded deliberately, the steep downwards motion indicating that it had first been raised to a height, showing intent.

The moral of the story? Even in a heated argument it is extremely unlikely that someone will risk harming themselves by advancing onto the blade of a knife. Self-preservation will almost always override everything.

CHAPTER 29

MAINTAINING THE ETHOS

The moment you know for certain that your design concept is successful is when competitors begin to emerge, influenced by your work. However, for us, our greatest challenge in business was actually the disappearance of a competitive marketplace, as the police copied our concept and, almost unanimously, developed their own in-house graphics departments, financed, at least in part, by the Crown Prosecution Service. This was a particularly bitter pill to swallow, given my creation of the entire concept, and even put us temporarily out of business.

Our clients were non-comprehending and powerless against the new *diktat* that courtroom graphics were now an in-house matter for preparation by police staff, rather than a proven specialist provider. Nor were they appeased by the justification of 'budget cuts', given the multiple permanent salaries that outweighed the previously more economical 'per case' fee.

Still, there were also causes for celebration.

* * *

I had been working full time in our business as a graphic designer since 2003 and, alongside this, studying for qualifications in graphic design and small business management. In 2007 my graphic design qualification formalized my legal status as designer of the images I was creating for the courtroom, and enhanced my creative skills; and in 2008 my business qualification acknowledged the skills and ideas I had been steadily introducing, including management of the office, publicity, strategy and measures for best practice.

In the next few years we found we had an option to amalgamate into the evolving body-mapping fraternity. We chose not to join, given that it required adherence to a set of strictures and limitations which were dictated by an overarching body with no allegiance to small business. In essence, it would have meant our forensic medical product being judged by many people, none of whom had medical qualifications – the pathologist for whom it had been prepared being the last to receive it, potentially when it had been altered out of all recognition. We weren't prepared to lose the essence of our product, or relinquish control of our tried, tested and successful business operations. We had an ethos to maintain.

We have never once regretted the decision to opt out. For a start, we saw an increase in the degree of professional wrangling surrounding the presentation of body mapping in court. For example, one barrister would request a particular style, while another would show a preference for its polar opposite, with consequential time-wasting and confusion. Added to which, the purpose for which body mapping was intended was being drowned out in favour of pressure to follow personal whims. In this way we saw a leaning towards the sacrificing of cutting-edge technology for images so basic that 20 years of advancement in this area were being disregarded. What most rankled, however, was the indifference shown towards the Home Office pathologist's right to govern how their expert evidence was presented in court; no longer was body mapping to be aligned with the preference of the qualified expert, but subject to an open forum that dictated how, and which, injuries were to be shown. It was inexplicable that medical findings were to be dictated by the non-medic, and for ourselves, as graphic artists with decades of forensic medical experience, the constant changes to accommodate the varying impulses of each party created its own chaos. You don't change a winning formula.

In fact, there is good reason for aligning body mapping with the pathologist's post-mortem report. It has become a statutory requirement for the pathologist to receive remuneration for time spent approving injury placement, and they largely take ownership of such graphics as a true and accurate representation of their findings. Having undergone many years of extremely thorough medical training, they have acquired an exceptionally broad anatomical expertise and are required to meticulously investigate every part of the deceased's body. Their evidence is the primary focus from the outset of an investigation of death and it stands to reason that they are the final authority on whether the accompanying body mapping illustrates that evidence. At the same time, the body mapping should be able to stand alone, particularly as the jury will eventually deliberate without the presence of a pathologist to provide further explanation.

Over the years at Guy's we acquired our own expertise, working alongside the pathologists. This has been reflected in the high level of trust shown to us by them, when preparing their forensic graphics.

Another area for conflict in the field of body mapping is injury representation itself. For the body of the deceased we use a computerized avatar. For the injuries we hand-craft replications, using drawing and painting techniques. We have never felt it necessary to change these design features, and have frequently been complimented on our depictions of injury, which are very lifelike. Barristers have claimed they could not possibly have been painted, and must have been cropped from an original photograph, which is not the case, as this, too, goes entirely against our ethos.

The cut–paste–blend method has, however, long been a route adopted by those who have entered this field without forensic or medical expertise. The simple 'cut' part of this operation involves cutting injuries from the actual electronic post-mortem photograph and pasting them onto the avatar. While this still avoids showing the body of the deceased, the fact remains that the real injuries are actually then being shown in court. You can see this, particularly when the injuries are facial, and recognizable features of the deceased are apparent, which is not ideal. There is always the risk that these real injuries – being presented in a forum where the relatives of the deceased are present – will upset them. Apart from the obvious fact that the family may recognize a facial or bodily feature of their deceased relative, they may be devastated that they are viewing the actual injuries sustained, along with everyone else present, not least in a public setting. It essentially contravenes the purpose for which body mapping was created.

The painted graphics and computer-generated bodies we produce have no realistic identity and are, of course, designed to sanitize the real injuries, as originally intended. There has, so far, been no overt opposition to them, from either a legal perspective or a bereaved family.

A point of contention in the legal profession is, however, the type of avatar used for body mapping. In short, the demand for a particular type can be as varied as the sources requesting it. As a rule, currently barrister preference tends to take precedence, with the result that a richly detailed avatar may be whittled down to its most basic format.

It is our practice to select an avatar applicable to each case. First and foremost, we choose according to age: is this an adult, an adolescent, a child or a baby? Then we choose according to the apparent sex of the individual, though male genitalia are not generally included, unless relevant to the site of the injury. Bearing in mind non-binary consider-ations, we tend to maintain neutral elements to some extent. For instance, removing distracting features often includes removing genitalia altogether, and if we are demonstrating injury to an arm we will avoid showing a breast.

We do not adopt a one-size-fits-all approach, though, as it is sometimes necessary to closely mirror the size and shape of the deceased's body. Certain features have more relevance in this regard: a shorter or longer body; a heavier or lighter frame.

Largely, it is anatomical markers which require adaptation. By 'anatomical markers' we mean nipples and genitalia. When, for instance, a stab wound is described by the pathologist as being at a certain distance from the nipple, the size and shape of the deceased will be significant. It is then essential to adapt the frame of the avatar accordingly, so that we are placing the wound on the curve of the breast, for example, rather than the side of the body, or, on a lean avatar, close to the armpit.

When it comes to facial features, while we do not alter our avatars to resemble the deceased, there can be a need to slightly alter nose shape. This is generally so that multiple injuries can better fit. However, we reserve the greatest flexibility for the neck. This is essential when, sadly, multiple injuries are evident in this area. In order to incorporate them all, we may need to lengthen and/or widen the avatar's neck. Without such adaptability – in principle, as much as in software – it would hinder the presentation of injuries to the required degree of accuracy.

Perhaps the most contentious issue surrounding body mapping, though, is the one of ethnicity. We have always chosen an avatar purposely to reflect a deceased's colour and ethnicity. This has come under fire on occasion, but there are reasons for it. Apart from the obvious right of the victim to be represented according to their ethnic origin, the fact is that body shape can vary according to the ethnicity of a deceased. Furthermore, pathologists have observed a strong sense of ethnic pride in grieving relatives. In one instance of which we were made aware, the pathologist related that, had ethnicity not been referenced in the avatar representing the deceased, he was in no doubt that considerable offence would have been caused to the bereaved relatives.

For us, adaptability in the use of avatars has been indispensable in other ways. Both our software and our adaptability allow us to incorporate features which others have been unable to produce. For instance, it has been recognized that our graphical capabilities are often better matched to infants, children and teens. This has been of particular consequence in cases of starvation, where the avatar requires a drastic reduction in shape and size. This type of work features heavily in child protection trials, and we can provide a range of associated specialist images entirely for this purpose.

The fact that everyone has their own opinion about producing forensic injury body mapping means of course that it is a thought-provoking field of expertise. It has become a routine requirement in the early stages of courtroom preparation in the majority of British murder trials. It is also used in cases of clinical wounding, including road traffic accidents and rape. It perhaps goes without saying that it is far preferable to show such injuries in this way, particularly when sustained by a living victim, rather than showing the real injuries in the public setting of a courtroom with the victim present.

In summary, body mapping is designed to allow each member of a jury to become informed enough to reach a personal opinion on wounding and intent. The aim of the

British court is to weigh all the evidence and reach a conclusion, whether that is the guilt or innocence of the accused. In such emotive, and often complex, circumstances, the use of injury body mapping to convey medical and anatomical information in an uncomplicated way is paramount.

Since Pauline and I started working in forensics, major strides have been made in a variety of analytical techniques which were, at the time, still in their infancy. It has been gratifying to be involved in such developments and to work in such a fascinating area. Despite the interest our children have in the work we perform, however, they have all realized their own aspirations in very different ways.

Ross is still a collector of Second World War memorabilia and an entrepreneur, renovating an assortment of classic, vintage and prestige cars; once more buying and selling, this time in his own highly successful business.

Gemma continues to spend her time drawing, colouring, painting and crafting, having qualified as an art teacher at Canterbury Christchurch University and gone on to become head of art and head of year. Her musical skills also found an outlet as the singer in a band.

Rowan won a scholarship and went on to gain an honours degree in commercial music at Canterbury Christchurch University (Broadstairs campus). His tutors, initially unaware of his preference for heavy metal, caught right up when he mistook an assignment for a contemporary drumming piece — they were treated to the unforgettable sound of his death metal band! Operational support might be his day job, but his first love will always be composing and drumming with his band at gigs across the south-east.

Amber found the perfect outlet for her love of gruelling physical and mental challenges during a gap year, as an activity instructor in the summer camps she so loved as a child. After graduating from the University of Glasgow in zoology, she followed her heart into the world of doggy daycare. Along with studying to be a canine behaviourist, she is developing her own dog-related business, having gained valuable experience in doggy daycare and designing/running puppy socialization classes.

Looking back, we ourselves have found, on a personal level, that our experiences at Guy's and beyond have made us more philosophical, more *laissez faire* and free-thinking. At the same time, we are constantly reminded of the fragility of the human body; the fragility of life itself. Such information could easily take its toll emotionally, though fortunately our thirst for knowledge in this arena, and our understanding of it, tend to prevent such thoughts from taking hold. Still, we have long been aware of the need for a sound philosophy to keep us in a good mental place while performing a job in which we observe photographs of deliberately inflicted injury, usually with fatal results.

After all you have read, it may not come as a surprise to learn that the philosophy to which we adhere has a scientific component to it. The nervous system, the senses, the gut, the heart – each of these is comprised of vibrant, living mechanisms which constantly influence and shape our life, whether or not we recognize it. Science has recently demonstrated provable links between a thought and the biological processes reactive to it; in other words, how a change in the way we think – whether that affects our emotional state in a positive or a negative way – impacts our resultant life experience. Scientific studies have monitored the heart and brain simultaneously, and revealed that the heart anticipates the outcome of a stimulus before the brain reacts to it. In other words, the heart knows first, or predicts.

Our philosophy reflects this. It is simplicity itself, but powerful and dependable in any given situation. Summed up in the language of the body, rooted in science, and understood by everyone on a subliminal level, it is: *Listen to your inner voice, trust your gut instinct and follow your heart.*

And finally, in a book written about our livelihood – because we could never really think of what we do as 'work' – our guiding principle is: *Do what you love … and you'll love what you do.*

ACKNOWLEDGEMENTS

Setting out our story has reminded us again of how fortunate we have been to work with a group of professionals who have given so freely of their time and encouraged us to excel in, and enjoy, our work. A strong work ethic – including the resilience necessary in the field of forensic medicine – tends to begin at home, through the example set by parents. We are both incredibly lucky to have received unstinting support from our own. Spending a large part of our working lives in a closed environment, occasionally shrouded in secrecy, we valued the constant support of our families, even though, at times, they knew almost nothing about the situations we faced or the high-profile cases in which we were involved. We are therefore grateful that our literary agent and publishers have given us this opportunity to pass on the full extent of this information, not only to yourself, the reader, but to our families – through the medium of a book.

Our literary agent, Robert Smith, believed in our book from the outset, and we are greatly indebted to you, Robert, for caring about our manuscript and your professional expertise in finding the perfect publishing house.

Commissioning editor Kelly Ellis, Simon Gerratt, Jessie Meenan, Hattie Evans, Tom Dunstan, Claire Ward, Steve Leard, Rhys Willson, Mark Rowland, Dean Russell, Fionnuala Barrett, Charlotte Brown, Sarah Burke, Graham Holmes and the rest of the HarperNonFiction team, we are so grateful that your vision for this book aligned with our own and we appreciate you accepting a full, and sometimes hair-raising, account, rather than a purely scientific one. In particular, Kelly, you have shown such enthusiasm, and we are very appreciative of your professional insight and kind hospitality. Thanks, too, to our copy-editor, Lizzie Henry – what a fantastic job you have done, bringing out the best in our content while being an absolute hoot to work with – and to James Ryan and Mark Bolland, for your additional expertise. Our intention was to create a book everyone could enjoy, especially the non-medic, and HarperCollins has proven the perfect fit, placing our book on shelves where everyone can find it.

Charlotte Atyeo, literary agent – this book wouldn't be what it is without your invaluable guidance at just the right time. Thank you so much.

John Hughes, thank you for being our early-version proofreader. You were full of surprises, not the least of which was divulging that your home locations always seemed to be in rather close proximity to some of the most high-profile British murders referenced in this book. Is there something you want to confess, John?

Professionally, we are both especially grateful to the Australian pathologists Dr Kevin Lee and Professor Stephen Cordner. You transformed our work environment into a place of sheer entertainment, on all levels, and presented us with opportunities that proved to be major stepping stones in the progression of our respective roles and supported the realization of our ambitions. Every day in your company was both a privilege and a joy.

We are indebted to the incredible pathologist team we worked with during our time at Guy's forensic department and beyond, in particular the renowned pathologist – and personal friend – Dr Dick Shepherd. Thank you so much for agreeing to write our Foreword. You have always been a huge source of encouragement, and Derek is particularly indebted to you for your recommendation of the Open University as a means of cementing his professional status through becoming a graduate imaging scientist. Thank you for your foresight.

Our departmental heads at Guy's all played an integral part in our story, especially those who are sadly no longer with us: Professor Keith Mant, Professor Keith Simpson, Dr Alan Grant and Dr Iain West. All were influential, but Dr Iain West, in particular, with whom we both worked closely, made a huge impact on our professional lives. In seizing the opportunity to have his own PA accompany him everywhere – as had, decades earlier, Professor Keith Simpson – he gave Pauline the chance to live her dream. We will also always be grateful to Iain for a chance conversation about replicating injury for a television audience leading to Derek's creation of the forensic injury body mapping, for which we are, arguably, most recognized today. We feel sure he would have appreciated the speed at which his concept took off and became a routine legal requirement for courtroom preparation, as seen in murder trials across the whole country. Without Iain's foresight, there would also have been no National Injuries Database and, without the National Injuries Database, Derek wouldn't have received exposure on such an epic scale to patterned injury. It has been a privilege to be taught in depth about the injury process by leading forensic pathologists, including Dr Nat Cary, Iain West's successor as head of department. Nat has always been a huge supporter of our business venture, and we will always be grateful to him for his loyalty.

No acknowledgement of those who have helped us along the way would be complete without mentioning the collective Guy's pathology team. All were a pleasure to work, and socialize, with. Particular thanks go to Dr Vesna Djurovic, Dr Ashley Fegan-Earl, Dr Rob Chapman, Dr Nick Hunt and Dr Peter Jerreat. We also owe our thanks to the steady stream of pathologists who arrived one by one, over the years, from Hong Kong, and made such an impact on us, not least in whisking us off for Dim Sum or dinner in Chinatown at least once a week. Thank you David, Mike, Stevie, Alfred, Philip and Bobby.

Sonya Baylis, you have always been such a wonderful and loyal colleague and friend, and a pleasure to work with, both at Guy's and up and down the country as we promoted and utilized the National Injuries Database. Your professional and personal support has been invaluable. Thank you.

Derek is particularly indebted to the late Joe Dawes, former curator of the Gordon Museum, who took on a 15-year-old with no technical experience and gave him exceptional training. We are also indebted to the museum's current curator, Bill Edwards. As well as being a great friend, you have given us incredible support, appreciated by our whole family. We also thank you for the permission to use an image of the Gordon Museum in this book. We both also extend our thanks to Westminster Council, who kindly gave us permission to revisit Westminster mortuary after all these years. We are particularly grateful to the superintendent and mortuary team, who so kindly gave up part of their lunchtime to give us a guided tour around the excellent mass disaster management suite dedicated to Dr Iain West.

Most of our content was compiled at Elliott's Harbour Kitchen in Whitstable. We would like to thank our busy waitress, who kindly kept up a constant supply of teacakes, coffee and green tea … and possibly overheard snippets of conversation which are not a natural accompaniment to breakfast!

Finally, we want to thank our children, who have shown great patience while waiting to read the content of our book. To you all, we want to say we both had the most incredible and rewarding of jobs, but being at home with you was always the best part of every day.